A WORLDLY AFFAIR

A WORLDLY AFFAIR

NEW YORK, THE UNITED NATIONS, AND THE STORY BEHIND THEIR UNLIKELY BOND

PAMELA HANLON

Empire State Editions

An imprint of Fordham University Press

New York   2017

Fordham University Press has no responsibility for the persistence or accuracy of URLs for external or third-party Internet websites referred to in this publication and does not guarantee that any content on such websites is, or will remain, accurate or appropriate.

Fordham University Press also publishes its books in a variety of electronic formats. Some content that appears in print may not be available in electronic books.

Visit us online at
www.empirestateeditions.com
www.fordhampress.com

Library of Congress Cataloging-in-Publication Data
available online at http://catalog.loc.gov.

Printed in the United States of America
19 18 17   5 4 3 2 1
First edition

Contents

Preface

Since the mid-1970s, East Midtown Manhattan has been my home. It's a neighborhood I originally chose because it was within easy walking distance of my office, then on Park Avenue in the Forties. The fact that the United Nations' world headquarters was a mere block from my apartment never struck me as particularly remarkable. And while I had always been a believer in the UN and its ideals, my interest in the UN as a *neighbor* centered mostly around the pleasure of taking a walk in its landscaped North Lawn, in those days open to the public.

Then in the early 2000s, my perspective started to change. I became more active in local community affairs, and in 2007 wrote a book about the history of Manhattan's East Midtown, the area called Turtle Bay. It was then that I began to better appreciate the fact that the eighteen acres of international land in the center of one of the world's largest and most multicultural cities was truly unique, and not without some controversy. And I came to recognize that the decades-long relationship between New York and the UN speaks volumes about the greatness of the city. That the world's huge peace organization, with its thousands of international workers, diplomats, and visiting foreign dignitaries, has carried on its business in the middle of Manhattan without overwhelming even its nearby surroundings seemed to me a wonder. I was curious to know more about the history of the bond between the two.

I might have been satisfied to simply read a book on the subject. But I found that no book had been written that addresses the decades-long interconnection between New York and the UN. So I began to research the background of the relationship—how the two have accommodated each other, benefited each other, and quarreled with each other. My starting point was the extensive online archive of the *New York Times*, where a year-by-year search from the 1940s to the present provided great detail of the evolving city-UN partnership. With that, and what I culled from biographies and memoirs of New York mayors and UN officials, I began to piece together the New York–UN story. At the same time, I looked at the origins of the relationship and the world body's initial search for a headquarters site. The United Nations Archives and Records Management Section was key to this, and I spent many days there in late 2008 and early 2009, with some very experienced, and patient, UN archivists who helped me pore through boxes of yellowed memos and verbatim reports that led me to other resources.

After putting aside my New York–UN work for a couple years while I was involved in other writing projects, I got back to the story with a search of the archived papers of the city's mayors since the mid–twentieth century, and other collections, books, periodicals, and interviews.

Since its founding, countless books have been written about the UN— its goals, challenges, programs, and leadership. And some have covered the organization's early days in New York, such as *A Workshop for Peace* by George A. Dudley (MIT Press, 1994) and *Manhattan Projects* by Samuel Zipp (Oxford University Press, 2010). A more recent work, *Capital of the World* by Charlene Mires (New York University Press, 2013), tells of the scores of locations that competed to become home to the UN headquarters, leading up to New York's surprising selection in late 1946. *A Worldly Affair* looks beyond that, to the partnership between New York and the UN that now spans more than seven decades and the terms of ten New York mayors and nine UN secretaries general.

I hope readers find *A Worldly Affair* both informative and entertaining, and will see that beneath an often rocky relationship lies a metropolis so resourceful and resilient that it has been able to host the world body over these past many decades without sacrificing its own special character, while providing the cultural diversity and inclusiveness essential for an assembly of diplomats striving to achieve their global goals.

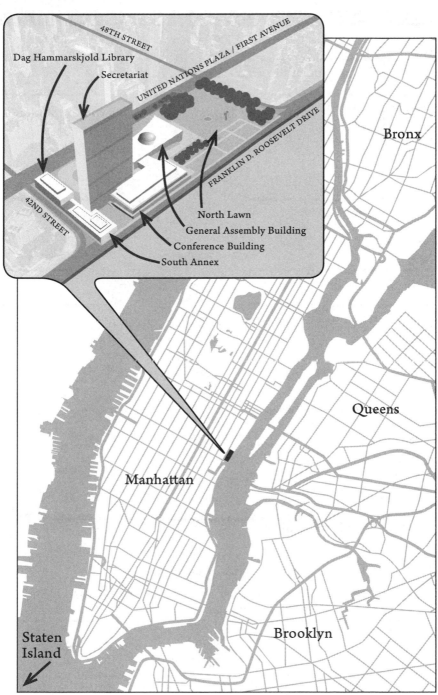

48TH STREET

Dag Hammarskjold Library

Secretariat

UNITED NATIONS PLAZA / FIRST AVENUE

FRANKLIN D. ROOSEVELT DRIVE

42ND STREET

North Lawn
General Assembly Building
Conference Building
South Annex

Bronx

Queens

Manhattan

Brooklyn

Staten
Island

THE UNITED NATIONS IN NEW YORK

NEW YORK CITY MAYOR	UN SECRETARY GENERAL	MEMBER STATES
1946 William O'Dwyer*	Trygve Lie	51
1950 Vincent Impellitteri		59
1954 Robert Wagner	Dag Hammarskjold	60
	U Thant	
1966 John Lindsay		117
	Kurt Waldheim	
1974 Abraham Beame		135
1978 Edward Koch		149
	Javier Pérez de Cuéllar	
1990 David Dinkins		159
	Boutros Boutros-Ghali	
1994 Rudolph Giuliani		184
	Kofi Annan	
2002 Michael Bloomberg		189
	Ban Ki-moon	
2014 Bill de Blasio		193†
	António Guterres	

* Mayor Fiorello La Guardia's term (1934–1945) overlapped with that of UN Preparatory Commission head and Acting Secretary General Gladwyn Jebb, who served from UN charter ratification in October 1945 until Lie's appointment in early 1946.

† In addition, the Holy See and Palestine hold non-member observer status.   *Date of listing: 2017*

Prologue

For more than seventy years, New York City and the United Nations have been neighbors, the boundary between them a mere six-block stretch of First Avenue on one side and the banks of the East River on the other. That they share a postal zip code and telephone area code is all but taken for granted. And the world body's headquarters has become a fixture along storied Forty-second Street, like the city's Broadway theaters, the Public Library, and Grand Central Terminal. Yet in 1946, when the nations of the world made an eleventh-hour decision to choose Manhattan as their global meeting place, it was a stunning development. The fifty-one founding members of the UN had been looking for a vast swath of land in the countryside, where they planned a self-contained international community of meeting halls, homes, and schools. So, many wondered, how could the unlikely pair ever coexist—a crowded, bustling metropolis and an enclave of diplomats located squarely in its midst?

Indeed, as the United Nations has grown over the years—to 193 member states by 2017—New York and the world body have had their share of conflicts. Each has suggested, more than once and often not so subtly, that the organization might find another place to meet. But their quarrels seem always to have been worked out, or papered over, or forgotten, before any foreign envoys have picked up and left. The two have stuck together—the ever-confident city, never wanting to appear overly enamored of its international guest, and the UN, never intimidated by its cosmopolitan host.

Over the decades, New Yorkers have grumbled about the UN's presence in the center of their town—the traffic-snarling motorcades, scofflaws hiding behind diplomatic immunity, member nations' controversial policies, and provocative foreign guests. But the benefits to the city can hardly be ignored. Today, more than sixteen thousand employees work at the UN, its agencies, affiliates, and missions in New York, and the annual boost to the local economy is estimated to be $3.7 billion.[1] That's some ten times the economic impact of hosting a major party's political convention, a one-time event for which U.S. cities, New York among them, compete vigorously. The General Assembly session held each fall has been referred to as a kind of "Diplomatic Olympics" that most cities would be pleased to host just once, let alone every year.

And perhaps more significant, if less tangible, is the prestige that being the "capital of the world" brings with it. Regularly, the UN attracts kings and queens, and presidents and prime ministers, and their presence in the city adds to the grandeur and excitement that has become the hallmark of New York. Some two hundred foreign correspondents are assigned to the UN, their news reports reaching every corner of the world and adding to the aura of the city as the global center of gravity.

Back in the 1940s, when a newborn UN proclaimed it had no interest in a New York home, Mayor Fiorello La Guardia, ever proud of his city, remained convinced the world body would change its mind. "When it comes down to the final analysis of what is needed, then it is New York," he said at the time, "because there is only one New York City. Yes, there is only one New York City in the whole world and there is nothing like it."[2]

By the twenty-first century, many diplomats and employees posted to the UN headquarters agreed. They say they like the city's diverse population, its culture, its freedoms, its energy. One of the organization's earliest employees, a Briton who went on to a distinguished career as UN Under Secretary General, Brian Urquhart, remembered the world body's initial resistance to a New York home. Years later, he called the city "the UN's greatest blessing."

"New York is a grand, hard, gritty place where no one underestimates their own importance or overestimates anyone else's," he said in 2010. "In other places, diplomats see themselves as the biggest fish in the little pond, but in New York they have to swim around like all the other fish, and no one will fail to criticize them if they deserve it."[3]

This book is the history of New York City's unlikely partnership with the United Nations and the story of the people who have shaped the bond between them. At times it has been a complicated affair, influenced by diplomatic, political, financial, legal, and personal dynamics. Yet as the United Nations marked its seventieth anniversary in 2015, and as the organization completed a massive restoration and modernization of its iconic headquarters buildings, it was clear the world's meeting place would be in New York for years to come. Many may offer reasons for the lasting relationship, but in the end, it may be that Mayor La Guardia was precisely right about his great city: There is nothing like it.

1

City Rebuffed

After twelve years in office, Fiorello La Guardia was about to leave City Hall. The candid, tough-talking mayor of New York had chosen not to run in the latest election, and on New Year's Day 1946, he would turn over the reins of government to William O'Dwyer. But until then, La Guardia was finishing out his third term with the same passion for his city that New Yorkers had come to expect from their colorful mayor. He had become well known for his regularly scheduled Sunday afternoon *Talk to the People* radio broadcasts, chats with constituents that he peppered with doses of news, opinion, humor, and counsel. And so it surprised no one that in one of his last radio shows before leaving office, La Guardia had some advice for the incoming mayor.

"I am not going to peddle New York, and I hope that my successor will not either. I advise strongly that we wait and let all the other cities peddle themselves," La Guardia told his listeners. "I am sure that when everything is considered—the facilities and communications, and everything that is needed—the United Nations Organization will come to New York City."[1]

Over the past few weeks, boosters from cities throughout the United States had been converging on London. Armed with glossy brochures, fiery speeches, and liberal expense accounts, mayors and high-powered public relations men were arriving in the British capital from Chicago, San Francisco, and Philadelphia, from Atlantic City, Boston, and even Rapid City, South Dakota—all hoping to catch the attention of the world's new peace organization. The charter of the United Nations had been ratified in October, and now, after a long drawn-out debate at the UN's temporary meeting hall in London, a delegates' committee had tentatively voted to locate the UN's permanent headquarters in the United States. The news set off a flurry of lobbying, with scores of U.S. municipalities bidding for the chance to become the new "center of the world."

New York City was noticeably absent from the London lobbying frenzy. And while reports circulated that Mayor-elect O'Dwyer was considering making the trip, La Guardia remained adamant that the city should stay away. "I am not going to put my city in a position of bidding for it the same as a small-sized city would bid for a national political convention or for the Elks convention or something like that," La Guardia told constituents in another of his radio talks. "I think it is unbecoming."[2]

O'Dwyer didn't go to London. Instead, he started working with La Guardia on the outgoing mayor's plan to bring UN headquarters to New York. For months, La Guardia and his park commissioner,[3] Robert Moses, had been quietly strategizing on how to make that happen. Moses had prepared a formal proposal for the United Nations. Now, the two mayors and Moses would wait for the opportune time to present UN officials with their two-foot-high, blue leather-bound book filled with twenty-six pages of renderings, photographs, and maps of a spot of land in the borough of Queens that they were convinced should be the new center of the world.[4]

Search for a Continent

Where the United Nations would locate its permanent headquarters had been talked about for years. But once delegates from some fifty countries[5] met in San Francisco in the spring of 1945 to draw up a proposed charter for the new world body, speculation surged. Whether the UN's home would be in Europe or America was the immediate question, an emotional issue that drew strong opinions from proponents of both.

Great Britain favored Europe, and believed Geneva, home of the pre–World War II League of Nations, was the choice location. The British felt that to move the new peace organization out of Europe, where war had left such devastation, would shift the focus from work that needed to be done there. France also favored Europe, and held that the United States, which was to be one of the five permanent members of the Security Council, shouldn't be considered because the home of the UN ought not to be in the territory of a permanent council member. And at a practical level, many believed Europe was simply more convenient to most countries than the United States. In addition to Geneva, places often mentioned were Brussels, Paris, London, the three Scandinavian capitals, and even islands such as Madeira and Rhodes.

But other UN countries, such as the Republic of China[6] and the Soviet Union, contended that America, in particular the United States, would represent a "new spirit." A home in the United States would not be laden with the failures of the old League of Nations, which had been unable to prevent World War II and which the United States had never joined.[7]

Probably most important, the pro-U.S. contingent believed that locating the new organization within U.S. boundaries would ensure that the United States would remain fully engaged in the workings of the new body, and not return to its previous isolationist tendencies. Mayor La Guardia, the son of Italian immigrants and an Army veteran of World War I, strongly supported that view. "Not until a world crisis takes place, do we [Americans] seem to show any interest in international affairs," he said in another of his weekly WNYC public radio talks. He believed locating the UN in the United States would "bring right home to us the troubles and the problems of the entire world, and also bring home to us our responsibility."[8]

The United States government remained neutral on the issue, but said it would welcome the world body if the other members decided they wanted to come to U.S. shores.[9]

The decision rested with the United Nations Preparatory Commission, set up to carry through on UN planning after the charter was signed in late June of 1945, just weeks after Nazi Germany's surrender and weeks before the Japanese surrender ending World War II. The commission met in London, at Church House, next to Westminster Abbey. Of all its critical work, nothing drew quite as much attention as did the question of a permanent site for UN headquarters.

In the United States, local leaders were quick to recognize the prestige and economic benefits of hosting the UN, and they flooded the Commission with cables, letters, brochures, and motion picture films urging the new international organization to settle in their midst.

South Dakota was among the first. Early on, the Dakotans teamed up with neighboring Wyoming and Nebraska to make an ambitious offer of up to one hundred square miles of the Black Hills region. Philadelphia, too, was an early bidder, along with San Francisco, Boston, Chicago, Atlantic City, Detroit, and scores of others. Mayor Hubert Humphrey of Minneapolis urged that his city be chosen because of its "ideal climate" and "internationally minded" people. The state of Tennessee put forward an offer, as did the Great Smoky Mountain region of the Appalachians. Serious invitations came from at least forty U.S. locations, and by one estimate, some 150 localities publicly expressed interest in becoming the new capital of the world.[10] One of the more significant early offers came from the Hudson River community of Hyde Park, New York—home of President Franklin Roosevelt, who had died in April, just weeks before the UN charter conference had convened. It was Roosevelt who had championed the UN's formation and had dedicated so much time during his final months to assuring that the worldwide peace organization would become a reality.[11] A group of Roosevelt's friends and neighbors suggested that the headquarters be located on his estate and much of the land surrounding it, a proposal backed by the president's widow, Eleanor, and privately favored by President Truman.[12]

In October 1945, a preliminary, and nonbinding, tally of the Preparatory Commission's fourteen-member Executive Committee showed a preference for the United States. Though only a straw poll, it boosted the hopes of the U.S. communities, whose representatives now rushed to London to shower Committee members with their bids. South Dakota businessman Paul Bellamy arrived with an oversized sixteen-page brochure promising that "no large city will absorb your identity."[13] Soon, a Philadelphia delegation was in London, followed by Boston, and then a high-powered duo representing San Francisco—Mayor Roger Lapham and Governor Earl Warren of California. The U.S. government, with its neutral stance on the location, tried to discourage them. But before long, more than twenty localities had sent representatives across the Atlantic, all roaming London hotel lobbies, restaurants, bars, and meeting halls to buttonhole commissioners with plugs for their city. "Be it said they were liberal hosts," recalled Trygve Lie, then a member of the Norwegian delegation and soon to be named the first UN Secretary General.[14] A British member of the Preparatory Commission's team was less kind: "Typical American high pressure methods . . . alright for corralling national conventions, but . . . not dignified enough for the United Nations."[15]

The U.S. government became so concerned by the impression being left by the backroom lobbyists that it persuaded the Commission to set up a special venue where the city promoters could make formal presentations.[16]

Some New Yorkers began to think the city should be represented in London. But La Guardia remained firm. "A scramble of cheap competition between American cities," he called it. "If they come here and look around, they will naturally come to New York City," the confident mayor assured New Yorkers.[17]

Meanwhile, the "Europe versus America" debates dragged on. The United States was among those increasingly concerned that a United Nations left "homeless" would be less effective in its early work,[18] and it soon backed off its position of neutrality. In early December 1945, both houses of Congress passed a resolution inviting the UN to come to the United States.[19]

On December 15, the UN's full Preparatory Commission—after a tense and emotional session in which a ballot for Europe was narrowly defeated by just two votes—finally gave the nod to the United States. The vote was thirty to fourteen with six abstentions.* Then the British, who had held out for Europe to the end, seconded a motion by Canada to make the result unanimous.[20]

Days later, the selection was narrowed to a site in the northeastern United States. But, in a blow to the departing Mayor La Guardia, the Commission stated firmly that the site "should not be located within or too near a large metropolitan district."[21] Instead, the UN said it would search for a vast multi-acre site in the countryside—at least forty square miles—on which it would build a self-sufficient headquarters and fully serviced international community.

By all accounts, New York City was out of the running.

Undaunted

Like La Guardia, his successor, William O'Dwyer, dearly wanted the United Nations to settle in his city. It was, he said, "the one great thing that would make New York the center of the world."[22] A brawny, blue-eyed Irishman who had immigrated to New York in 1910, O'Dwyer was a policeman before going to law school and rising to become Brooklyn District Attorney. When La Guardia chose not to run for a fourth term in 1945, O'Dwyer, a Democrat who also ran on the American Labor ticket, won easily.

The New Yorkers that O'Dwyer would govern were optimistic and proud of their ever-growing and multicultural city. One-quarter of New

---

*Voting against were Belgium, Canada, Denmark, France, Greece, Iraq, Lebanon, Liberia, Luxembourg, Netherlands, Norway, Saudi Arabia, Union of South Africa, and the United Kingdom; abstaining were Colombia, Ecuador, Ethiopia, New Zealand, Syria, and the United States. No vote was registered for Costa Rica.

York's population of more than 7.5 million people was foreign-born, the city was more populous than most of the UN member nations, and annually its public transit system carried more than the total of the world's population. A tourist brochure encouraged visitors to explore dozens of ethnic neighborhoods, from the Italian, Russian, Syrian, German, and Spanish quarters, to Chinatown and the "Push Cart and Bargain Town," a predominantly Jewish section on the Lower East Side. The city's second airport, Idlewild, was about to open, easing congestion at La Guardia Field, and the Brooklyn–Battery Tunnel would soon offer a new, much needed, connection between Manhattan and the city's largest borough.[23]

Still, the positive outlook was marred by an acute housing shortage facing the city, as war veterans were returning home and refugees arriving. Easing the crisis had been a key plank of O'Dwyer's campaign platform.

As the mayor took office on January 1, 1946, a seven-man UN inspection team was preparing to fly from London to the United States to begin scouting rural regions in the Northeast. Their Pan American Airways flying boat would land at La Guardia Field, and O'Dwyer was planning a welcome worthy of visiting heads of state and royalty. The fact that the Preparatory Commission had eliminated a metropolitan area as home to the UN didn't faze him. He and Commissioner Moses still planned to present the team with the city's hefty leather-bound proposal offering land in Flushing Meadow Park in Queens, site of the 1939 World's Fair.* Moses had enlisted a group of architects intimately familiar with the fairgrounds to draw up the offer. They included Aymar Embury II, who had designed the New York City Building for the 1939 Fair, and Wallace Harrison, whose work included the Fair's thematic center point, the Trylon and Perisphere, and who had close ties to the wealthy and influential Rockefeller family.[24]

On hand to receive the team was the city's longtime official greeter, Grover Whalen—known to most New Yorkers as simply "Mr. New York." Before a throng of reporters and photographers, the ever gregarious Whalen invited the group to City Hall to meet with the mayor. He then whisked them into five waiting limousines for a speedy transit— with police motorcycle escort—to a VIP check-in at the luxurious Waldorf Astoria Hotel in Midtown Manhattan.[25]

On January 8, after a trip to Washington where they were greeted by President Truman, the UN representatives were back in New York for

---

*In 1964, the name was changed from Flushing Meadow Park to Flushing Meadows–Corona Park.

their meeting with the mayor. The group was led by Stoyan Gavrilovic from Yugoslavia.* The tall, slim fifty-year-old had fled Belgrade in 1941 ahead of the Nazi invasion, and since 1943 had been living in the United States with his wife and young son.[26]

O'Dwyer asked some of the most prominent and influential New Yorkers to join the meeting, members of what he called his "Committee on a Permanent Site." They included Herbert Bayard Swope, the longtime *New York World* editor; Bernard Baruch, financier and close confidant to the late President Roosevelt; Frederick Ecker, chairman of Metropolitan Life Insurance Company; Thomas Watson, head of IBM; and a young, energetic member of the Rockefeller family, Nelson, who was now back in New York after a stint at the State Department in Washington. Whalen and Robert Moses also attended.[27]

Despite the high-profile help, the meeting did not go well. When the mayor emerged from the half-hour session, reporters observed that he appeared "flushed" and "testy."[28] O'Dwyer reflected later that after that first meeting, he thought the chances of ever getting the United Nations in New York were poor. "I clashed almost immediately with the committee chairman whose attitude was so arrogant and demanding that it was almost impossible to deal with him," he wrote of his meeting with Gavrilovic.[29]

Gavrilovic had made it clear that the city would not be considered for the permanent site. But he said New York might be considered as a temporary location, and he asked O'Dwyer if the city was prepared to house the UN for three to five years, while the permanent headquarters were being constructed elsewhere.

"Could we do it?" O'Dwyer paraphrased Gavrilovic's question for reporters. "The answer is 'yes,'" he said. "Would we do it? That's another story."[30]

The city's blue leather-bound book of architectural drawings had not gotten much of a reading. O'Dwyer said the city would now put its plans "in the safe and file them away carefully against the time that the UNO† will give further consideration to this matter and perhaps come back and ask us what we have."[31]

---

*In addition to Gavrilovic, the UN group included Francois Briere, France; Awny el-Khalidi, Iraq; Shu Hsi-hsu, China; Don Julio A. Lacarte, Uruguay; Georgi Saksin, the Soviet Union; and Kenneth Younger, Great Britain.

†In its early days, the United Nations was known as the United Nations Organization, or UNO.

Moses was incredulous. "I can't believe that the better balanced and more influential people of the UNO will blunder so egregiously as to the site," Moses wrote to Swope, adding that he saw "no earthly excuse for a huge compound ... where people of all nationalities will get into each other's hair, will never get away from each other, will create neighborhood dissensions, and will cut themselves off from the life around them."[32]

As the master planner in New York State and New York City for most of the past two decades, Moses could anticipate probably better than anyone the complexities of building, from scratch, a multi-mile self-contained compound of buildings in the countryside. Throughout La Guardia's administration, Moses had served as the city's park commissioner and as a member of the City Planning Commission, wielding great power over city planning and construction. By the time O'Dwyer took office, Moses, then fifty-seven, had been responsible for hundreds of public works projects, from playgrounds to parks, to parkways, bridges, and tunnels. Now, the new mayor had asked him to take on an even more influential role. He named him city construction coordinator, a kind of "umbrella" title that gave Moses authority over virtually every public building project in the city.

Moses and O'Dwyer didn't completely close the door on serving as the temporary headquarters, and they asked Gavrilovic for details of what the United Nations might need for interim offices and housing. Still, the two remained openly cool to the idea. Without at least the possibility that the United Nations would eventually settle permanently in New York, they didn't believe having the UN in town for just a short while justified the expense and disruption to residents and businesses. Most troubling was the city's housing crisis. Thousands were in need of homes and apartments, office buildings were filled to capacity, and hotel space was at a premium. With the mayor having made housing a top priority of his new administration, how could he now justify making room, on a temporary basis, for the thousands of staff and delegates that the United Nations would bring with it?

In mid-January, O'Dwyer sent a polite but tepid response to Gavrilovic's request for interim quarters. Carefully drafted by Moses and Whalen, and reviewed by Nelson Rockefeller, the letter continued to make a case for the *permanent* site to be in the city—in Flushing Meadow Park. "You will pardon us ... but we do not entirely grasp the reasons for seeking a location in some large and remote area dissociated from the centres of population," the letter read. "To create in the wilderness, so to speak, an entire new city ... is a formidable task requiring years for completion."[33]

However, O'Dwyer said, if the United Nations still believed it needed spacious seclusion, its inspectors might like to take a look at Staten Island. As for the city serving as temporary quarters, the mayor said again that the city's housing crisis was the obstacle. Then the letter closed with a kind of afterthought, a suggestion that a Sperry Corporation plant in Nassau County on Long Island might work for temporary quarters. The modern facility—three enormous buildings on 147 acres of fenced-in land in Lake Success—had been built in the early 1940s and was an important manufacturer of gyrocompasses and other high-tech equipment during the war. Owned by the federal government's Reconstruction Finance Corporation, it soon would be available to rent.[34]

The letter "is on its way to the gentleman from Yugoslavia," Moses wrote the next day to Swope. "I doubt whether the committee will even visit the Sperry plant."[35]

But the inspection team did ask to see the Sperry plant. "Grover and I will take them around," Moses told O'Dwyer. "I think they are just going through the motions and really no longer have any interest in this neck of the woods," he said. "Perhaps it is just as well."[36]

A Change of Heart

Soon, the city's reluctance to being the UN's interim host began to change. By the time of the Sperry visit in late January, Moses and O'Dwyer had started to warm to the idea of serving as temporary quarters. It was said to be Nelson Rockefeller who sparked the change in mindset. The third of the six children of John D. Rockefeller Jr., the thirty-seven-year-old Nelson was becoming increasingly active in city affairs. The previous summer, he had left his job as assistant secretary of state for Latin American affairs, in a Washington shakeup. Now, he had been named chairman of his family's huge Rockefeller Center complex. And as an avid art collector, he would soon move back into his role as president of the city's prestigious Museum of Modern Art, a position he had held before his Washington interlude.

Rockefeller knew many of the UN delegates from his time at the State Department and from his days attending the UN charter conference in San Francisco. There, the charming young heir to the Rockefeller fortune had mingled with the other conferees, and even threw a party for them at the exclusive St. Francis Yacht Club, an extravagant evening of champagne, cocktails, and entertainment provided by the nightclub singer Carmen Miranda, the "Brazilian Bombshell."[37] Now, Rockefeller believed

New York could gain a foothold in its bid to host the United Nations permanently if it would first be named to serve as interim headquarters. He convinced O'Dwyer and Moses that once UN personnel and delegates had a chance to live in the city and experience its hospitality, they might start to look more favorably on Flushing Meadow Park as a permanent home.[38]

Yet, to be a serious contender for the interim site, New York would have to offer more than just the Sperry plant. So Rockefeller told O'Dwyer he was prepared to provide—rent-free—the 3,500-seat Center Theatre in Rockefeller Center for the large General Assembly sessions.* With that offer in hand, the city looked for other meeting venues and within days had lined up space at the Whitelaw Reid House, or Villard Houses, on Madison Avenue, and possibly City Center on West Fifty-fifth Street and Manhattan Center on West Thirty-fourth Street. The Hotel Association of New York City agreed to hold rooms for UN delegates and staff during the General Assembly session.[39]

The other two contenders for temporary quarters—Boston and Atlantic City—couldn't compete with the city's offer. In early February, by a five to two vote, New York found itself the preferred interim home of the new United Nations.† Meanwhile, for the permanent site, the inspection team selected a large swath of suburban land north of the city—in Fairfield County in Connecticut and in New York State's adjoining Westchester County. The UN General Assembly, still meeting in London, supported the recommendations and set up a new committee to work out the long-range plans for the U.S. suburban "mini-city."[40] For the interim arrangements in New York City, the Assembly put the newly elected Secretary General, Trygve Lie, directly in charge. "The temporary headquarters problem was dumped squarely in the lap of the Secretary General," Lie later recalled.[41]

For New York, the "dumping" proved to be good fortune. Lie, a Norwegian whose father was a carpenter, was known to be pragmatic. Educated as a lawyer at Oslo University and active in Labor Party politics, he had gone on to serve as Norway's foreign minister during the war, when the government was in exile in London after the German inva-

---

*The Center Theatre, at the southeast corner of Sixth Avenue and Forty-ninth Street, had opened in 1932. Originally called the RKO Roxy, the building was demolished in 1954.

†Iraq's Awny el-Khalidi voted for Atlantic City, and France's Francois Briere dissented for a technical reason.

sion of Norway. Lie had a good rapport with O'Dwyer. The mayor once described the six-foot-one, 240-pound Lie as a "big, affable, charming Scandinavian."[42] And from the beginning, Moses and Lie had a mutual respect for one another. Some said their personalities were similar, abrasive at times but always decisive. But most important, and unbeknownst to O'Dwyer and Moses at the time, Lie believed the permanent home of the United Nations should be in New York City. "The huge metropolis and international crossroads would in many ways offer the best contact with the world at large," he later wrote of his thoughts at the time. And although he didn't say so publicly, he thought that once temporary UN headquarters were established in New York, "human inertia—and the high cost of moving" would make it more likely the city would eventually be selected for the permanent site.[43]

The "Girls from Hunter"

New York had not a moment to spare in firming up space for the UN. Almost immediately, Secretariat staff started arriving, and the Security Council, which needed space for up to one thousand delegates and staff, translators, stenographers, and the press, was set to open in just weeks. Less urgent was a location for the larger General Assembly, since it wouldn't open until the fall, and it was generally assumed it would use Rockefeller's Center Theatre.

It soon developed that two key locations were not going to work out. The Sperry plant that O'Dwyer and Moses had suggested wouldn't be available to rent on such short notice, and space at the Reid House was simply too small. Now Bronx Borough President James Lyons, who earlier had lobbied for the Riverdale section of the Bronx to be the permanent site, suggested the Bronx campus of Hunter College—known as Hunter-in-the Bronx.* The two-year women's college had been taken over by the Navy during the war and used as a training camp for WAVES. Now the college was scheduled to reopen. But instead, Lyons thought its four main buildings, constructed as a project of the Works Progress Administration (WPA) in the early 1930s, would be the "ideal place" for the UN Security Council and Secretariat offices.[44]

The UN agreed. "It suits almost perfectly," said Lie's British executive assistant, David Owen, when he first saw the college's stately ivy-covered halls.[45]

---

*Hunter-in-the-Bronx became Lehman College in 1968.

But the president of Hunter and his women students didn't see it that way. With postwar school facilities at a premium, Dr. George Shuster called the plan "disastrous," and the president of the student council immediately circulated a petition to stop a UN "takeover." Students were particularly worried that a short stay might be extended, or even made permanent, a concern that Lyons only encouraged by repeatedly suggesting that the UN would be so pleased with the Bronx it would never want to leave. At Hunter's main campus in Midtown Manhattan, three thousand students rallied in protest, teachers joined in, and petitions with 3,500 signatures against the Hunter takeover were delivered to O'Dwyer's office.[46] Soon, pickets went up around City Hall.[47]

Lyons tried to reason with his constituents, and former Mayor La Guardia, who since leaving office was keeping a close eye on the UN search, urged the "girls from Hunter" to take "the big stand of world affairs."[48]

By the end of February 1946, with the Security Council scheduled to open in less than a month, the United Nations still had no place to meet. "U.N.O. officials are at their wit's ends," the *New York Times* reported.[49]

After a flurry of meetings with education officials—and with no serious alternatives—O'Dwyer agreed to back the UN-Hunter plan. The Board of Higher Education gave its blessing and in early March, the United Nations signed a lease to rent three of Hunter's four buildings through the middle of May.[50]

Now the city had little more than two weeks to turn Hunter's gymnasium into a respectable Security Council chamber. Construction crews worked round the clock, in three eight-hour shifts. The head electrician moved a cot into the building and slept there while he and his men installed some ten miles of wiring for power and what he said was ten times more for other more sophisticated communications systems. Concrete blocks atop steel girders were set over the swimming pool to make way for a press room. Open space was partitioned into meeting rooms, classrooms were converted into offices, and one large room—luxuriously furnished in a modern style and outfitted with a twenty-foot bar—became the Delegates Lounge, where a scotch whiskey would be offered for fifty cents and a martini for thirty-five.[51]

On Monday, March 25, 1946—with workmen still sweeping up wood chips and testing communications equipment—the historic first New York meeting of the Security Council got under way. Forty-five seats were promised to the public, and New Yorkers started lining up at the entrance to the gymnasium the night before the meeting, most satisfied to simply catch a glimpse of the world's leaders coming together to begin their "experiment in peace."[52] Just days before, former British Prime Minister Winston Churchill had declared that an "iron curtain" was descending across Europe, signaling the start of the Cold War between the United States and its allies and the Soviet bloc. Now, catching a glimpse of the dour young Russian delegate, the former Soviet ambassador to the United States, Andrei Gromyko, was considered a coup among the city's growing set of curious Kremlin watchers.

Lie was pleased with the gymnasium-turned-council space. However, he remained troubled by what he referred to as the "emotional outburst" from the Hunter students. "It had its source, I am sure, in isolationist, anti-European tradition and was exaggerated out of all proportion by the newspapers," he later wrote.[53]

But Lie found some comfort in what he called a "fitting answer" to the outbursts. It came from one of the workmen who crafted the first ballot box for the Security Council. When the box was opened up just before the first vote, a piece of paper was found inside. It read:

> May I, who have had the privilege of fabricating this ballot box, cast the first vote?
>
> May God be with every member of the United Nations Organization and through your noble efforts bring lasting peace to us all—all over the world.
>
> Paul Antonio, Mechanic[54]

"From Pillar to Post"

For now, the quandary of where to house the Security Council had been resolved. But it was hardly the end of the United Nations' space problems. Throughout the city, delegations were working from cramped, makeshift offices, mostly in hotels. Lie and a few others were based in a small number of offices at 610 Fifth Avenue in Rockefeller Center. Shuttling back and forth between hotels, to the Bronx for Security Council matters, and to Rockefeller Center for Secretariat meetings proved exhausting and confusing. "We spent most of the time dashing about and getting speeding tickets," remembered Brian Urquhart, a young Britisher and one of the earliest UN employees.[55]

And when an Assistant Secretary General, China's Victor Hoo, showed up late for a meeting with Lie at 610 Fifth Avenue, he explained that he had mistakenly thought the meeting was in Room 610 of the Waldorf Astoria. He knocked on the door, the good-natured Hoo later told Lie, to find it was the room of a hotel guest, an elderly woman who told him, "Oh, no laundry today."[56]

The city tried to cajole the federal government into giving up some of its 440,000 square feet of office space in the Empire State Building, but the government insisted that its workers needed to stay in Midtown.[57]

Then soon, a glitch arose in the plans to hold the General Assembly session in the space offered by Nelson Rockefeller, Center Theatre in the Rockefeller Center complex. Olympic skating champion Sonja Henie and her partner, Arthur Wirtz, had a long-standing contract with Rockefeller Center to produce nightly ice skating shows in the theater. Henie and Wirtz said they were willing to turn over the space to the United Nations, but the ninety-two skaters, twenty-four musicians plus stage-hands—all members of Local 802 of the Federation of Musicians—would have to be paid for the time they were not working.[58]

Far more serious was the fact that Nelson Rockefeller had made the offer without consulting with his father, John D. Rockefeller Jr. Although Nelson had recently been named to head Rockefeller Center operations, the elder Rockefeller still was firmly in charge of family affairs. Two days after the UN announced it intended to use Center Theatre for General Assembly sessions, Nelson found himself writing a memo to his father, explaining how the deal would work. His father didn't agree with abrogating the long-standing contract—Sonja Henie's ice shows had been playing there since 1940—and Nelson was in the embarrassing position of not being able to deliver on his offer.[59]

Meanwhile, in the Bronx, Hunter College was not living up to expectations. The UN had an option to extend its lease, but most of the Security Council delegates and Secretariat staff were living in Manhattan, and they found the campus inconvenient. Even more troubling, with summer approaching, the buildings weren't air-conditioned. And, finally, the students of Hunter-in-the-Bronx continued to agitate to get their campus back.[60]

Still, Bronx leaders tried to persuade the UN to bring even more of its operations to their borough. With Center Theatre out of the picture, they suggested that Kingsbridge Armory, a nine-story castle-like structure dating back to 1917, be converted into a General Assembly Hall, or that a temporary auditorium be built on a swath of open green space on the Hunter campus.[61]

Others suggested the ballroom of the Waldorf Astoria Hotel. And former Mayor La Guardia was convinced the City Building on the old World's Fair grounds in Flushing Meadow Park was the best option. The long, low Embury-designed structure had been turned into a city-run roller and ice skating rink after the 1939 Fair closed. Now La Guardia encouraged O'Dwyer and Moses to convert it into a temporary General Assembly Hall.

The protracted site search became the butt of jokes around town. When the New York City press corps put on its annual "Inner Circle" show lampooning local politicians and officials, the United Nations was satirized in a parody portraying an inspection team in search of burlesque dancers, with a parade of high-kicking "can-can" show girls auditioning before a frustrated and furious Stoyan Gavrilovic.[62]

More serious commentary came from others. In an editorial, the *New York Times* took the federal government to task for not playing more of a role in helping the United Nations find meeting space. "This spectacle of representatives of the world's greatest nations traveling around like business agents seeking housing . . . is one of which we as the host people should be totally ashamed," the *Times* said. "It may be democracy . . . to have New York City school girls passing resolutions of non-welcome, but it certainly isn't consonant with our dignity as a host city." The newspaper called on President Truman and Congress to assume responsibility.[63] Others echoed that sentiment, including town planning expert Frederick Gutheim. "The U.N. has been harried from pillar to post, and left strictly to the tender mercies of the city of New York," he said.[64]

The "tender mercies" continued into early April when Whalen escorted Lie and most of the Security Council delegates on a tour of the Sperry plant, which now would soon be available to rent. The plant's four-story Administration Building—with over two million square feet of office space—was modern, came with office furniture already in place, plenty of parking, good cafeteria facilities, and was air conditioned.[65]

While Lie was said to be impressed, most of the Security Council members were not. The plant didn't have space for the huge General Assembly, it was an inconvenient seventeen miles from Midtown Manhattan, and some simply questioned whether it was appropriate for the new global body to be meeting in a converted factory building.

Delegates started to agitate for giving up on New York altogether. Some suggested the temporary site could be moved to San Francisco, where—based on memories of that city's fine hospitality during the charter conference—the search for accommodations surely would be easier.[66]

But the General Assembly had given Lie sole responsibility for deciding on temporary quarters, and Lie wanted the United Nations in New York City. Over lunch with Whalen on Wednesday, April 10, Lie laid out the issues: The Sperry plant's Administration Building would be fine for the Secretariat and the councils. As for the General Assembly, he would like to use the City Building at Flushing Meadow Park, but the United Nations couldn't afford the expense of remodeling the building. He wanted to know if the city could help.[67]

The city acted fast. Mayor O'Dwyer invited Lie to City Hall the next morning, and after a ten-minute meeting, the plan was set. Within an hour, O'Dwyer had Board of Estimate* Executive Committee approval, and before noon, he announced to the press that the General Assembly would meet rent-free in the City Building at Flushing Meadow Park and the city would spend $1.2 million† to remodel the building and improve the grounds around it; the UN would rent the Sperry plant from the federal government for Secretariat offices and the councils; and it would extend its Hunter-in-the-Bronx lease until mid-August, when necessary modifications to the Sperry facility would be finished.[68]

"Little Orphan Annie" has at last found a home, the *Times* reported on April 13, 1946. Indeed, the long months of hunting for interim space had finally come to an end. But most UN delegates were lukewarm to the plans. "Under the circumstances, the general feeling is that the [temporary] headquarters will have to be housed where it can be housed," was the sentiment of the Chinese delegation, shared by most of the others.[69]

Now the focus turned to the bigger issue—the UN's choice of a permanent home in the suburbs north of New York City.

*The city's Board of Estimate existed until 1990, when a new city charter moved most of its responsibilities to the City Council.
†All dollar amounts throughout the book, unless otherwise noted, are accurate for the time period being addressed.

2
Suburbia Unnerved

On Wednesday, January 30, 1946, with the next day's edition of the *Greenwich Time* about to go to press, the newsroom phone rang. Bernie Yudain, managing editor of the daily paper serving the well-to-do town of Greenwich, Connecticut, took the call. It was Prescott Bush, a Greenwich resident and prominent Wall Street banker,* calling from his Manhattan office. He had just learned something he thought Bernie and his brother, Ted, the editor, might like to know.

When Bernie hung up, he yelled across the newsroom: "Jesus, I've got a beauty . . . we've got to bust open the paper."

"Nobody busts open any paper," his older brother shouted back.

"Well, you will for this one!"

His brother did, making way for a banner headline streaming across the front page: "Greenwich 'Near Top of List' of UNO Sites." Bernie's story, citing a "source of unquestionable reliability," reported that the town of Greenwich was likely to be selected as the new home of the United Nations, part of a forty-two-square-mile swath of land embracing sections of both Fairfield County in Connecticut and Westchester County in New York State.

Bush had gotten hold of a draft report of the site inspection team. While it would not be formally announced until Saturday, the "reve-

---

*Bush, later elected a U.S. Senator from Connecticut, was the father and grandfather, respectively, of Presidents George H.W. Bush and George W. Bush.

lation," Bernie wrote in the *Greenwich Time*, "will come as a veritable bombshell to this town."[1]

Greenwich resident John Gray didn't have to wait to read Bernie's "bombshell" in the next day's paper. An attorney with one of New York's leading law firms, Gray had a friend serving as an advisor to Gavrilovic's site inspection group. His friend called him at his home on the evening of January 30. "John, I want you to know that I was wrong when I told you last month that there was no risk of Greenwich being the UNO headquarters site," he told him. "Your house on Middle Patent Road is slap in the middle."[2]

Meanwhile, James Hopkins, town supervisor of historic North Castle in Westchester County, showed up at the Waldorf Astoria Hotel in Manhattan on January 30. He had heard talk that North Castle was being seriously considered as part of the UN site and now he wanted to see Huntington Gilchrist, an American aide to the inspection group, which was meeting in the hotel. Gilchrist confirmed the report. As disturbed as Hopkins was by the news, something else alarmed him even more. Gilchrist told him an engineer-consultant to the United Nations had prepared a report showing how the forty-two-square-mile site could be extended—to up to 140, or even 172, square miles.[3]

By the time of Gavrilovic's formal announcement three days later, the initial shock of the Fairfield and Westchester townspeople had turned to outrage, and a high-powered, well-organized protest was already under way.

From "Thunderclap" to Protests

The countryside that the United Nations was about to select included some of the region's most valuable and picturesque land, with historic villages dating back to the early 1700s and large estates owned by many of the country's wealthiest and most influential families. Scattered among golf clubs, polo grounds, and riding clubs were the estates of countless corporate magnates, bankers, lawyers, and publishers, including those of *Time* publisher Henry Luce and his wife, Congresswoman Clare Booth Luce; American Telephone and Telegraph president Walter Gifford; and *Washington Post* publisher and soon-to-become president of the World Bank, Eugene Meyer. Benny Goodman, the jazz musician and band leader, lived in the area, as did retired heavyweight boxing champion Gene Tunney.[4]

Even before the choice was announced, Gray and his law partner and neighbor, Wilkie Bushby, had organized a protest movement. They gathered some two hundred Connecticut residents at the Greenwich Country Day School and obtained 930 signatures on a petition that they rushed off to the UN General Assembly in London.[5]

On the New York side of the border, the reaction was no less swift. Hopkins and the supervisors of five nearby towns—from Pound Ridge to Bedford—issued a statement to the press objecting to the site because of its excessive size, the hardship it would pose to residents, and the lack of prior consultation with county and town officials.

The UN decision, Hopkins said, was like a "thunderclap" to residents. "Many families had owned their homes for generations; they could not comprehend why they should be ousted . . . or where they would go."[6]

The seven-man inspection team had made its choice after a dizzying two-week tour of thousands of miles of countryside in the northeastern United States, a trip that had taken them through parts of New Jersey, Massachusetts, Rhode Island, Connecticut, and New York. In all, they looked at some fifteen vast tracts of land, several more than once. They met with governors, mayors, local promoters, and community groups, and received briefings from the Regional Plan Association of New York, New Jersey, and Connecticut. While the U.S. government remained neutral on the choice of a site (the Truman administration wanted to avoid the political ramifications of taking sides), Washington did provide assistance to the team. Allen Dulles from the State Department served as the group's legal counsel, and he was assisted by department staffer Alger Hiss, who had worked on the early plans for UN formation and had been in charge of managing the San Francisco charter conference.[7]

During their whirlwind trip, the inspection group was careful to keep their deliberations confidential. But at one point the opinion of the French team member, Francois Briere, made its way into the Parisian press. He said he thought Hyde Park's "beauty, view of the Hudson and possibility of big buildings along the plateau of the river" made it the only spot that could rival his country's original choice, Geneva. Quickly, news spread around the world that the Roosevelt estate was likely to be selected.[8]

But the chosen spot was not to be Hyde Park. In the end, the UN Committee feared that the estate's connection to the Democratic president would have negative connotations for the country's Republicans at a time the UN needed all the support from the United States that it could muster. "We might be wise not to become involved in a domestic quarrel," Briere, the champion of Hyde Park, reluctantly told his colleagues.[9]

Instead, the UN's more than forty-square-mile choice was centered some thirty-five miles northeast of Manhattan, at approximately the tiny hamlet of Banksville, New York, on the Connecticut–New York border. Slightly more than half the land was in Connecticut, the rest in New York. Some five thousand people lived directly on the tract of land. Dulles and Hiss had assured the United Nations that the federal government would acquire the affected properties for the United Nations through eminent domain.[10]

The inspection group said that residents whose homes were not immediately needed could remain as tenants of the United Nations, and it promised adequate compensation for the property taken and for the loss of tax revenues. But that was of little comfort to those living there. "My home is 150 years old," said ex-boxer Tunney, one of the earliest and most vocal opponents of the UN plan. "Naturally, we are all for the UNO. But so many communities elsewhere are clamoring for the headquarters site, communities that . . . do not have a lot of people who would lose their homes."[11]

The protest group organized by Gray and Bushby came to be known as the "Greenwich People's Committee." Bushby was its chairman, and they asked Amadee Cole, an advertising executive with J. Walter Thompson, to handle the group's publicity. Soon, they called for a town-wide referendum on the matter, and mailed some 21,000 flyers to registered voters telling them how and why to vote against the United Nations coming to Greenwich.[12]

Angry telephone calls poured into town halls. Informal groups sprang up seemingly everywhere, meeting almost round-the-clock in private homes, community rooms, restaurants, and street corners. Opponents used scare tactics and alarmist stories about what would become of Greenwich if the United Nations came to town. A doctor appeared at one meeting to suggest that exotic diseases would be spread by foreign germs, others said camels and maharajahs with elephants would wander the streets, and still others spread the word that nests of spies would live among them.[13] "It will be like living in the middle of a World's Fair!" said the town's tax assessor.[14]

Polls showed residents objected to the UN plan by as much as seven-to-one. Yet, there were pockets of support for the United Nations. The "sort of nice, gentle liberals, you know," Bernie Yudain said later.[15]

Alton Ketchum, who lived in the quiet, historic Greenwich neighborhood of Cos Cob, was one of them. A self-described "internationalist," Ketchum—a former United Press foreign correspondent and now in the advertising business—said he personally could see no other course than to support the UN coming into the area. "The debates were really hot," he remembered, "Whewww . . . you have no idea the bitterness."[16]

The Macy chain of newspapers in Westchester, including the *White Plains Reporter Dispatch*,[17] came out in support of the UN, and a contingent of Greenwich businesspeople, recognizing the UN could be good for the local economy, began to openly support the choice.[18]

This troubled Cole, whose PR campaign was taking hold with almost every other Greenwich constituency. With the referendum on the UN plan scheduled for March 2, Cole couldn't risk letting the pro-UN business sentiment grow, so he resorted to what he called a simple little "trick."

"We hired two 'Syrians,'" he recalled many years later. "One of them had a fez and neither of them could speak Syrian . . . the other was an Irishman. We gave them cameras, chalk, tape measures and on Saturday morning, they entered the business district . . . went down Greenwich Avenue . . . and they would talk back and forth in pig Latin to each other."

One acted as if he were surveying buildings, Cole explained, while the other drew chalk marks on the sidewalk. When shopkeepers asked what they were doing, "They would shake their heads and just go on measuring things," he remembered.

The sentiment within the business district began to turn around. "That was $50 well spent," Cole boasted of the sum he paid the two men. "I think it bought us probably several hundred votes on the referendum."[19]

Towns started to turn against each other. When the Greenwich referendum to oppose the UN plans passed handily, the neighboring town of Stamford, Connecticut, let it be known that it would welcome the United Nations even if Greenwich would not. The Greenwich People's Committee quickly shot back with the threat of another round of protests and pamphlet mailings, this time in Stamford. "It's none of Greenwich's business," snapped Stamford First Selectman George Barrett, who called the Greenwich referendum "a case of insolent snobbery and a narrow-minded and bigoted view. . . . If they [the UN] are going to be pushed around by this little group, what chance have they got to settle a squabble in the Balkans?"[20]

New Team, Fresh Start

Increasingly, UN delegates and staff members—now arriving in New York City as they prepared to set up shop at Hunter-in-the-Bronx—

were disturbed and confused by the reports of antagonism toward the United Nations. Gavrilovic seemed baffled. "You should have seen the . . . deputations which came to London, all begging that we choose their areas," he said, recalling the presentations he chaired at Church House just months earlier. "The present change in attitude I can only attribute to international differences."[21]

Secretary General Lie, too, was troubled by the suburban reaction, and he blamed the UN's process itself. He thought the inspection team had been forced to squeeze too much work into too few weeks, and had had little time to deal with residents' concerns.[22] By the late spring of 1946, less than four months after the Greenwich Time's "bombshell" headline, the UN General Assembly had formed a new committee—nine members this time, and now called the "Headquarters Commission." This team was headed by a congenial, distinguished-looking Briton, Sir Angus Fletcher. Sir Angus was committed to being a good listener. He said he wanted to hear all the local citizens' points of view.

As a member of Fletcher's team, the French government selected a celebrated, influential modernist architect named Charles-Edouard Jeanneret. Known as Le Corbusier, or simply "Corbu," the fifty-eight-year-old designer was an icon of his time. Born in Switzerland but a French citizen for many years, he was recognized throughout the world for his visionary buildings and prolific writing on urban planning. The eccentric and often cantankerous Corbu was proud of his UN appointment and he took up his duties with great enthusiasm.[23]

The Russians, too, sent a highly regarded representative to join the Fletcher team. Nikolai Bassov, a structural engineer, was well known in engineering circles for his World War II endeavors, when he headed a mass transfer of Soviet factories to the Ural Mountains in the face of a German invasion. The stocky, middle-aged Russian was asked to join Le Corbusier in heading two subcommittees looking into basic space and building requirements of the UN headquarters. The two men conversed only through interpreters, but they got along well together and their conclusions—not made public for several months—would prove of considerable interest not only to their commission colleagues, but to Fairfield and Westchester residents and to New York City officials as well.[24]

The new UN team represented a "fresh start" for the concerned suburbanites, who were particularly relieved when Sir Angus announced that his men would look at sites as small as just two square miles. While he said the UN still held out the possibility of a larger forty-square-mile site, discussion of a smaller option calmed residents' nerves, and initial meetings with the new commission were cordial.

But within just a few weeks, a level of frustration began to build, bubbling over at the second meeting of the new UN team and a group of Connecticut representatives on Thursday, June 27. In an act of goodwill, the Connecticut group—appointed by Governor Raymond Baldwin and headed by Kingsley Gillespie, publisher of the *Stamford Advocate*—traveled to Secretariat offices at Hunter College in the Bronx for the meeting. They were divided on the question of the United Nations moving into their neighborhood, but they had resolved to put their differences aside for the day, and simply try to help the new UN team with its task.

"We are at your service," Gillespie announced as the meeting opened.

The distinguished-looking Le Corbusier, in his signature bow tie and heavy round-rimmed eyeglasses, suggested that the Connecticut visitors point out on a wall map the places that it felt would be best for the United Nations. When no one came forward, he tried again. "I asked the Secretariat to provide us with some pencils and crayon," he explained, "and if any of [you] gentlemen would kindly draw on the map . . . I think it would be helpful."

But the Connecticut representatives pointed out that it was difficult to do that, considering the wide range of sizes being studied, and besides, one of them said, "We do not know much about what the area will include in the way of railroads, airports, buildings, etc. Could you give us an idea?"

The UN team responded that first it wanted to know of some suggested sites. Le Corbusier: "I wish members would draw on the map . . . You went through a lot of trouble to come here [to Hunter College] . . . I think it would be excellent . . . it would be a good idea that each one mark with the charcoal a certain place, and give us some facts about it."

Finally, Gillespie came forward with his crayon. "I am ready to draw a place of eight to twelve miles . . ." he began, before he was stopped by a fellow committee member who reminded him that half of the Connecticut contingent was opposed to having a United Nations site of *any* size *anywhere* in Connecticut.

Gillespie objected. ". . . If you do not think they are wanted . . . it is not the time to talk about that today!"

"It seems to me we are just where we started from," Le Corbusier quipped. The meeting adjourned.[25]

"Three Tailors of Tooley Street"

At the end of July 1946, the Fletcher commission announced it had narrowed its choice to fifteen specific sites, ranging from a compact two-square-mile tract at Harrison and Rye in New York to a forty-square-mile area that was almost identical to the original Fairfield/Westchester site considered earlier in the year.[26]

Greenwich People's Committee chairman Wilkie Bushby, who had been confident the United Nations "wouldn't repeat its old mistakes," was stunned. Of the fifteen sites suggested, Greenwich was included in seven of them. "It is difficult to understand how the United Nations could again be considering [Greenwich]," he said, and he vowed to fight the United Nations "by every lawful means."[27]

On the New York side of the border, too, the news brought a furious reaction. "I will fight to the last ditch to keep the United Nations away, and my friends will do likewise," said Helen Frick, daughter of the wealthy industrialist Henry Clay Frick and owner of a large estate in the affluent town of Bedford.[28]

Sir Angus remained unflappable, and announced he would begin a "listening tour" in the communities. His commission prepared a fourteen-point questionnaire that asked town leaders how the UN presence might affect their neighborhoods.

Greenwich leaders were ready with a long list of answers. They cited serious problems of "water supply, sewage disposal, transportation, highway traffic, recreational facilities, education, future growth of the town, condemnation proceedings, and displaced persons."[29]

The United Nations seemed to get the message. When it announced its five final choices two weeks later, Connecticut was not among them. The two- to forty-square-mile sites were all in New York State, in Westchester County—areas in and around Harrison, Yorktown, Somers, and Cortlandt.[30]

Now, the ensuing uproar from Westchester residents made the earlier Greenwich protests look cordial. Opposition groups sprang up in virtually every Westchester town. At raucous gatherings in overpacked meeting halls, petitions were signed, resolutions passed, and polls taken, all showing overwhelming opposition to the UN plans. At a stormy meeting in Harrison, only one out of 120 voters sided with the United Nations, and a county-wide group, The United Westchester Citizens Committee to Save our Homes, stepped forward to take legal action—to the U.S. Supreme Court if necessary, it said.[31]

Fletcher and UN commission members sat in on the turbulent meetings. In Yorktown, one resident hollered out that the United Nations would bring nothing but "racetracks, touts and brothels," to which the ever-composed Sir Angus finally rose to object. "I want to congratulate you on the fine, healthy democratic meeting you are conducting . . . but don't think our people live solely for night clubs. It is not a fair inference." At the end of the evening, the vote was 293 to 85 against the UN plans.[32]

But it was in Somers—a town that prides itself in being the "home of the circus," the birthplace of Hachaliah Bailey—where tempers finally flared out of control. Some eight hundred residents literally howled down a United Nations' legal adviser, an American named William Roseborough, when he tried to answer their questions. He could not be heard above the hissing and booing and he finally gave up. When a vote was taken, only twelve in the room wanted the United Nations to come to their town, and the evening left more than one observer wondering what Bailey would have thought of the performance.[33]

The United Nations did have supporters in Westchester, albeit quieter. When the particularly vocal Harrison's People's Committee sprang up to "represent the people" in opposing the United Nations, the Reverend William Prunty of the town's St. Gregory Parish cabled Sir Angus: "Many years ago in London, there were three tailors of Tooley Street who believed they had a common grievance against the crown. They prepared an elegant petition and it opened, 'We the people of England . . .' and that incident is since known as the 'three tailors of Tooley Street.'"

Sir Angus cabled back the same day: "The entrance of the three tailors of Tooley Street into our rather baffling problem has done much to relieve the burden of my day, and I am very grateful to you."[34]

Increasingly, the U.S. State Department was being called on to abandon its position of neutrality and get involved in the search. Secretary General Lie himself sought guidance from Senator Warren Austin, U.S. delegate to the United Nations, when he visited Austin at his Vermont home during the summer. Lie later wrote that all he got was "a wealth of information on the crossing and grafting of the apple trees in his beloved orchard, but not a hint of his stand on the Headquarters question."[35]

In Westchester, both sides soon called on the federal government to step in. Harrison's UN supporters sent a telegram to President Truman likening the U.S. position to that of a host who invites an overnight guest and then tells him to "locate his own lodgings."[36] Harrison opponents announced they were heading to Washington to voice their concerns to anyone who would listen. And a coalition of eleven national organizations, led by the American Association for the United Nations (AAUN) and including the International Chamber of Commerce, League of Women's Voters, American Jewish Committee, and American Veterans Committee, called on President Truman to appoint a U.S. "high commissioner" to aid in the problem of establishing the United Nations in the United States. Signed by the head of the AAUN, Clark Eichelberger, the highly publicized letter read, "The confusion which has arisen . . . with the consequent impression that areas in the United States are hostile to the United Nations, could result in a situation that would be a national disgrace if not met satisfactorily by the intervention of the Federal Government."[37]

3

Cosmopolitan Charm

While the suburbanites were hissing and booing and "fighting to the last ditch" to keep the UN out of their midst, New York City found itself with a problem of a different sort. Mayor O'Dwyer had hoped that Nelson Rockefeller was right—that by hosting the United Nations temporarily, the delegates would warm to the city and want to stay permanently. But it wasn't working out that way. To the contrary, the United Nations' first weeks in New York brought a chorus of complaints from the foreign visitors. Cramped office quarters scattered all around Manhattan, traffic hassles, inadequate hotel accommodations with less-than-friendly staff, the city's high costs, and continuing inhospitable treatment from the Hunter-in-the-Bronx students made for some serious discontent among the UN staff.

The city was on the defensive and officials worried that New York's reputation around the world was being damaged. A report prepared for Grover Whalen warned that with New York now on the "world stage," it was in the "interests of the city and its citizens to have the . . . visitors return to their homes applauding New York," not finding fault with it.[1] O'Dwyer said the city had to show the UN that it was "not a distant, impersonal metropolis, and not . . . too big, cold and inconsiderate."[2]

Clearly, if the city held out any hope of becoming the permanent home to the United Nations, it was going to have to come up with a new strategy.

Rich and Famous Lend a Hand

In late March 1946, O'Dwyer sent a telegram to hundreds of New York's most prominent businessmen, philanthropists, and leaders in the entertainment industry: "It gives me great pleasure to appoint you a member of the 'United Nations Committee of the City of New York,'" the cable read, and it asked the recipients to get back to Whalen with their acceptance.[3]

Almost overnight, the city had more than one thousand of its best and brightest ready to work to persuade the foreign guests that New York wasn't such a bad place after all. From the New York Times publisher Arthur Hays Sulzberger, to retailing giant Bernard Gimbel, banker Winthrop Aldrich, RCA's David Sarnoff, and Broadway producer Billy Rose—all were on board with the mission of bringing the UN to New York. Even John D. Rockefeller Jr., Nelson's father and patriarch of the wealthy family, made an exception to his policy of refraining from committee memberships. "Of late years, I have found it necessary to decline, practically without exception, membership on all committees," the seventy-two-year-old Rockefeller wrote Whalen. "However, because I feel that in the UNO lies the hope of the world and that every citizen should do his utmost to support it, I am happy to accept the committee membership thus offered."[4]

O'Dwyer chaired the committee, Nelson Rockefeller served as a vice chairman, and Robert Moses headed a group to deal with office space and housing issues, the "Committee on Plan and Scope."[5]

Soon, many of the city's society-page names joined the crusade. Harriet Aldrich, wife of Winthrop Aldrich and Nelson Rockefeller's aunt, was named to head a women's group, and Eleanor Roosevelt was honorary chair. Scores of New York's most socially prominent women pitched in, including Mrs. Vincent Astor, Mrs. Walter Hoving, Mrs. Cornelius Vanderbilt, Mrs. Ogden Reid, the wives of three of the Rockefeller brothers, Nelson, John, and David, and the women's mother-in-law, Mrs. John D. Rockefeller Jr. And the gossip columnist and celebrated party-giver, Elsa Maxwell, added her own special flair to the cause.[6]

The women entertained UN staff and their families at teas, luncheons, cocktail parties, dinners, and even weekend stays at their country homes. They invited them to Broadway shows, the opera and concerts, and arranged to have the city's best galleries and museums open their doors for private showings. They hosted parties at the American Museum of Natural History's Hayden Planetarium, the Metropolitan Museum of Art's Cloisters, and the Museum of Modern Art, and a formal supper dance for the UN guests was a highlight of New York's spring social season. Like so many events for the UN guests, it was held at the Waldorf Astoria Hotel.[7]

The Waldorf Astoria, in fact, played a special role in helping to keep the top UN folks happy in New York. Not only was the luxury hotel the venue for many social events, but it was where higher-level visiting UN workers usually lodged, and many of its suites had been converted into temporary offices for the world organization. But more significant, perhaps, was the fact that the hotel's owner and operator, Lucius Boomer, was married to a Norwegian-born American, Jorgine, known as "Georgia." The Boomers were well connected in New York society, and with Georgia's Norway ties to the Lies, the couple took it upon themselves to introduce the Secretary General and his wife, Hjordis, to some of the most influential people in town. "These two dear friends received us with a warmth and enthusiasm that is hard to describe," Lie later said of the couple. "The Boomers seemed to regard it as their special mission to make us acquainted with . . . leading figures in business, politics and industry—men and women whose support could mean much for the United Nations."[8]

Elsa Maxwell, too, introduced the Lies to her circle of friends. She once took the couple and their young daughters, Guri and Metta, to a performance at Carnegie Hall, where she brought the handsome young Frank Sinatra to their box for a chat. Unfortunately, Lie misheard the introduction and thought the popular singer was Maxwell's son, until his embarrassed daughters, in their early twenties, interjected to straighten him out.[9]

Nelson Rockefeller and his wife, Tod, made a regular practice of entertaining UN men and their wives with dinner and performances at Radio City Music Hall, always with a backstage visit to chat with the Rockettes and Corps de Ballet dancers.[10]

But it was Mrs. Vanderbilt who hosted the international visitors at what became the most publicized, and undoubtedly grandest, party of them all—a five-course formal candlelight dinner at her twenty-eight-room mansion, a French Renaissance–style home at 1048 Fifth Avenue, an event that ended up as a picture story in *Life* magazine.[11]

Some practical assistance came from Mrs. Aldrich's women, as well. Working out of space provided rent-free at the exclusive Metropolitan Club on East Sixtieth Street, they enlisted volunteers to answer basic questions for the newcomers, such as how to hire a babysitter, where to shop for a sari, and where to buy baklava. An information center set up at the Commodore Hotel on East Forty-second Street, and later in a bigger space on Duffy Square at Broadway and Forty-seventh Street, offered everything from package-wrapping services to a desk where Broadway producers gave away free tickets, a particularly appealing perk in mid-1946, with Irving Berlin's "Annie Get Your Gun" premiering on stage and Rodgers and Hammerstein's "Carousel" and "Oklahoma" enjoying long runs.[12]

Housing Dilemma

But parties and theater tickets were not enough. The UN staff needed places to live. The hotel situation had turned messy. Some hotels were not keeping to their commitment to hold rooms for the United Nations, and reports of discrimination began to circulate. Hundreds of homeowners in Queens and Nassau County finally answered an urgent plea to rent out spare rooms to the UN employees, while Moses worked on longer term housing needs, for the three to five years the UN was expected to be in New York.

Moses focused on Queens. He devised a plan for a privately financed apartment complex on a forty-acre undeveloped site adjoining Kew Gardens. The land was conveniently located midway between the Sperry plant in Lake Success and the City Building at Flushing Meadow. A group of twenty mutual savings banks financed the project, called Parkway Village, and construction of the 685-unit colonial-style development began in the summer of 1946. The United Nations leased the entire complex for three years, with an option for another two. It then sublet the apartments to its delegates and staff.* Veterans groups protested the exclusive deal with the United Nations because, they said, at least some of the Parkway Village apartments should have been held for returning GIs.[13] Still, the city paved the way for the UN to enter into agreements for even more apartment space. At a large New York Life Insurance project being built on the old Fresh Meadow Golf Course in Jamaica, Queens, some of the first units were reserved for UN renters. On Long Island, apartments were rented to UN staff in new buildings going up at Great Neck Plaza in Great Neck and hundreds of rooms were leased at the Lido Beach Hotel, a Moorish-style place in Long Beach. And, in Manhattan, some 600 units in Metropolitan Life's huge new housing

---

*One of the earliest residents of Parkway Village was the UN's Ralph Bunche, winner of the 1950 Nobel Peace Prize and later Under Secretary General for Special Political Affairs.

complex on the Lower East Side, Peter Cooper Village, were set aside for the UN, a deal that later would prove controversial.[14]

Now, with the UN's immediate housing needs easing, with New York's elite entertaining the foreign guests regularly and lavishly, and with the remodeling jobs for temporary office and meeting space moving along on schedule, O'Dwyer and Moses turned their attention to longer-range plans.

Flushing Meadow Park, Second Time Around

Despite the fact that the United Nations had narrowed its choice for a permanent site to five multi-mile tracts of land in Westchester County, the city was quietly moving ahead with a plan to offer the UN one-half of a square mile, 350 acres, in Queens. It was the same Flushing Meadow Park location the UN had flatly rejected earlier in the year. But this time, the city's proposal would be fully designed with new buildings, roadways, and landscaping.

Moses, in particular, was determined to make the case for Flushing Meadow Park. For years, he had been trying to reinvent the park, a plot of land that had never fully recovered from a less than glamorous past. In the early 1900s, the once peaceful meadow on the banks of Flushing Bay had the misfortune of being turned into a huge dump for burning all the garbage of Brooklyn. It came to be known as the "Corona Dumps" and had become a symbol of society's decay, the "valley of ashes" in Scott Fitzgerald's 1925 novel *The Great Gatsby*.

In the mid-1930s, Moses, then city park commissioner, had seized on the idea to clear the dump and fill it in for the site of the 1939 World's Fair. Grover Whalen had been president of the Fair and he recalled that when he turned over a "shovelful of hardened muck" at the Fair's ground-breaking ceremony in 1936, "it was half tidal silt and half refuse. Beyond and above the smell, which was evil enough, there were mosquitoes of a size you couldn't believe existed."[15] And Moses famously said the rats at the dump were "big enough to wear saddles."[16]

Still, the grounds had been magically transformed into gardens, lakes, futuristic buildings, and breathtaking sculpture for the enormously popular Fair. But after the Fair closed in late 1940, the land began to deteriorate, its trees and shrubs dying, and even the rats were coming back.[17] Developing the land for the United Nations was an expedient solution to the problem.

Behind closed doors, Moses put together a high-powered architectural group to work on the offer. Once again, he chose Embury and Harrison, both of whom had worked on the World's Fair plans and on the city's original UN proposal. But this time he added Gilmore Clark and John Hogan to the team. Clark had designed the Fair's landscaping, and Hogan was with the engineering firm Parsons Brinkerhoff, which had devised the network of roads for the Fair.

The city planned to keep its proposal confidential until the fall of 1946, when it would be unveiled to UN delegates as they arrived for the opening General Assembly session. Planning was so tightly held that the president of the Queens Chamber of Commerce, James Lundy, had heard nothing about it when he started to try to lure the state-sponsored World Trade Center to his borough's Flushing Meadow Park. On learning of Lundy's plans, Moses put a stop to it with a letter to Lundy that soon made its way into the press. By July 15, Moses' UN work no longer was a secret.[18]

About the same time, San Francisco, too, was involved in some behind-the-scenes work. In August, a San Francisco banker, Belford Brown, quietly checked into the Waldorf Astoria to begin what he called an "underground movement" on behalf of San Francisco's Mayor Lapham. Buttonholing UN delegates wherever he could find them, Brown let it be known that his city was prepared to offer the UN several sites, each one larger than New York's 350 acres. Soon, Lapham himself came to town, and then California's Governor Earl Warren.[19]

San Francisco's renewed bid opened up the floodgates to others, and suddenly, once again, the United Nations found itself deluged with propaganda from cities all over the country. Many were the same locales that had lobbied so intensely in London months earlier.

Still Bound for Westchester

Reports of New York's "secret" plan and renewed offers from around the country didn't distract Sir Angus and the UN Headquarters Commission members. During the late summer of 1946, they prepared their formal report to the General Assembly on the five final Westchester County choices. The Assembly, scheduled to meet in October, could either approve the Commission's recommendations or choose another location altogether.

In mid-September, the Commission sent Lie an advance copy of its 142-page report. The Secretary General had long understood the troublesome aspects of proposing a multi-mile enclave, and now, he was particularly struck by something he read in the report. He sent a memo to Sir Angus: "... I note that although the report was adopted 'nemine contradicente' [unanimously], the Annexes include two Special Opinions of the French and U.S.S.R. members."[20]

Indeed, Le Corbusier and Nikolai Bassov, the illustrious French architect and the Russian engineer, each had written a minority view on the gigantic tracts of land that were being considered. In a long illustrated analysis of the requirements of the United Nations, Le Corbusier said that such a large site was not necessary: "... our needs are for one square mile," he concluded.[21] And Bassov questioned a large site that would create a "rural, new city."[22]

Westchester residents applauded. And New York City officials, too, might have praised Le Corbusier's finding were it not for another observation in his special report: "... Flushing Meadow is not the site for the headquarters of the United Nations because Flushing Meadow is inescapably a suburb of New York ... to implant its headquarters in the very shadow of the skyscrapers of Manhattan is inadmissible," he said, and he went on to call New York "terrifying" and "menacing. . . . We are not wrong in keeping at a distance."[23]

Moses fired off a letter to the *New York Times* objecting to Le Corbusier's opinions.[24] "Caustic," he once called the architect.

Even more irritating to Moses were the recurring, less than flattering, comments about Flushing Meadow's past as a filled-in garbage dump. The Headquarters Commission let it be known that it was concerned not only about nasty marsh odors that were said to float above the former dump, but there was talk that unstable ground conditions on the landfill would not support large buildings.[25]

Moses was not sure where the reports were coming from. "A good many laymen who don't know a pile from a spread footing have suddenly become foundation experts and authorities on subsoil conditions," he shot back. "To those of us who ... have had to wrestle with infinitely more difficult foundation problems on the East and West Sides of Manhattan Island, the gloomy predictions of these critics are so much vapor."[26]

Still, the foundation issue was not to be put to rest.

Golden Key and a Formal Offer

By the late summer of 1946, arrangements for the UN's temporary New York stay were moving ahead and Secretariat employees relocated from their Hunter-in-the-Bronx offices to the converted Sperry plant at Lake Success. The Security Council's move to Lake Success wasn't quite so easy. Much of the Council's Hunter-in-the-Bronx home had to be dismantled to be reused at the Sperry plant—especially the vital communications equipment—and the Council was forced to wait out the reinstallation at yet another interim location, the ballroom of the Henry Hudson Hotel on West Fifty-seventh Street, a boxy twenty-four-floor structure originally built in 1929 to house the American Women's Association.

But transformation of the City Building in Flushing Meadow Park from skating rink to General Assembly Hall went smoothly, and on Friday, October 18, 1946, five days before the Assembly was to open, the city turned over the building's key to the UN in a ceremony that gave the public the first glimpse of the remodeled hall—a panoply of color with blue velour-draped walls and some three thousand seats upholstered in pink, blue, and green. Behind a huge rostrum hung a sixty-by-forty-foot gold and blue illuminated world map, a north polar projection that had been designed as a delegates' badge for the San Francisco conference but soon was to become the United Nations' distinctive logo.[27]

It was the Manhattan borough president, Vincent Impellitteri, who turned over the city's foot-long golden key to Lie. Mayor O'Dwyer was in California under doctor's orders to rest after the death of his wife, Catherine, and his own health concerns. "May I repeat, in Mayor O'Dwyer's own words, that the United Nations is heartily and unreservedly welcome in New York City," Impellitteri told the delegation.[28]

He then presented Lie with an elaborate brochure of renderings, photographs, and sketches—the city's formal offer of Moses' fully re-designed Flushing Meadow Park as the site of the UN's permanent quarters.

The proposal called for the City Building to be razed to make way for a domed General Assembly Hall that would be connected to two long low-rise buildings, with another building to house UN missions. A ceremonial entrance drive would lead motorists from the Grand Central Parkway to a courtyard and pylon-bordered plaza at the foot of the General Assembly. The 350 acres were offered as a gift, which the city said was worth some $7 million on top of $20 million that had been spent when the grounds were converted from a dump to the World's Fair site. The proposed cost of construction of the buildings, to be paid by the United Nations, was estimated at $65 million.[29]

Showing off the Town

Its offer now public, New York City kept pouring on the charm. Hundreds of delegates were arriving for the General Assembly session, set to open October 23. Many were coming to New York for the first time, and the city saw a chance to show them just how warm and friendly New Yorkers can be. Grover Whalen boarded the RMS *Queen Elizabeth* at her Hudson River pier and shook hands with some 150 arriving delegates. At La Guardia Field, the city worked with Pan American Airways to turn a hangar into a reception hall where city officials met the delegates and sped them through immigration and customs clearances. Hotels were on the alert to treat the visitors with special care. And on the Sunday before the session opened, the cover of the *New York Times Magazine* featured a well-timed story by Robert Moses with a personal appeal to the UN to come to Flushing Meadow Park. In making his case, Moses dismissed the UN's choice of a big enclave in Westchester County: "The disadvantages of a great international compound . . . are so obvious that they hardly require extended comment," he wrote. And then he ruled out another location that was beginning to be rumored as a preference by some delegates. The United Nations should not be located in Midtown Manhattan, he said: "Certainly this would not be a proper, dignified and practical location in the light of congestion, atmosphere and cost." The only spot for the United Nations, he assured readers, was Flushing Meadow Park in the borough of Queens.[30]

Yet, on Wednesday morning of the opening General Assembly session, when the city's charm offensive was to go into high gear, it was played out almost entirely in Manhattan. Grover Whalen arranged for a motorcade of ninety-six cars and four buses to deliver the delegates to the City Building in Queens via a route through the heart of Manhattan. Led by a limousine carrying Whalen, Lie, Soviet delegate Andrei Gromyko, and Assembly President Paul Henri Spaak of Belgium, the procession started at the Waldorf Astoria and made its way to Bowling Green where they were joined by mounted police and the Fort Jay Army Band for a ticker tape parade up lower Broadway, then a stop at City Hall, and back uptown to the Waldorf Astoria for lunch before finally heading to Queens. There, President Truman awaited the delegates in the converted skating rink, where he formally welcomed the world body to the United States, and Impellitteri proudly proclaimed, "New York City today has become the center of the hopes of the world."

Then it was right back to Midtown Manhattan again, where President

Truman and the first lady, Bess Truman, hosted an evening reception in the Waldorf Astoria's Starlight Room.[31]

The partying continued. The following Saturday, Nelson Rockefeller and his wife, Tod, invited one thousand delegates and notable New Yorkers to a luncheon at their spacious Pocantico Hills estate in the woodlands north of Tarrytown, New York. After most of the chauffeur-driven cars got lost in the maze of country roads, leaving only about 350 to enjoy Rockefeller's extravagant lunch of "typical American fare,"[32] Robert Moses—one guest who did find his way—began to think it was time for a change. "The top people at the United Nations are, I believe, fed up with the endless dinners, dances and entertainment," he wrote to a friend, as invitations to yet another ball at the Waldorf Astoria were about to be mailed.

Moses decided a different style of entertainment was in order. He had learned that the Secretary General was an avid hunter, a favorite sport since Lie's teenage years back in Norway. So Moses arranged for Lie to go duck hunting on Long Island. It was better, Moses told a friend, than "a lot of superfluous food and drink and endless speeches and ceremonies."[33]

At the same time, some wealthy New Yorkers found a quite practical way to make Lie feel at home: They bought him one. Lie had been staying at the Waldorf Astoria since arriving in New York, but with a wife and two daughters, and entertainment obligations that came with his position, he needed a more permanent place to live. In the fall of 1946, Winthrop Aldrich and his friends bought a house in Forest Hills, Queens, that they then rented to the United Nations for the Secretary General's use. Located at 123 Greenway North, the fourteen-room brown brick and granite structure with a turret had been built in 1925 for Albert Armour, inventor of the telephone booth door. It was called Granston Tower. Nelson Rockefeller, then president of the Museum of Modern Art, arranged for Lie to furnish the house with his choice of art loaned from MOMA.[34]

At times it seemed there was nothing New York City wouldn't do to make the UN feel welcome.

Starting the Search All over Again

When Lie addressed the General Assembly at its opening session, he referred to the first months of the United Nations as a "wandering existence."[35] Indeed, over the past year and a half, the United Nations had met at the Opera House in San Francisco, Church House and Central

Hall in London, Hunter College in the Bronx, the Henry Hudson Hotel in Manhattan, and now in the old skating rink in Queens and a former factory on Long Island. And so when the United States finally reversed its "neutral" stance and agreed to take on a bigger role in helping the UN find a permanent home, the delegates wholeheartedly welcomed the news. "We have missed you," the Iraqi, Awny el-Khalidi, said to his U.S. counterparts.[36]

But within a few weeks, some were wondering if the United Nations wasn't better off without the U.S. help. Very quickly, the whole question seemed to have been turned upside down. On November 1, U.S. delegate Warren Austin proposed that in addition to the Westchester sites, New York City's Flushing Meadow Park and the Crystal Springs area south of San Francisco should be given serious consideration.[37] The Ukrainians then moved to include locations in Europe as well. The British objected to the U.S. proposal and the U.S. objected to the Ukrainian proposal. The Russians sided with the Ukrainians. Four days later, the British did an "about-face" and urged that the field be opened up to include even more U.S. cities than the United States itself was proposing.[38]

And so it was that on November 18, 1946, a newly organized subcommittee of eighteen men boarded a train bound for Philadelphia to begin the search for a permanent United Nations home all over again. From Philadelphia, a chartered American Airlines DC-4 shuttled them across the continent to San Francisco, back to Boston and on to New York. This time, they were led by the chairman of the Assembly's Permanent Headquarters Committee, an affable Colombian named Eduardo Zuleta Angel. Le Corbusier and Nikolai Bassov again were part of the inspection team, which, for the first time included a representative of the United States, Isaac Stokes, a State Department employee.[39]

By the time they completed their inspections two weeks later, they had toured Philadelphia's Belmont-Roxborough area; San Francisco's Presidio, an Army base in park-like grounds overlooking the bay, and nearby Crystal Springs; the Blue Hills and sites in Framingham and the North Shore near Boston; and in the New York area, Flushing Meadow Park, White Plains and Harrison, as well as Mohansic Park on the Taconic Parkway in Westchester County's Yorktown. Mohansic Park had been a last-minute suggestion of a Westchester group, eager to find any opportunity to reduce the amount of private land the United Nations might take if it settled in their county.[40]

Once again, the UN inspectors' conclusion was less than decisive. They reported they were equally enamored with two of the sites—Philadelphia's Belmont-Roxborough section and the Presidio in San Francisco. But on one point, they were clear: New York City's Flushing Meadow Park was no longer in the running.

Just a few weeks earlier, New York City officials had seemed confident in the prospects for the Queens site. On November 6, in fact, Moses had organized a meeting to finalize project costs and work out a detailed construction schedule.[41] But discontent with New York had been growing among the UN visitors. The lack of adequate office space was particularly irritating. Nelson Rockefeller, who kept in close touch with many of the delegates, repeatedly warned O'Dwyer and Moses that deficient office space was impairing chances the UN would stay in the city.[42]

And many delegates were echoing Le Corbusier's opinion of Flushing Meadow—that the UN shouldn't be in what he had called "inescapably a suburb of New York . . . in the very shadow of Manhattan."

But in the end, it was Flushing Meadow Park's former past as the "Corona Dumps" that doomed it.

When O'Dwyer, Moses, and Whalen joined twenty-six other city leaders to make one final appeal to the United Nations on Saturday, November 30, they were pointedly asked about the "ground conditions" of the former garbage refuse. O'Dwyer and Moses remained puzzled by the UN's fixation with the soil issue. Only later did they learn that the UN, with the help of the U.S. State Department, had hired an engineer, Lazarus White, who raised questions about the feasibility of building on the filled-in "soft" land. O'Dwyer immediately cabled the Secretary of State: "I am astonished that we were not given an opportunity to see and refute these statements."[43]

Two days later, the United States announced that President Truman would ask Congress to offer the Army's Presidio to the United Nations free of charge. Like other delegations, the Russians—long opposed to a West Coast location—interpreted the offer as an indication that the U.S. government supported San Francisco. At a December 5 session of the Headquarters Committee, the Soviet's representative, Georgi Saksin, charged the United States with "maneuvering," and interfering "inexcusably" with the site debate. In an angry tirade that brought a sudden hush to the stunned delegates, Saksin said, "The U.S.S.R. delegation will not, under any circumstances, countenance the selection of the San Francisco site, and will not go there." If the United Nations were to move to California, he said, it would become a second rate organization with only second-rate delegates whose efforts "cannot lead to anything."[44]

Once again, for more times than anyone cared to count, the debate had reached an impasse.

The chaotic, topsy-turvy disputes were reported daily in the city's press. So New York real estate developer William Zeckendorf was well aware of the controversy. But on Friday, December 6, as he sat at the breakfast table of his Upper East Side apartment reading the *Times* story of the past day's bitter squabble, it occurred to him that maybe he himself had a spot for the UN headquarters. He turned to his wife, Marion, and said, "I'm going to put those bastards on the platform!"

"Which bastards on what platform?" she asked.

"The U.N.—I am going to put them on the platform over the slaughterhouses!"

"Oh, my God, how are you going to do that?"

Indeed, the idea seemed like a long shot, at best. William Zeckendorf's firm, Webb & Knapp, held an option to buy one of Manhattan's most unsightly properties—roughly six blocks of dirty, smelly slaughterhouses and old tenements between the East River and First Avenue, on landfill that once was a little cove called Turtle Bay. Zeckendorf had hoped to build a huge multi-use development on the site, to be raised up on a platform over street level. Now, with his plans coming together slowly, and his option to buy the land expiring in just five days, he thought maybe he could interest the United Nations in the land.

Zeckendorf had no immediate response to his wife's incredulous reaction. "I wasn't sure just how we would pull it off," he later wrote. But he would start with a call to the mayor's office.[45]

4

Rockefellers to the Rescue

By Saturday, December 7, 1946, Mayor O'Dwyer had come to realize that the 350 acres in Flushing Meadow Park were not going to be chosen as the "center of the world." It appeared that Philadelphia would be selected the following week, when the General Assembly's Headquarters Committee was scheduled to take up the question once again.

Still, O'Dwyer refused to concede. He asked Moses to come up with some last-minute alternatives. Moses found five: Governors Island, just off the tip of Manhattan and then serving as home of the U.S. First Army (President Truman was willing to give away the Army's Presidio in San Francisco, so it was assumed he would do the same for Governors Island); an area south of Washington Square bounded roughly by West Third and Houston streets, and McDougal and Wooster; the Midtown Manhattan slaughterhouse land that William Zeckendorf had phoned O'Dwyer about just the day before; a Flushing Meadow site, vastly expanded from 350 to 550 acres; and a portion of the Rockefeller family's 3,300-acre estate at Pocantico Hills, on the Hudson River north of New York City. In a memo to O'Dwyer, Moses wrote, "I don't know if Mr. Rockefeller would entertain the idea of giving this area to the UN," but if it were deemed a serious solution, he said, "I should be glad to talk to one of the Rockefeller sons about this."[1]

Pocantico Hills Takes a Turn

Three days later—on Tuesday morning, December 10—when John D. Rockefeller Jr., the head of the Rockefeller fortune, arrived at the family's suite of offices on the fifty-sixth floor of Rockefeller Center's RCA Building, he was told that his sons Nelson and Laurance (Nelson's younger brother) were eager to see him.

He wasn't able to meet with them until shortly after noon. "The boys then proposed the offer of the Rockwood Hall property in Tarrytown," their father recounted, in a memorandum he wrote some days later.[2]

The Rockwood Hall area that Nelson and Laurance were talking about was a two-hundred-acre portion of the family's lush, rambling Pocantico Hills estate. It had been the property of their great uncle, William Rockefeller, younger brother of the late patriarch of the family, John D. Rockefeller Sr., and cofounder with him of the Standard Oil Company. For years, William and his wife lived in a 204-room mansion on the Rockwood Hall property. In the years after William's death in 1922 at the age of eighty-one, his huge house was demolished, and the land recently had been passed on to thirty-six-year-old Laurance.[3] Now, Laurance had agreed to donate it to the United Nations.

The two brothers now turned to their father, still very much at the helm of family affairs. Only a few months earlier, Nelson had experienced the elder Rockefeller's paternal grip when he was forced to reverse himself on the offer of Rockefeller Center's Center Theatre for UN General Assembly sessions.

Nelson had begun to focus on Rockwood Hall over the weekend. He had been in Texas on a short hunting vacation enroute back from a business trip to Brazil and Mexico when he got word of the UN's last-minute scramble. He flew home on Sunday, and immediately went into a meeting with O'Dwyer, Moses, Austin, and Secretary General Lie.[4] Lie told them that of the five last-minute alternatives Moses had put together, he was certain the UN delegates would be most receptive to Zeckendorf's East River site. But it was assumed the cost was prohibitive. At the time, reports were circulating that the asking price was some $25 million.

Now Nelson and Laurance explained to their father that unless New York could come up with something fast, it looked like Philadelphia was likely to be selected at the UN's session the next day. They proposed the family offer Rockwood Hall instead.

Their father had reservations: "I said at once that if such an offer were made and accepted, we might as well face the fact that this would mean our all giving up our homes in Pocantico Hills, for the Rockwood Hall area would be only the beginning, and, if accepted, would lead to our being asked for added gifts of Estate property since a much larger area would be required."

Nelson countered that boundary lines could be drawn. But, his father said, "I told him that even if ... these boundaries provided an adequate area, should the great central gathering buildings be built on the Rockwood Hall property, they would completely dominate the foreground of our view of the Hudson; that should the thousands of people connected with the United Nations organization take up residence in the general area, the whole character of the countryside would be so changed, that its peace and quiet for us as a country home would be gone, that even if our hilltop residences were not disturbed, they would no longer be the beautiful and secluded homes they now are."

He wasn't necessarily arguing against offering the Pocantico Hills property, John Jr. told his sons, but he wanted them to "realistically face the facts."

Laurance had to leave for another appointment, but Nelson and his father continued to talk. John Jr. suggested that the Harrison area, already on the UN's list, would be a better choice for the organization than his family's land. "It is higher and cooler, getting the breeze both from the Hudson and the Sound," he told Nelson, "and secondly ... it is more rolling, far less rocky and rough than our land and would lend itself better and less expensively to the [UN's] desired development."

He asked Nelson to take a closer look at both sites and, if indeed it turned out that land from the family's estate was to be donated, to find out what other adjacent or nearby tracts of land might be acquired in order to enlarge it.

Their meeting ended, and Nelson stayed in the office, working feverishly on his father's requests ahead of the UN's deadline the next day.

"At half past seven that evening, just as we were going out to dinner, Nelson telephoned me. He was still at the office," John Jr. recalled. By now, Nelson had been joined by several family advisors, including John Lockwood, the Rockefellers' chief lawyer; Frank Jamieson, the family's public relations man; and Wallace Harrison, the architect who had been a close friend and advisor to Nelson since he helped design Rockefeller Center years earlier, and who most recently had been working with the city to design its proposed Flushing Meadow Park site for the UN.

Nelson told his father that while he agreed that the Harrison area would be a better choice for the UN, it was available only for a purchase price of $9 million. As for land near the family's Rockwood Hall property, he had learned that some one thousand acres might be available for purchase.

Nelson also told his father that he had gotten in touch with two other of his brothers, John and David, and both had agreed to give up their Pocantico Hills property to enlarge the Rockwood Hall offer. (David was the most reluctant. Before consenting, he reportedly asked, "Couldn't I give money instead?") Nelson's other brother, Winthrop, was out of the country, in Venezuela, and not available to consult.

Then, the elder Rockefeller recalled, "I asked Nelson what he thought was the *ideal* site, quite irrespective of whether our homes were involved or not."

Nelson knew from his Sunday meeting with Lie that the UN delegates would prefer the Zeckendorf site in Midtown Manhattan, but that the cost was prohibitive. So now, his reply was quick and to the point. "The East River site from Forty-second to Forty-eighth Street is without any question the ideal site," he told his father.[5]

Blot on the Riverfront

The land that Nelson was sure the UN would covet was approximately six blocks of industrial landfill along the river in Midtown, from First Avenue to the East River. Covered mostly with stockyards and slaughter-houses, as well as some tenements, a depot for refilling fuel oil trucks and a tiny strip at the north end where Italian neighbors played bocce, it was considered a blot on the riverfront. The stench from the site, along with soot belching from smokestacks of a nearby electric generating plant, was so overwhelming that when the last large development had been built in the area, an apartment complex called Tudor City, its river-facing side was designed with virtually no residential windows.

The land was in an area of Manhattan called Turtle Bay, once a pleasant neighborhood named for a crescent-shaped cove that ran along the East River from just north of Forty-fifth Street to south of Forty-eighth Street. But in the 1860s, the bay had been filled in and the resulting land-fill had attracted some of the city's dirtiest industries.

In recent years, the area had been enjoying a slow renaissance, with renovation of a cluster of brownstones called Turtle Bay Gardens that at-tracted some celebrated residents, including the Academy Award–winning actress Katharine Hepburn. And to the north, quiet Beekman Place was home to other illustrious names, among them, songwriter Irving Berlin, who recently had bought a townhouse there. And two of Nelson Rocke-feller's siblings, his brother John and his only sister, "Babs," each lived in apartments in a fashionable building at One Beekman Place.

But still, the slaughterhouses remained. They were owned by the Swift and Wilson meatpacking families of Chicago, and had been there so long that "they seemed almost untouchable," Zeckendorf once commented. But by late 1945, Swift and Wilson were ready to sell, and they approached Zeckendorf's firm, Webb & Knapp, which agreed to put up $1 million for a one-year option to buy the property for $6.5 million. Under terms of the deal, the option would expire on December 11, 1946.[6]

Zeckendorf, never one to think small, had a grand vision for the property. He viewed it as the site of a complex rivaling the then twenty-two-acre Rockefeller Center, and he hired one of its architects, Wallace Harrison, to design it.

Zeckendorf's mega-development—its working name was "X City"—would comprise four forty-story office towers at the south end, three thirty-story apartment buildings at the north, and in between, two fifty-seven-story towers, one with offices and the other a hotel with more than four thousand rooms. In between the two tallest buildings Zeckendorf proposed a concert hall and home for the Metropolitan Opera, which at that time was planning to leave its West Thirty-eighth Street address. The development would also have an airline terminal, and out over the water, Zeckendorf hoped to build a floating nightclub and marina.[7]

But as the year moved on, Webb & Knapp had trouble finding investors for the project. One of the best possibilities was the Aluminum Company of America, Alcoa. But the head of Alcoa wanted to name the whole project "Aluminum City." Zeckendorf didn't have much faith in aluminum's use as a building material, plus he thought the name would drive away other potential investors.

On December 6, when he read about the ever-increasing confusion over the UN's land search, he was just five days away from expiration of his option on the property.

He called Mayor O'Dwyer and told him his firm would offer the United Nations the approximately seventeen acres of the East River waterfront for "any price they wish to pay."

O'Dwyer was skeptical of his open-ended offer. Zeckendorf later explained his reasoning: "Unless I said price was no object, they [the UN] would think this was a trick by a real estate operator to stop their Philadelphia negotiations, and then hold them up for millions. It had to be carte blanche."[8]

Moses was skeptical too. He was not convinced that Zeckendorf's Webb & Knapp actually controlled the site. Still, they passed on news of the offer to Lie.

An Overnight Deal

The elder Rockefeller recalled that when Nelson told him over the phone—in "definite and unqualified" terms—that the UN would prefer Zeckendorf's East River site, his first words were, "But this site would cost some $25 million, would it not?'"

Nelson turned to Harrison, Zeckendorf's X-City architect. While Harrison had no direct knowledge of what Zeckendorf might accept as payment, he was familiar enough with the developer's situation to make a good guess. He told the elder Rockefeller he thought it could be bought for $8.5 million.

"Why should we not acquire it and give this site [to the UN]?" his father responded.

Hearing a gleeful Nelson on the other end of the line, John Jr. was decisive: "All right . . . I authorize you to secure it and offer it from me."

He set three conditions, which he outlined to Nelson over the phone: that Zeckendorf provide a thirty-day option on the property; that the city agree to close the streets that crossed the property, turn over the river frontage, and "round out" the tract by adding small parcels of surrounding land to the north and south; and that his gift be free of taxes. (In 1927, when he had given $2 million to the League of Nations for its library in Geneva, he had paid a huge federal gift tax.)

Then John Jr. and his wife, Abby, left their Park Avenue apartment to go out to dinner. If the deal worked out, not only would the Rockefeller family make a huge contribution to the new peace organization that John Jr. had called "the hope of the world," but Rockefeller Center would lose a potential competitor, the huge X-city project. He asked Nelson to get back to him later that night.[9]

As Zeckendorf's architect, Harrison was the logical choice to deal with the developer, and along with Jamieson, he tracked down the real estate giant and his wife at the Monte Carlo nightclub at Madison and East Fifty-fourth Street. It was not surprising that Zeckendorf would be at the Monte Carlo. Webb & Knapp, which owned the building, had taken over the club when the club's cash-strapped operator could no longer pay the rent. Zeckendorf dined often at the Monte Carlo, where he had his own corner table. On this evening, Zeckendorf and his wife were celebrating their wedding anniversary and the birthday of one of his partners, Harry Sears.

"Sit down, have a drink," Zeckendorf said when Harrison approached his table. But Harrison—a map of the slaughterhouse site bulging from his pocket—had other things on his mind. Pulling out the map, he asked the flamboyant real estate developer if he would consider selling his East River land for the UN's home for $8.5 million.*

Zeckendorf grabbed Harrison's map, drew a line around the property, and wrote that the land within the boundaries was under option to the United Nations for thirty days. "I'd had a lot of champagne by that time," Zeckendorf later recalled, "but I had drawn the property line clearly." He handed it off to Sears, who agreed that everything looked right, and then they both signed.[10]

Harrison raced back to Nelson's office, and Nelson called his father. It was now close to midnight, less than twelve hours before the Headquarters Committee was scheduled to take up the Philadelphia offer. John Jr. was skeptical of the "informal and unorthodox" way in which the document had been signed—a handwritten scrawl on a neighborhood map transacted over champagne toasts in a boisterous nightclub. "I asked how legal the offer was," John Jr. remembered. Lockwood, the trusted family legal counsel, got on the phone. He admitted to having never seen anything like it, but he explained his logic to the elder Rockefeller, concluding that because of the high-profile nature of the transaction and the harm to his reputation that Zeckendorf risked if he backed out, he believed the real estate developer's word could be relied upon.

Over the phone, Nelson read to his father, paragraph by paragraph, a draft letter to the UN's Zuleta Angel and accompanying documents, as his father made revisions. "After Nelson again read them as revised, I approved them," he later recounted. By now, it was shortly before one o'clock in the morning. John Jr. asked Nelson, Lockwood, and Jamieson to be at his apartment early the next morning when he would review the papers once again and sign them.

They arrived at the apartment at 7:30 a.m., December 11, papers in hand. Again, the elder Rockefeller and Lockwood discussed the legalities of the situation, and by shortly after 8 a.m., everything was signed. As Nelson and his colleagues departed, John Jr. grabbed his son and whispered into his ear, "Will this make up for the Center Theatre?" It was a reference to the public embarrassment Nelson had felt months earlier when his father reversed Nelson's plan to temporarily house the UN General Assembly in Rockefeller Center's Center Theatre.[11]

---

*Approximately $106 million in present-day funds.

Within two hours, O'Dwyer and Moses had given the city's all-out support to Rockefeller's conditions, Austin and Secretary of State James Byrnes had been notified, and the general counsel of the Bureau of Internal Revenue had given the opinion that no taxes would be levied on the gift.

Meanwhile, after Nelson Rockefeller and Harrison briefed Zuleta Angel, in ill health and recuperating at Columbia Presbyterian Hospital, the diplomat left his hospital bed to personally preside over the Headquarters Committee meeting. There, he called on Austin to make a "very important statement." Austin began reading John D. Rockefeller Jr.'s letter to an increasingly startled committee:

Dear Dr. Zuleta Angel:

I have followed with deepest interest the effort of the United Nations to find a permanent home in the United States. New York is a center where people from all lands have always been welcomed and where they have shared common aspirations and achievements. It is my belief that this city affords an environment uniquely fitted to the task of the United Nations and that the people of New York would like to have the United Nations here permanently.

For these reasons I have ventured to obtain a firm offer covering property located on the East River in the midtown area, which, should it serve your purpose, I would be glad to give to the United Nations. If this property can be useful to you in meeting the great responsibilities entrusted to you by the people of the world, it will be a source of infinite satisfaction to me and my family.

I am enclosing a memorandum setting forth the terms and conditions of my offer.

Sincerely yours,
John D. Rockefeller Jr.[12]

About the time Austin was reading the momentous letter, Zeckendorf got a call from Nelson. "We've been up all night patching up the details, but it's going to work," Nelson reported.

"I couldn't believe it," Zeckendorf later recalled. He was so surprised he asked his switchboard operator to check to see if the call truly had come from Nelson Rockefeller's office.[13]

Center of the World, at Last

Over the next forty-eight hours, a UN group of delegates visited the
site, accompanied by Moses and other city officials;[14] the Headquarters
Committee approved a resolution accepting the gift; and on December 14, 1946—just eight days after Zeckendorf first called O'Dwyer about
a possible land deal—the UN General Assembly voted to make New York
City its permanent home.*

As Mayor La Guardia had predicted, as O'Dwyer had so desired, and
as Lie had always hoped, the city was to become the new "center of the
world."

Though some, particularly supporters of competing cities, objected
that the decision was made too hastily, the generosity of John D. Rockefeller Jr. was applauded widely throughout the world. But Lie, for one,
knew that without the unwavering efforts and influence of Rockefeller's
son Nelson, it would not have happened. "I know that we owe this to
your energy and devotion," he wrote Nelson shortly after the gift was approved. "We could not have done better, and you are the man primarily
responsible for our good fortune."[15]

*The vote was forty-six to seven. The Arab League countries—Egypt, Iraq, Leba-
non, Saudi Arabia, and Syria—voted against New York, as did Australia, which clung
to its choice of San Francisco, and El Salvador.

5

Rise of a Cityscape Icon

After a weeks-long spell of damp, dreary weather, New Yorkers awoke to a warm, sunny Mother's Day in 1947. Families flocked to the city's parks, strolled the avenues, and set out to discover one of the city's newest attractions, an excursion boat that circled Manhattan Island, offering breathtaking views of the skyline. But the Circle Line's mid-morning Mother's Day departure carried a less likely group of passengers as well. Some of the world's most distinguished architects were on board. They were members of an international team of designers planning the United Nations headquarters buildings. Now, their work nearing completion, they were eager to catch a glimpse of a six-block stretch of riverbank on Manhattan's East Side where, within just months, their creation—three strikingly modern glass and marble buildings—would begin to rise up against the backdrop of Manhattan's majestic skyscrapers.

Among them were Le Corbusier of France and Russia's Nikolai Bassov. The men knew each other well from working together the previous year when they represented their countries during the UN's long search for a permanent site. Now they had been called upon by their governments again, this time to join eight other prominent architects as members of the UN Board of Design.[1]

Choosing the Team

A New Yorker had been selected to lead the design team. In January, Secretary General Lie had named architect Wallace Harrison the UN's

Director of Planning. Some said that Harrison "went with the deal"—a reference to his close association with the family that had donated the land to the UN.[2] Indeed, the fifty-one-year-old Harrison was a Rockefeller confidant—he had known the family since the 1930s when he worked on the Rockefeller Center design—and he had played a key role in persuading the United Nations to settle in New York. While Lie was said to have considered other architects as well, he surely recognized that in Harrison he not only would have a designer with the Rockefeller family's approval, but a man who knew New York City intimately and had a solid working relationship with Mayor O'Dwyer and Robert Moses, both key to the project's progress.

Harrison had gotten into building at an early age, in his native Worcester, Massachusetts, where he worked as an office boy at a local construction company. After serving in the Navy during World War I, he studied at the Ecole des Beaux Arts in Paris before returning to the United States and settling in New York City. He was a partner with Helmle, Corbett, and Harrison in 1929 when the Rockefeller family commissioned the firm to help design the monumental Rockefeller Center complex. There, Harrison worked closely with the Rockefellers, particularly with Nelson, whose father had given him a significant role in the Center project. In 1940, shortly after Harrison completed his high-profile work on the 1939 World's Fair design, he joined Nelson in Washington as his deputy in what would become the State Department's Office of Inter-American Affairs. Returning to New York in early 1946, he formed a partnership with the architect Max Abramovitz, and almost immediately got a call from William Zeckendorf, who wanted him to design his huge "X City" project on the old slaughterhouse site on the East River. About the same time, Robert Moses asked Harrison to work with the city on plans to offer the UN a plot of land in Flushing Meadow Park in Queens, the same site Harrison had helped transform into the picturesque World's Fair.[3]

In choosing architects for the Design Board, it was decided that ten key areas of the world should be represented. Each UN member state was asked to make suggestions, and, with Lie's agreement, Harrison made the final selections: Gyle Soilleux of Australia; Gaston Brunfaut, Belgium; Oscar Niemeyer, Brazil; Ernest Cormier, Canada; Liang Sicheng, China; Le Corbusier, France; Sven Markelius, Sweden; Howard Robertson, United Kingdom; Julio Vilamajo, Uruguay; and Nikolai Bassov, Russia. They would be paid a $5,000 honorarium, plus travel expenses. Seven others would serve as special consultants, and three New York architects—Louis Skidmore, Gilmore Clarke, and Ralph Walker—provided local expertise.[4]

The appointment of Le Corbusier had been controversial. Harrison had known him for years, and was well aware that the architect was egotistical, opinionated, and temperamental. Trying to get some of the most creative minds in the world to work together would be difficult under any circumstances, but having the iconoclastic "Corbu" on the team could generate its own set of problems. Still, Harrison felt Le Corbusier belonged on the Design Board. Like many in the architectural world, he believed Le Corbusier had been treated unfairly in a design competition held back in 1927 for the League of Nations headquarters in Geneva. While it was generally believed Le Corbusier's strikingly modern and unconventional entry had been superior to the others—and it had received the most votes in early tallies—it was later eliminated because his design used the wrong ink, a technicality many thought was contrived by opponents of the modernist movement. A traditional palace-like structure was selected instead.[5] Now, Harrison said Le Corbusier should be on the UN team, in part to make up for what he told a colleague was "the screwing he got from the League of Nations."[6]

Another Board selection that caused some hesitancy was Nikolai Bassov. The pragmatic, self-assured Russian had, like Le Corbusier, worked tirelessly for the UN during the site selection process. Yet he was known for his engineering prowess, not for his architectural skills. But after Harrison conferred with the Soviets' UN representative, Andrei Gromyko, he was convinced that because in Russia the scope of the two professions overlapped, Bassov was right for the Board.[7]

About the time Lie appointed Harrison, Mayor O'Dwyer announced that Robert Moses would represent the city in all its dealings with the United Nations' building project. Even positions that didn't report to Moses in his job as city construction coordinator would now work through him on UN business. "A single individual must be responsible for the coordination of all the complex legal and construction problems" of the UN's settling in Manhattan, O'Dwyer wrote to Moses in asking him to take on the job.[8]

Critics All Around

In typical fashion, Moses moved swiftly. By January 23, 1947—a full month before the UN Board of Design architects had even held their first meeting—Moses presented Harrison with the city's plans for improving the area surrounding the UN site. "Moses was getting the jump on any Board of Design architects, going right on the record with New York

City's 'givens,'" recalled George Dudley, a young architect from the firm
of Harrison and Abramovitz, whom Harrison brought in to assist the
Board and keep notes of its meetings. Dudley knew Harrison well. They
had worked together in Nelson Rockefeller's Office of Inter-American
Affairs during the war. Now, the thirty-two-year-old Dudley, who held
graduate degrees from Yale University and had organized Yale's first
course in City Planning, would become an astute observer of the design
team's interactions with the city.[9]

Moses' plans were, for the most part, intended to ease traffic around
the site. Initially estimated to cost some $15 million, they called for broad-
ening Forty-second Street between First and Second avenues at the approach to the UN property; constructing a tunnel under First Avenue
between Forty-second and Forty-seventh streets to minimize noise and
congestion on the top level; and creating a grand approach to the UN by
widening one block of Forty-seventh Street between First and Second
avenues, from 60 to 160 feet, to allow for two 30-foot roadways separated
by a 12-foot-wide mall, with a narrow landscaped park to the south.
Moses also called for rezoning some of the city blocks in the immediate
vicinity of the UN site to restrict them from manufacturing use.[10]

Moses' "givens" were almost immediately met with criticism from
local architecture and civic groups, who argued they didn't go far enough.
And the United Nations itself was disappointed. As word got out about
the plans, Moses received a memo from Abraham Feller, the UN's general
counsel. Feller was a native New Yorker who had joined the UN in London and now was in charge of coordinating with the city on the land
swap deal. Moses' plans were "too cautious," he wrote. "Pardon me if
I express the view that the zoning plan as a whole seems not to have
taken into account the enormous potentialities for the entire area."

Feller had particularly harsh words for what he called the "eyesore" on
the Queens side of the East River across from the UN site—the "jumble
of industrial plants, warehouses and dilapidated dwellings" that he said
would detract from the views from the United Nations' new offices. And
he objected to the big advertising signs, some electrically lighted, that had
become the hallmark of Long Island City's factories and plants. Among
them was an enormous 122-foot-long Pepsi-Cola sign that had been
standing atop the company's bottling plant since the 1930s.[11]

Feller's letter found its way to the New York Times, which sided with
the UN official. In an editorial, the newspaper said, "We can scarcely dis-
miss these comments as the effort of a group of foreigners to tell us what

to do with our own city. We also are a part of the United Nations." The *Times* called on Moses, the "bold dreamer, and doer," to dream a little bigger.[12]

While Moses did agree to broaden and expand the scope of the re-zoned area to some forty city blocks, from Thirty-fourth Street to Fifty-ninth Street as far as Second Avenue, and to take up the matter of the Long Island City signage, that didn't satisfy his critics. The American Institute of Architects (AIA) called for rezoning some 130 blocks, from Thirty-fourth Street to Sixty-first Street, all the way over to Park Avenue. Moses' ideas were "picayune," the Fine Arts Federation told a City Planning Commission hearing in early March.[13]

But others attacked Moses for going too far. Businesses and residents on the Queens side of the East River were more than a little annoyed that Feller had called their area an "eyesore." And now that the city was working to restrict the huge billboards, they inundated Mayor O'Dwyer's office with letters and petitions, protesting that signage was simply the symbol of a prosperous and growing neighborhood, an example of free enterprise at its best. In a reference to the Rockefeller family oil fortunes, a Long Island City plant manager wrote, "If the Standard Oil Company . . . had been prohibited from placing signs in all sorts of public places, Mr. Rockefeller would not now be in a position to make such a magnificent gift [to the UN]."[14]

"We like those signs!" wrote Long Island City resident Elsie Boeker, whose father had represented the district in the State Assembly. "Why don't they look at their desks, and not out the windows?"[15]

Meanwhile on the Manhattan side of the river, on Forty-seventh Street between First and Second avenues, protests were brewing as well. Residents began to realize what Moses planned for the street. His vision for a sweeping entrance to the United Nations called for the buildings on the entire south side of Forty-seventh Street to be demolished so the roadway could be broadened.

The block housed some factories, including a period furniture manu-facturer that had been in business since the turn of the century, and a red brick church at the west end of the block, St. Boniface Roman Catholic Church, built in 1868. Now St. Boniface and its nearby rectory and pa-rochial school, as well as the factories, were to be razed. The parishio-ners fought the plan, petitioning the mayor and protesting along Second Avenue after Sunday morning mass. They are "praying and crying in de-spair," Peter Albano, owner of the neighboring furniture factory, wrote to

O'Dwyer. "I agree . . . that all of us citizens . . . must show our gratitude to the UN for having accepted the invitation to locate here, but if it is going to be a success, it will be a success without this destruction."[16]

The St. Boniface worshippers appealed to the archbishop of New York, Cardinal Francis Spellman, but didn't get much of a reception. Indeed, Moses was working closely with Spellman on the issue, rather than the parish priest who, Moses said, "does not get the whole picture."[17]

As Moses' planning moved ahead without delay, he faced persistent criticism from both sides.

Meanwhile, the UN Board of Design, too, was under attack. Many influential members of the architectural community believed an international competition should be held to select the design team for the new headquarters. The AIA and the American Society of Planners and Architects led the charge, calling the method in which the Board of Design was selected "unworthy of such an important assignment." Thomas H. Creighton, editor of *Progressive Architecture*, was particularly vocal. The magazine said a competition was "the only reasonable and professional way" to handle the UN design.[18] But Lie was determined not to repeat the mistakes of the old League of Nations, when 377 architects had submitted more than ten thousand plans in a competition that resulted in years of wrangling over the headquarters design, including the Le Corbusier "ink" controversy.[19]

Still, the cry for a competition would continue, even as Harrison and his Board of Design got well into their planning.

"Tout Manhattan"

The Board of Design first met on Monday, February 17, 1947. But Le Corbusier made his presence known weeks earlier. In a telegram from Paris, he informed Harrison that he agreed with only four of the ten choices for the Board—himself, Bassov, Robertson, and Niemeyer. Harrison remained firm, retaining the Board membership he and Lie had planned. Still, the episode was an omen of what Harrison could expect from Le Corbusier in the months ahead.[20]

In all, forty-five formal meetings would be held before the design group concluded its work in June. They met on the twenty-seventh floor of the RKO Building, above Radio City Music Hall at Rockefeller Center. A central workroom was set up with a huge six-by-twelve-foot model of the site and the Turtle Bay neighborhood surrounding it. Chairs faced a long pin-up wall, where architects' conceptual schemes were dis-

played. In an adjacent room, a group of talented young draftsmen—
the "backroom boys" they were called, despite the fact that one was a
woman—stood ready to turn the concepts into renderings and clay models. Harrison asked his partner, Max Abramovitz, to serve as his deputy
director, and a junior architect in the firm, Harmon Goldstone, to join
Dudley in assisting the Board.[21]

Except for Russia's Bassov, all the architects spoke either English or
French, and the two languages were used interchangeably. Bassov attempted a little English—limited to "okay" if he liked a design and
"nokay" if he didn't—but otherwise he relied on his longtime translator,
Serge Wolff, or sometimes on an unassuming young Soviet, Valentin Gubitschev, whose name would leap into New York headlines two years later,
as the game of spy and counter-spy played out on city sidewalks. While
Le Corbusier, too, preferred to use an interpreter, he was known to inter-
rupt her whenever he didn't like how his French was being translated.[22]

Harrison saw his role as that of a manager and consensus builder, a
combination he found trying at times. At the Board's first meeting, he
had barely begun to speak about the broad parameters of the project,
when Le Corbusier tried to take over. "*Tout Manhattan . . . is our concern . . . the heavy traffic . . . rapid transit . . . pedestrian traffic . . .*" he pro-
nounced.[23] As the weeks unfolded, it became clear that Le Corbusier
wanted to be seen as the architect of the United Nations. "In so many
ways, Corbu was all but impossible to deal with," Harrison's partner,
Abramovitz, remembered. "No sooner had he arrived than he sought to
take charge of the entire operation."[24]

And one of the backroom boys assigned to work with Le Corbusier, New York designer Thaddeus Crapster, said years later that Harrison
"probably regretted [selecting Le Corbusier for the team] at times," and
then added, "Well, probably *all* the time."[25]

Still, Harrison was determined that the meetings remain a team effort.
Dudley likened them to "psychotherapy sessions."[26]

Niemeyer's Breakthrough

Early on, it was agreed that the complex should be designed to accommodate an additional twenty member nations beyond the original fifty-one,
and some seven hundred meetings a year. It would comprise three main
buildings—a General Assembly Hall for the large gathering of delegates;
a Conference Building that would house conference space and the Security Council, Economic and Social Council, and the Trusteeship Council;

and a tall office building for UN Secretariat employees. Two other high-rise buildings were included in the initial planning—potential space for UN diplomatic missions, the organization's specialized agency offices, and housing for UN staff.[27]

A New York engineering firm specializing in foundations, Moran, Proctor, Freeman and Mueser, was brought in to gauge the bedrock beneath the surface, the Manhattan schist on which most of the city's skyscrapers are built. Their studies showed that between Forty-sixth and Forty-seventh streets the bedrock dips to more than sixty feet below sea level, the area that was the deepest water of Turtle Bay before it was covered with landfill. To avoid the high costs of sinking deep pilings into the soft land, the UN buildings would be situated either south or north of what Le Corbusier referred to as the "Turtle Bay hole."[28]

One of the first plans that drew praise from the majority of the team was indeed a Le Corbusier concept. As far back as 1922, he had designed a scheme for a "contemporary city" of glass-encased skyscrapers in a park-like setting. Now, he sketched for his fellow UN architects a thin slab skyscraper, oriented north and south, located toward the site's southern end and rising out of a large low building that would house the General Assembly and Conference buildings. Others, too, came forward with ideas. To Harrison's delight, Bassov, the engineer, showed his architectural sensibilities early on, referring to the need to maximize the "scenic beauty" of the site.[29] The Chinese representative, Liang, clung to the idea that the buildings should be oriented east to west, a tradition followed in China for thousands of years. Robertson, from Britain, favored inward-looking buildings, facing courtyards like those at Oxford and Cambridge. And the Swedish architect, Markelius, a city planner back in Stockholm, took the most all-encompassing approach. His scheme extended the UN site, via a bridge, to Welfare Island (later renamed Roosevelt Island), where he proposed housing for UN staff, and via a grand boulevard all the way to Fifth Avenue.[30]

One bright young architect on the team didn't arrive in New York until the sessions were well under way. The Brazilian, Oscar Niemeyer, was an avowed member of the Communist Party ("a man from the Left," he called himself),[31] and the United States held up issuing his visa until Secretary General Lie finally asked the U.S. UN ambassador, Warren Austin, to intervene. Harrison was particularly eager for the Brazilian's contributions. Just four years earlier, Niemeyer had gained international recognition for his modern "Pampulha" complex of buildings in the Brazilian city of Belo Horizonte, a design that was highly acclaimed when it was exhibited at the Museum of Modern Art in New York. And even earlier, Mayor La Guardia had been so impressed with the imaginative Brazilian Pavilion co-designed by Niemeyer for the 1939 World's Fair that he had awarded him the keys to the city.[32]

But once the thirty-nine-year-old Niemeyer got to the UN Design Board meetings, he appeared reluctant to participate. Some of his earliest training had come when he worked with Le Corbusier on two projects in Rio de Janeiro. Now, he seemed to shy away from asserting himself in the presence of the master he considered his mentor, and he later said Le Corbusier had asked him not to submit an independent design.[33]

It was not until Le Corbusier was called back to his Paris office on business that Niemeyer—at Harrison's urging—finally began to sketch. By April 25, the architects' thirty-second meeting, Niemeyer was ready to present a scheme. Dudley described it in his notes as a "breakthrough" for the architects. "First reactions were beyond words," he remembered.

Niemeyer had used Le Corbusier's basic concept, but separated the Secretariat, General Assembly, and Conference Building. "As different as day and night," Dudley observed. "In Niemeyer's refreshing scheme the site was open, a grand space with a clean base for the modest masses standing in it," compared with Le Corbusier's "set of intersecting spaces in [a] unitary block."[34]

A "spell" had been cast over the team of architects, Dudley observed.

Winners and Losers

Le Corbusier was not pleased with Niemeyer's plan to separate the buildings, and he once drew the concept as a nude woman with dismembered head and legs.[35] But the Board of Design's summer deadline for getting plans to Lie was nearing, and Harrison knew that the city, Moses in particular, was anxious to see some results. Now, Harrison needed all the leadership skills he could muster. At their April 30 meeting, he told the team they had two ways to proceed. "There can be a decision by a vote—or I can make a decision," he said. "I have explained the difficulty of a vote. After a vote, you have the winners and the losers. If I make a decision, I am the only loser."

And then he made his decision. "I conclude the only scheme that gets complete satisfaction is an early idea of Le Corbusier, as carried out, drawn up, by Oscar Niemeyer," he said, in a clear appeal to Le Corbusier's vanity. "This seems like a good compromise to me," Harrison continued. "Any objections?"

Le Corbusier's response was the one everyone waited for. "I am very happy about what I have heard," he said.[36]

While this was hardly the end of Harrison's troubles with Le Corbusier, for the moment it got the planning on track, so the architects could work out the details and deliver the final design to the General Assembly on time.

Within days, by Friday, May 9, 1947, Harrison felt comfortable enough with the plan to invite Lie to take a closer look. That evening, the Secretary General and aides joined Harrison and his wife, Ellen, at their apartment on Fifth Avenue and then Harrison took them to the RKO Building's Radio City Music Hall, which, he pointed out, was approximately the same size as the proposed General Assembly Hall. Then they went up to the twenty-seventh floor where for the first time, the top UN officials got a close look at what would take shape in the years to come. The architects' drawings and models showed a high-rise Secretariat office building to the south, a low swoop-roofed General Assembly Hall slightly north, and a long, low Conference Building at the river's edge.[37]

It was two days later that the architects boarded the Circle Line boat to make their way around Manhattan. As they cruised up the East River past the site of the UN's new permanent home, still dotted with dirty slaughterhouses and old tenements about to be razed, they leaned over the rail. And from there, they could visualize their drawings and clay models transformed to a complex of stately buildings that would hug the water's edge.[38]

The Boulevard to Nowhere

Once a week at Gracie Mansion, the mayor's residence on Manhattan's Upper East Side, Harrison and Lie met with O'Dwyer and Moses. And Harrison had at least one other weekly meeting with Moses, usually lunch at Moses' office on Randall's Island under the Triborough Bridge or at one of his other offices at the Central Park Arsenal or at 270 Broadway. Moses and Harrison had a good rapport, but still, Dudley remembered, "Robert Moses wielded a heavy hand."[39]

Indeed, Harrison tried to shelter his creative designers from the pragmatic, often brusque, city planner. And years later Moses would talk disparagingly about his work with the UN architects. "One experience with massed artistic genius is enough for a lifetime," he said, calling the team of architects "a congress of Kilkenny cats—all flying fur and little harmony."[40]

Moses had particular disdain for Le Corbusier, who had flatly rejected Flushing Meadow as permanent home for the UN. Not surprisingly, Moses most appreciated the no-nonsense Russian engineer Bassov. "The smartest and most helpful," he recalled. Still, he thought Harrison would have done better on his own. "He never should have had all those other fellows with him," Moses said.[41]

Even after the Board of Design held its last meeting on June 9, and as Harrison prepared his final report for Lie and the General Assembly, influential architectural groups still clung to their demands for an international competition for the UN design. And Moses remained under attack for his less than visionary ideas for the UN surroundings. The objections to offensive signage had been partly resolved when the Board of Estimate voted to prohibit new large advertising billboards in Queens and Manhattan that were visible from the UN.[42] But the Board was facing such public opposition to Moses' plans for development and zoning around the site that it delayed a meeting scheduled to approve them. By now, another player was speaking up, the same man who just months before had sold his options on the East River frontage that Rockefeller Jr. donated to the UN, the real estate mogul Bill Zeckendorf.

Zeckendorf called Moses' plans for the area around the UN a "travesty," and came up with his own proposal—a grandiose approach to the United Nations that would be created by razing and redeveloping into one huge superblock the land from Forty-sixth Street to Forty-ninth Street, from the UN site to Third Avenue. He envisioned a gigantic concourse housing two forty-story office buildings, an opera house, a concert hall, eight theaters, and twin groupings of four tall apartment buildings, all ending north of the UN at the East River with a tall steel pylon rising from a fountain and sunken plaza.[43] It would be "one of the architectural jewels of the world," he said, and would replace what he called the "seedy and uninspired" East Midtown area.[44]

But the "seedy" East Midtown was becoming a popular home for a growing number of well-known actors, musicians, and leading publishing figures. They lived in an elegant compound of townhouses, Turtle Bay Gardens, that had been stylishly redesigned in the 1920s. It was located right in the center of the tract Zeckendorf now wanted to destroy. Among the celebrated residents were two influential writers, essayist and *New Yorker* columnist E. B. White and journalist Dorothy Thompson. And they knew how to make headlines.

White warned of the "stuff that Turtle Bay residents are made of" and Dorothy Thompson wrote a blistering attack on Zeckendorf in a long letter to the *Times*. "If the city . . . tries to expropriate us for the benefit of Mr. Zeckendorf, the residents, most of whom are socially minded people, may recall that the Constitution declares that the right to bear arms shall not be abridged," she wrote.

Zeckendorf responded in the *Times*. He said he regretted that his first "skirmish" with the brilliant Dorothy Thompson had "inspired her to fall back on her right to 'bear arms,'" but still, he argued that his plan for a 320-foot-wide, two-block-long concourse was far superior to Moses' 160-foot-wide, one-block-long approach to the UN.

Soon, another plan was on the table. The AIA's New York chapter proposed replacing what it called Moses' "piecemeal" approach with an underground roadway beneath a 150-foot-wide mall running from First Avenue to Lexington Avenue between the north side of Forty-fifth Street and the south side of Forty-eighth Street. The Turtle Bay Gardens homes would be spared under the AIA's concept.[45]

In the days leading up to the delayed Board of Estimate vote on Moses' plan, now scheduled for late August, civic and architectural groups weighed in, virtually all opposed to the Moses plan. It would result in "haphazard and unrelated improvements . . . that would . . . impede and hamper any efforts [to improve the area] in the future," the Real Estate Board of New York said, in a view shared by the New York Board of Trade, Regional Plan Association, Municipal Art Society, and others.[46]

The Board of Estimate meeting was, the *Times* reported, "one of the bitterest debates" in City Hall history. But at the end of the session of name-calling ("liar" was a favorite), Moses' plan was approved. Neither Zeckendorf's proposal nor the AIA plan got much of a hearing. "A cry in the wilderness," the developer called the whole effort.

Years later, Zeckendorf wrote, "Every time I go by the so-called approachway the city gave to the UN, I feel the old and righteous anger start to stir." He called the block-long approach nothing but a "dreary drying-out place for the drunks scattered among the few benches . . . An entranceway to the putative capital of the world it is not."[47]

Indeed, the approach that Moses envisioned began to deteriorate almost as soon as it was completed. The UN's final architectural plans called for the UN entrance to be oriented closer to Forty-second Street, and when First Avenue was converted to one-way northbound traffic in 1951, Moses' approach became, literally, a stub of a boulevard that led to nowhere. After the death of Secretary General Hammarskjold in 1961, the land was named Dag Hammarskjold Plaza in his honor. But not until the 1990s would the city, under pressure from the surrounding neighborhood, turn the widened street into a park space worthy of its illustrious name.[48] And then in the 2000s, in a notable coincidence, the Zeckendorf name would again surface in connection with the land, when William Zeckendorf's grandchildren—developers Arthur and William—broke ground for a luxury high-rise condominium facing the UN along First Avenue and bordering the plaza.[49]

The Essential Dome

The United States and the UN signed an agreement in late June 1947 defining the legal status and issues surrounding the UN headquarters' presence in New York City. And on July 8, Mayor O'Dwyer ceremoniously picked up a sledgehammer and hacked at bricks of a five-story tenement north of Forty-second Street, the first of some fifty buildings that would be demolished on the former slaughterhouse site. Only one building, a seven-story nondescript concrete structure at the south end of the site, was left standing. It recently had been completed as offices for the New York City Housing Authority, and now the city agreed to sell it to the UN at cost, $1.5 million.[50] It would serve as offices for UN workers and as the UN's library until it, too, was finally razed in the early 1960s. In its place, Harrison would design a long, low white marble and glass library, the fourth major building on the UN's campus. Financed with a grant from the Ford Foundation, it was named for Dag Hammarskjold, whose death in a plane crash in the Congo occurred shortly before its opening.

Some 270 residents of the old tenements on the site were relocated, in a plan paid for by the UN and carried out by the New York Bureau of Real Estate. Some were placed in buildings purchased and renovated by the Bureau, including four tenement buildings at the southwest corner of Second Avenue and Fifty-fourth Street. Others took a cash settlement and found housing on their own.[51]

Harrison's final architectural plan was ready for Lie by June 1947. It was estimated to cost some $84 million, a price that the Secretary General found a "shock . . . too high, far too high."[52] Harrison quickly went about shaving some $20 million from the estimate. He trimmed the Secretariat from its planned forty-five stories to thirty-nine; reduced the scope of the General Assembly Building; eliminated space in the Conference Building; cut the number of underground parking spaces from 2,000 to 1,500 (the minimum the parking space-deficient city would agree to at the time); and deferred installation of some of the communications equipment.[53]

UN-U.S. Headquarters Agreement

The tract of land on which the UN headquarters buildings are located is owned by the United Nations, but the territory remains part of the United States. Under terms of an agreement signed by the United States and the UN in June 1947, the laws of New York City, New York State, and the U.S. federal government generally apply within the headquarters district. But in order to protect the independence of the organization, the agreement calls for the district to be "inviolable," which means that no New York City, state, or federal authority may enter the headquarters territory without UN permission.

The accord also specifies that the organization's headquarters district may not be used as a refuge for anyone attempting to avoid arrest under city, state, or U.S. laws, nor by anyone trying to avoid extradition from the United States.

Under the pact, the UN land is not "extraterritorial" or "sovereign." Instead, the UN owns the six blocks along the East River—which it bought with an $8.5 million donation from John D. Rockefeller Jr.— while the land remains a part of U.S. territory.

The UN has its own fire-fighting and security forces, and, in accordance with the UN-U.S. agreement, New York City's fire and police departments may enter UN premises only at the request of the UN, or with its permission. Under the agreement, the United States is responsible for providing security from threats emanating outside the perimeter of the UN headquarters. And, like all properties in the city, public services—such as electricity, gas, and telephone—are provided for the headquarters district by local utility companies.

The agreement, which also addresses the diplomatic immunity status of UN officials and delegates, was signed by UN Secretary General Trygve Lie and U.S. Secretary of State George Marshall on June 26, 1947, at Lake Success on Long Island, then home to the Secretariat's temporary offices, and just days before work was to begin on the permanent site. After U.S. Congressional and UN General Assembly approval, it went into effect November 21, 1947.

In line with a later 1951 agreement, the UN has its own post office, and issues its own stamps, which can be used only at UN headquarters. The cost of a UN stamp is the same as a U.S. stamp. The UN's zip code is that of the surrounding Midtown Manhattan area.

Moses had a particular interest in enclosing the UN site with a fence. Neither the UN security staff nor the designers saw any need for it, and so Harrison told Moses if he wanted a fence, the city would have to pay for it. And if the city was to pay for it, Moses said he would pick his own architect. He chose Jacques Carlu, a Frenchman and head of MIT's School of Architecture, who designed an elegant, low fence to surround the UN complex.*[54]

One element, a dome for the General Assembly Building, was a late addition to the design. It was a bit of symbolism that the architectural team had resisted. Russia's Bassov, in particular, once told his colleagues that a dome on a building was only slightly less offensive than having a restaurant atop it.[55] But as it became clear that the UN would ask the U.S. Congress for a $65 million interest-free loan to pay for the headquarters, the U.S. got word to Harrison that a dome, an important symbol of government to much of America, should be incorporated in the design. "If you are going to get this loan request through Congress, the building should have a dome," Austin is said to have advised Harrison.[56] Harrison affixed the symbolic dome to the center of the Assembly Hall's elegant swooped roof, although he did not see the UN buildings as symbolic. "The world hopes for a symbol of peace. We have given them a *workshop* for peace," he once said.[57]

Whether the dome helped the case or not, Congress approved the loan and on September 14, 1948, ground was broken. Four leading New York construction companies were contracted to handle the work: Slattery Contracting, the George A. Fuller Company, Turner Construction, and Walsh Construction. And another New York firm, Syska Hennessy, was the project engineer.[58]

A little more than a year later, on Monday, October 24, 1949—four years to the day since the UN charter had been ratified—Harrison joined Lie, President Truman, Mayor O'Dwyer, and others at a dedication ceremony at the site's southeast corner. Some 16,000 diplomats, guests, workmen, and ordinary people from the neighborhood surrounded the scaffold-shrouded Secretariat to watch as Harrison helped Lie seal a metal container and lower it into a spot east of the Housing Authority building near Forty-second Street. It held the UN Charter, Declaration of Human Rights, and a copy of the program for the ceremony.[59]

---

*Moses' fence was replaced in 2005 with a taller, more secure fence, this one paid for by the UN.

Mixed Reviews

The first of the buildings to be completed was the slender, 550-foot-tall slab of the Secretariat, its two glimmering walls of glass—some 5,040 windows in all—facing the city to the west and the river to the east, and its northern and southern ends covered in white Vermont marble. By late August 1950, office workers began moving in. The Conference Building, a 400-foot-long, five-story structure oriented toward the river, was next, followed by the saddle-backed General Assembly Building with a striking north wall of English Portland stone—and, of course, topped with a dome.

The two high-rise buildings that had appeared in early design schemes—space for housing, and for UN agencies and missions—were never built. UN personnel preferred to find their own places to live, the fledgling specialized agencies could not afford the high cost of sharing a new office building, and the missions liked their independence, often sharing quarters with their countries' New York consulates.[60] But some said the truth lay more in the growing paranoia over espionage. "No country wanted to be right down the hall from another," the UN's Brian Urquhart said years later. "Fears of spying and wiretapping were becoming pervasive back then."[61] Instead, the north portion of the UN territory became a garden, known over the years as the North Lawn. It included a large patch of vibrant roses, a suggestion of the All American Rose Selections organization, which supplied the bushes. And Japanese cherry trees and thousands of white daffodils were gifts from the New York philanthropist Mary Lasker.[62]

Reviews of the UN buildings were mixed. The Secretariat, in particular, seemed to draw an opinion from everyone. "Not since Lord Carnarvon discovered King Tut's tomb in 1922 had a building caused such a stir," the *Architectual Forum* wrote. "A triumph of unadorned proportion," the American architect George Howe, head of the architecture department at Yale, said of the building, while Frank Lloyd Wright called it a "super-crate, to ship a fiasco to hell."

The rising young architect Philip Johnson deemed the UN design the "best modern piece of planning" he had seen. The president of the AIA's New York chapter said it looked like nothing more than "a sandwich on edge and a couple of freight cars." And the *New Yorker's* influential architectural critic Lewis Mumford, in six articles devoted to the design, expressed disappointment. He had never liked the location—he favored the area south of Washington Square, one of the city's last-minute alternatives—and he did not like the Secretariat's slab design, which he said "symbolizes the worst practices of New York, not the best hopes of the United Nations." And yet he warmed to the Secretariat at nightfall, calling it "chaste, startling, fairylike in its cold austerity, a Snow Queen's palace, exhaling by night a green moonlight splendor."[63]

Even Moses, ever-supportive of Harrison, was tepid in his reaction to the buildings. "Dear Wally," the candid Moses wrote to Harrison after the design was finalized, "While I have some reservations as to your UN site plan, I realize that you can not satisfy everyone."[64]

But over the years, the glass and marble Secretariat increasingly showed its architectural significance. Just a year after the UN tower was completed, Gordon Bunshaft designed the first all-glass-walled office building, Lever House, on Park Avenue at Fifty-fourth Street. And soon, glass towers were going up all across the United States and throughout the world. The architectural historian and Harrison biographer Victoria Newhouse called the Secretariat "a true symbol of Western civilization at mid-century."[65]

Rockefeller and Le Corbusier

Le Corbusier, meanwhile, had become increasingly vocal in claiming ownership of the UN design, and he wanted to take charge of its implementation during construction. In November 1947, months after the design team had completed its work and as Harrison was finalizing the project, Le Corbusier wrote to Harrison, Lie, and to Nelson Rockefeller, whom he had known since the 1930s when he visited New York on a trip sponsored by the Museum of Modern Art, where the young Rockefeller was then a trustee. "The project is 100 percent the architecture and urbanism of Le Corbusier," he wrote,[66] referring to himself in the third person, as he often did. He threatened to take the matter to the French government if he wasn't given due credit and paid a fee to come to New York to oversee its finalization.

In response, Rockefeller dictated a three-page letter to his secretary that read, in part: ". . . I feel obliged to say in all frankness that I think you conducted yourself throughout the entire period of planning in a manner unbecoming to a man of your ability and prestige and that a lesser man than Wally Harrison would have asked for your resignation at an early stage in the proceedings." He went on to say that if Le Corbusier still felt he needed compensation for his work, he should, as he himself was suggesting, "put the matter in the hands of your government."[67]

Rockefeller never sent the letter. Instead, he collaborated on a short, diplomatic reply that Harrison sent to Le Corbusier. "I am delighted that you feel that you are the one who designed the United Nations Headquarters. It pleases me equally that other members of the Board have that same satisfaction. After all, the combined work was to be symbolic of the unity and selflessness of the United Nations," he wrote, adding that a decision on carrying out the project would be made by the UN itself.[68]

Secretary General Lie made the UN position very clear, writing to Le Corbusier about the same time: "I see no possibility of associating you with Mr. Harrison in the future work."[69]

Then Rockefeller followed up with a short note to Le Corbusier. "There is nothing further I can contribute to the situation," he wrote.[70]

"In New York apparent kidnapping of the Le Corbusier UN project by USA gangster Harrison," Le Corbusier wrote in a letter to his elderly mother about the same time. "Yes, New York 1947 imitates, with variations on certain aspects, the scandal in Geneva 1927," he told her, referring to his elimination from competition for the League of Nations headquarters.[71]

Until his death in 1965 at the age of seventy-seven, Le Corbusier held himself to be the architect of the United Nations headquarters. As late as 1963, in a letter to an acquaintance in New York, he referred to the UN building as ". . . a bitter memory for me. I worked in New York for eighteen months, and my plans were not borrowed but stolen!"[72]

Many years later, the prominent Dutch architect and Harvard University professor Rem Koolhaas assessed the old controversy simply: The Secretariat, he said, was a "building that an American could never have thought and a European could never have built." It was a "collaboration . . . between cultures," appropriate for an organization of world nations.[73]

Solid upon "Manhattan Rock"

In 1952—on Thursday, October 9—Wallace Harrison stood with Secretary General Lie beneath the dome of the impressive General Assembly Hall to formally announce completion of the three main United Nations buildings. The surrounding grounds were yet to be landscaped, and the city's tunnel running under First Avenue in front of the UN was months from being ready for traffic. But with completion of the General Assembly, the UN's presence was now, as Lie put it, "solid upon the Manhattan rock."[74]

Five days later, on October 14, General Assembly delegates from the then sixty member countries gathered for the first time in their new meeting place. The mayor of New York was invited to address the opening session. But it was not William O'Dwyer, the mayor who believed the UN's decision to settle in New York had turned the city into the "center of the world." Shortly after his re-election to a second term in the fall of 1949, O'Dwyer had been confronted with a police corruption scandal and resigned the next summer.

And sadly, O'Dwyer's predecessor, Mayor Fiorello La Guardia, who had gone on to head the United Nations Relief and Rehabilitation Administration (UNRRA) after he left office, didn't live to see the United Nations headquarters completed. The popular three-term mayor who predicted the UN would come to the city because, he once said, "There is only one New York in the whole world and there is nothing like it," died of pancreatic cancer in September 1947 at the age of sixty-four. His funeral was attended by representatives of every diplomatic consulate in New York, a tribute to the charismatic leader who was so determined to bring the world capital to his town.

It fell to Mayor Vincent Impellitteri, the former Manhattan borough president who won a special election after O'Dwyer resigned, to address the UN session. "The city of New York is now indeed the world center of hope," he told the diplomats. "We wish you Godspeed in your work."[75]

It would be more than forty years before another New York mayor would cross over into the UN's international territory to address the world body. In 1995, on the occasion of the UN's fiftieth anniversary, Mayor Rudolph Giuliani was invited to appear before the General Assembly. And then just six years later, Giuliani was again asked to come before the annual assemblage of delegates, this time as a stunned city and the world reacted to the shock of 9/11.[76]

6
Smoothing out the Wrinkles

I t was an unlikely spot for Manhattan's borough president to meet two
secretaries general of the United Nations. Yet on a cold, windy day
in April 1953, Robert F. Wagner Jr., along with Robert Moses, joined
Trygve Lie and Dag Hammarskjold at a tiny children's playground in
Midtown Manhattan. Lie had recently resigned his post as UN chief, and
Hammarskjold had been elected to succeed him. Now, they watched as
the world body's blue and white flag was hoisted into the air to mark the
opening of a small park for city kids, located along the East River just
south of Forty-eighth Street on the UN's international territory.

Earlier in the day, the four had joined Mayor Impellitteri at a nearby
ribbon-cutting ceremony to officially open a tunnel beneath First Avenue
in front of the UN headquarters.[1] The underpass, part of Moses' plans to
improve the area surrounding the UN—now estimated to cost $25 mil-
lion—was intended to ease traffic on First Avenue.* The UN had welcomed construction of the underpass. But the little playground was another story. Despite its size—just one-third of an acre—its creation had
been controversial and it represented one of the first times the city and
its worldly partner found themselves in a public dispute. The uneasy marriage of New York and the global organization would face rockier times
in the decades to come—over espionage and political suspicions, race re-

*In 1952, the stretch of First Avenue from Forty-second to Forty-eighth Street, in
front of the UN, was renamed United Nations Plaza. Still, many would continue to
refer to it as "First Avenue."

lations, and everyday lifestyle frictions—but for now, the tiff would focus
on seesaws and swings.

The Seesaw Skirmish

Three years earlier, under pressure from citizens' groups for more parkland in the East Midtown area, Moses announced that a small playground
for Turtle Bay neighborhood children would be built on a parcel of land
at the northeast corner of the landscaped grounds of the UN's eighteen-
acre site.[2] Unfortunately, he seemed not to have notified Lie. "There
is nothing to the story," Lie responded confidently when the *New York
Times* asked for the UN's view of a playground being built directly on
its property.[3]

Lie and most of the UN delegates thought a playground would detract from the dignity of the UN's international domain. "I have great
admiration for my friend, Bob Moses, but if he sees a little bit of land . . .
he wants it at once for a playground or a swimming pool," Lie said of
the man who during his career opened more than six hundred city playgrounds and fifteen swimming pools. "I do not think there will be any
swimming pool or playground on the site of the UN," Lie told the press.[4]

But within a year Moses had managed to convince Lie that it would
be an act of goodwill to have a public park on the UN's land. After all,
the property had been donated to the UN with considerable cooperation from the city, and by now architects had decided that no other UN
buildings would be built on the northern end of the site. So, reluctantly,
Lie got the UN delegates to consent.[5]

As planning for the little space got under way, it was Moses' turn to
be rebuffed. Moses had intended that the park—to be built by the city,
but maintained by the UN—would be like all the other public playgrounds—filled with the Park Department's standard swings, slides, and
seesaws. But three wealthy women who lived on Beekman Place, a prestigious two-block residential enclave just north of the UN, had another
idea. Mrs. John D. Rockefeller III, Mrs. Thomas Hess, and Mrs. David
Levy ommissioned the highly regarded Japanese-American sculptor Isamu
Noguchi to design a futuristic playground that would be, they said, "befit-
ting the United Nations and the forward-looking standards which it sets."
The women were indeed to be taken seriously. Not only was Blanchette
Rockefeller the daughter-in-law of the man whose donation led to the
UN's purchase of its headquarters site, but Audrey Hess, a noted philan-
thropist, was married to the managing editor of the influential magazine

Art News. And lest money become an issue, the women promised to arrange financing for the park's construction.[6]

Noguchi designed a modernist sculpture-like park, with tunnels, climbing hills, spiraling paths, and a wading pool. "Instead of telling the child what to do—swing here, climb there," the playground will be "a place of endless exploration," the artist explained.[7]

Art News called the design "one of the most important integrations of modern art with daily life in recent years," and it was hailed by educators, civic groups, and child welfare specialists alike.[8]

But Moses, who had turned down another Noguchi park project in the 1930s, hardly agreed. "A hillside rabbit warren," he called the little sculpture park. "If they want to build it, it's theirs, but I'm not interested in that sort of playground."[9]

He brushed off critics who claimed he lacked imagination. But when even Eleanor Roosevelt questioned his judgment, he took the time to reply with a long, thoughtful letter. He told the late president's widow and now U.S. Representative to the UN Commission on Human Rights that, for safety reasons, he preferred a design that had "stood the test of rough usage." He suggested to Mrs. Roosevelt that Noguchi's design might be tried at a public housing project, perhaps one then being planned near Corlears Hook in Lower Manhattan.[10]

In the end, Robert Moses got his way. When he and the borough president joined Lie and Hammarskjold to open the city park on UN land, they looked out over a conventional design of green seesaws, orange-colored swings, slides, and a sandbox atop a slab of gray pavement.[11] But Noguchi's sculpture park was not entirely forgotten. A model of the futuristic playground was exhibited at the Museum of Modern Art, where the highly acclaimed design captured the imagination of the art world, and of parents and children who would never have the chance to explore its pleasures.[12]

"International Rhubarb"

Trygve Lie's skirmish with Moses over the playground may have signaled a turning point in the city's previously cordial relationship with its new neighbor. But for sure, the next episode—which found Moses pitted against the new Secretary General, Dag Hammarskjold—would lead to a change in the way New York addressed its partnership with the UN. And it would mark the end of Robert Moses' role as the city's chief liaison with the world body.

Moses and Lie had gotten on well. Lie once described Moses as an "imaginative and dynamic planner," and referred to him as a "pillar of strength" during the UN's entry into the city. And Moses praised the Norwegian diplomat as a "builder and a driver" with "bluff, hearty forth-rightness and tenacity."[13]

But the brusque, hard-driving Moses found the next UN chief diffi-cult to understand. Dag Hammarskjold was quiet and introspective. The son of a former Swedish prime minister, forty-seven-year-old Hammar-skjold held a degree in law and a PhD in economics, spoke five languages, and had been chairman of the National Bank of Sweden before being appointed to his country's Foreign Office in 1947. He would become one of the most effective and respected leaders in UN history, and would play a pivotal role in the city–UN partnership during his eight years in the post. But his first few months dealing with Moses were anything but smooth.

"We never had any trouble with Trygve Lie," Moses lamented shortly after Hammarskjold took over. The new Secretary General was "hard for us to comprehend," he said, and he once referred to him as a "mystic."[14]

Moses' differences with Hammarskjold arose over an issue that would plague UN–New York relations for years: the seemingly mundane matter of parking. In the postwar automobile boom, the borough of Manhat-tan was increasingly suffering from heavy traffic. From the mid-1940s to 1953, the number of cars entering and leaving Manhattan each day nearly doubled. During planning and design of the UN buildings, the subject of parking had been at the top of the city's agenda. Originally, the city and UN had agreed to an underground parking garage within the UN site for 2,000 cars. But when the project later was scaled back for economic reasons, the spaces were reduced to 1,500.[15]

Then in midsummer 1953, Moses got word that the UN planned to convert some 250 of those spaces into a storage room. With neighboring streets already overflowing with cars, he wrote to Hammarskjold, telling him he could see "nothing sillier" than eliminating parking spots. The UN action was, he said, "a rather poor way of repaying those who have been your friends."[16]

Before Hammarskjold had a chance to reply, Moses released the text of his letter to the press. "The city would never have . . . agreed to pay for the improvements around the UN," he wrote, "if there had been the slightest impression that the United Nations would break this agree-ment."

And he contended public opinion was at stake. One of the city's greatest problems since the UN settled in New York, Moses wrote, was trying to convince residents that the United Nations "is not an arbitrary, extra-territorial institution which pays no attention to the ordinary rules and practices of the government municipality in which it is located."[17]

The metropolitan newspapers recognized a good story, and made the most of it. "The UN has a new trouble spot on its crowded agenda," wrote the *New York Post*. "The Kingdom of Central Park and associated states over which Robert Moses presides has served notice it may sever relations with the world organization."[18]

The new Secretary General held his ground, replying to Moses in a statement—also released to the press—that a UN survey had found that 1,250 spaces were all that were needed for cars of UN delegates and official visitors. And so, he said, it seemed unreasonable that the UN should have to rent storage space outside its own facility when it could convert part of its garage for that purpose.[19]

The world's top diplomat soon got some negotiating advice from Mayor Impellitteri. At a chance meeting at a reception at the Pierre Hotel, the mayor suggested to Hammarskjold that he have a "face-to-face" chat with the City Construction Coordinator. That was usually the only way to settle differences with Moses, he told the Secretary General, whose agenda at the time was filled with a number of critical world issues, including an armistice agreement to end the UN Command's fighting in Korea.[20]

But a luncheon meeting in Hammarskjold's private dining room in the Secretariat did nothing to cool things down. Before long, Moses publicly accused Hammarskjold of giving him the "runaround." Moses thought the Secretary General had agreed to restore the 250 garage spaces for parking immediately, while Hammarskjold said he had agreed to return them only if they might be needed in the future. Moses called his meeting with the Secretary General "high diplomatic palavers," and said the language used by the Secretariat was "almost a foreign language. . . . one we don't understand on First Avenue and Forty-second Street."

But when Hammarskjold got the support of several UN representatives, including the U.S. delegation then led by Henry Cabot Lodge Jr., Moses retreated. The parking issue was left to fester in City Hall until a new mayor came to power, with his own ideas of how to deal with the new world body in the city's midst. Moses' role as the chief liaison with the United Nations had, in effect, come to an end. "International rhubarb," he called the whole affair.[21]

Discovering the Wrinkles

While to Moses it may have been "international rhubarb," to the next mayor of New York, former Manhattan Borough President Robert F. Wagner Jr., it was a serious problem. Soon after being sworn into office in January 1954, the forty-three-year-old Wagner—a Democrat whose father had been a four-term U.S. Senator from New York State—visited Hammarskjold at UN headquarters. When he left, he announced he would set up a committee of New Yorkers to work to strengthen the city-UN partnership. For sure, he said, he was going to resolve the parking controversy.[22]

Wagner's "United Nations Committee of the City of New York" was a prestigious group. He asked Richard Patterson Jr., a seasoned business executive and former diplomat whom he had appointed Commissioner of Public Events and Commerce, to lead it. The committee included Eleanor Roosevelt; David Rockefeller; Mrs. Arthur Hayes Sulzberger, wife of the *New York Times* publisher; and IBM chairman Thomas Watson. Noticeably absent from the committee was Robert Moses, though he still held considerable power within the new administration. Moses seemed pleased to be excluded. "I must say frankly that after my recent experience with the Secretary General on the parking question, I am not disposed to solicit further contact with the organization," Moses wrote to an associate.[23]

Patterson and his committee members soon learned that parking wasn't the only issue on the city-UN agenda. At their first meeting with Hammarskjold, they heard a litany of other sticky problems, including the lack of adequate schools for children of UN delegates and staff, confusion over local property taxes on real estate owned by foreign governments, and inhospitable behavior on the part of some New Yorkers who either didn't understand—or didn't want to understand—diplomatic immunity and privilege. Perhaps most troublesome, the UN was growing increasingly uneasy about race discrimination in the city, particularly in housing.[24]

Discrimination in the United States had been a concern of the UN since early Preparatory Commission debates over whether to settle in the United States or Europe. And as early as 1947, not long after the organization was firmly committed to locating in New York, the subject had been catapulted to the forefront when the UN found itself in dire need of more housing for its multi-racial staff. At the city's urging, the UN agreed to reserve 600 rental apartments for employees in Peter Cooper

Village, a housing complex being built by Metropolitan Life Insurance Company on Manhattan's east side just north of another of its projects, Stuyvesant Town.[25]

Under the deal, the apartments would be set aside for UN employees and the UN would subsidize the employees for 25 percent of their rent. But the insurance company held the right to decide who among the UN staff would be accepted as residents.[26]

The latter point was the problem. Metropolitan Life had a strict policy of segregation in its housing units. "Negroes and whites don't mix," the company's chairman, Frederick Ecker, had notoriously told the press.[27] It didn't take long for UN employees to recognize that Metropolitan Life's stand on race was clearly at odds with the very principles of the UN charter—"freedom for all without distinction to race, sex, language, or religion." And when it was pointed out that no employee was being forced to live at Peter Cooper Village, the workers argued that by guaranteeing a quarter of the rental fee, the UN was, in effect, encouraging employees to accept racial discrimination.[28]

Despite their dire need for housing, and the tempting location of Peter Cooper Village—within easy walking distance of the permanent UN headquarters site—the staff fought the deal. On July 24, 1947, some one thousand UN workers, from New York and countries around the world, turned out in front of the UN Secretariat offices, then located at the temporary Lake Success facility, to rally in protest of the agreement. While Metropolitan Life had the legal right to exclude blacks in its housing— segregation in the city's private housing wasn't prohibited until 1958 when Mayor Wagner signed the Sharkey-Brown-Isaacs bill—the UN workers' highly publicized stand would later be credited as an episode that contributed to the end of discrimination in the city's housing. And for Patterson and his committee members, it was a forerunner of problems they would find at the top of a long list of issues plaguing the city-UN relationship in the early 1950s.[29]

After his group's first meeting with Hammarskjold, Patterson wrote him to say that Mayor Wagner had instructed him to "leave no stone unturned" in "smoothing out the hundred and one wrinkles between the city of New York and the UN."[30]

For a time, relations did appear to improve. Wagner was known for his progressive position on race, and UN staff noticed when he appointed blacks and Latinos to senior jobs in his administration. He set up a group to look at property tax issues facing the UN community and formed a task force to address building development in the area surrounding the

UN (including blocking a plan by the National Sugar Refining Company to erect a huge "Jack Frost Sugar" sign across the East River from the UN). To educate future generations of New Yorkers about the world organization's work, Wagner recommended that every city high school student tour UN headquarters at least once, a program that was to become a fixture of New York's school curriculum for years to come. Eleanor Roosevelt, who had recently resigned as a U.S. delegate to the UN and was now volunteering with AAUN, was asked to head a group to coordinate New Yorkers' interactions with delegates. And he restored an annual tradition, dropped by the previous administration, of hosting a reception for UN delegates and New York businesspeople—taking advice from Hammarskjold that he skip the lengthy speeches and let the UN people and New Yorkers mingle and get to know one another. Even the Soviet Union's deputy foreign minister, Andrey Vishinsky, noticed a change in the city's approach to the UN. "At last, the ice has been broken," he observed after attending Wagner's get-together in October 1954.[31]

Tackling the Wrinkles

Soon, an attractive young redhead, Nina Rao Cameron, joined Patterson's committee as the chief liaison with the UN. A lawyer and the daughter of a federal judge who was influential in Democratic politics, she was hired to help UN delegates with advice on housing, schools, and transportation needs. But by all accounts, she especially enjoyed giving a good party. In one year alone, she reported to the mayor that she had hosted thirty-one events for the UN, ranging from a lavish day of swimming, dining, and a musical concert at Jones Beach, to a dinner dance on the SS Constitution, and a day at the zoo. "I love my job so much that I never take all my vacation," she proudly exclaimed to a *New York Times* reporter.[32]

But the number of nations joining the UN was increasing fast, and with each new country, problems between the host city and the world organization grew more complex. During the first two of Mayor Wagner's three terms in office, UN membership increased from 60 to 104 nations. The city itself was facing a multitude of troubling issues—from unbearable traffic tie-ups, lack of adequate schoolrooms, the need for homes and apartments, to racial conflicts. All were exacerbated by the influx of UN diplomats and their families. In 1960 alone, seventeen nations joined the UN. All but one of them were newly independent African countries, and as many had feared, their delegates learned firsthand that New York was still struggling with racial prejudice.[33]

Accustomed to a level of respect back home, many were unprepared for what they faced in the city. "In restaurants here they serve us reluctantly, or they take their time—in some way they let us feel we are not welcome," said one West African ambassador. "Policemen often are uncivil to us. Bus drivers are downright rude."

Some Africans took to wearing their national dress to distinguish themselves from New York blacks, the wife of one African delegate telling the press that her husband wouldn't let her wear American-style clothing because he was "afraid I would be taken for an American Negro and perhaps I would come to some harm."[34]

In 1962, not long after Adlai Stevenson became U.S. UN ambassador, he urged Mayor Wagner to strengthen efforts to deal with the growing New York–UN schism. Stevenson, a former Illinois governor and twice the unsuccessful presidential contender against Dwight Eisenhower, had first been associated with the UN back in 1945, when he was the country's deputy delegate to the Preparatory Commission. Now, he was disturbed by the growing tension between the host city and its international guests. The mayor soon signed an executive order forming the "Commission to the United Nations." He named Eleanor Clark French to the unsalaried commissioner post. Active in Democratic politics and a member of the New York City Commission on Human Rights, the fifty-three-year-old French had studied at Columbia, Harvard, and the Sorbonne, and was a former women's editor of the *New York Times.*[35]

Crowded Curbs

French found a deteriorating relationship between the city and the UN. Within months, she wrote the mayor that the "anti–New York sentiment in the UN is increasing rather than decreasing" and she warned that some in the UN were "grasping at every incident to stimulate a move to set up UN headquarters elsewhere."[36]

And in another memo to the mayor, headed simply "Problems," she said she was particularly disturbed that landlords and cooperative apartment buildings were turning down high-level UN diplomats who wanted to rent or buy. She suspected discrimination played a role, but the reason being given, she wrote, was "diplomatic immunity," bringing with it concerns that the UN people could walk away from their lease, or rent payments, or maintenance charges, without penalty.[37]

Diplomatic immunity was a legal concept with which French would become all too familiar. One of the oldest principles of foreign relations, and governed by international treaties, its intent is to ensure diplomats' independence when they are working outside their own country by allowing them to carry out their diplomatic duties without fear of violating local laws they might not fully understand.

The city was no stranger to the concept. Long before the UN came to town, New York had been host to foreign consular offices, some of whose employees, in varying degrees, enjoyed diplomatic privileges. But the world organization's arrival brought to New York three new categories of officials with some level of immunity—certain staff at the UN, diplomats at government missions to the UN, and various others associated with UN-related organizations.[38]

Diplomatic privilege quickly became the subject of resentment on the part of some New Yorkers, and the commissioner's office took to reminding residents that Americans, too, enjoy diplomatic immunity when they serve in posts around the world. Still, many believed UN personnel misused their immunity. French told the mayor that landlords were taking the attitude that UN delegates "crowd up elevators with their guests, and curbs with their DPL cars."[39]

"DPL cars"—automobiles with distinctive diplomatic license plates—were another of French's worries. Issued by the U.S. State Department, the plates are intended to provide easy identification of cars whose owners hold diplomatic immunity. But as French would learn, many New Yorkers viewed DPL cars as just another obstacle to finding parking spaces on the crowded streets of Manhattan.

Parking, the root of the Moses-Hammarskjold feud, now was exacerbated by the increase in UN member nations, coupled with a building boom under way just two blocks west of the organization's headquarters. On Third Avenue, the Elevated Rail Line, which had rumbled overhead since the late 1800s, was demolished in the mid-1950s. In its place, the city encouraged development of a midtown office district of high rises lining the avenue that, by the 1960s, provided welcome office space for foreign governments' UN missions. But that meant more traffic, more DPL plates, and fewer available parking spots for the public.

Trying to control the congestion, the city embarked on a plan to give each UN mission two parking spaces outside its building, suggesting that any further parking needs be met by using the UN's underground garage. But as more new office towers opened up, more missions moved in, and double parking—even at city bus stops—became the norm. By the mid-1960s, pedestrians were complaining bitterly about the dangerous conditions. Evoking a far-off war, Peter Detmold, a community leader in the Turtle Bay neighborhood, likened the risks of boarding a city bus on Third Avenue to "strolling in Vietnam's back woods."[40]

Some protests got vicious, with reports of cars with DPL plates having their tires slashed and left with insulting messages on their windshields. At French's urging, police stepped up ticketing the illegally parked cars. But many missions, shielded by diplomatic immunity, ignored the tickets.

"Laws are Meant for Other People," shouted a headline in a three-part *Daily News* story in June 1965. "Some of us are more equal before the law and get more equal protection—that is, if we work out of the UN," the story editorialized.[41]

By the time Commissioner French left office six months later at the end of Wagner's third term, diplomatic parking was still high on the list of problems that plagued city-UN relations, and it wouldn't be essentially resolved for many years.

Still, she knew it was hardly the only matter affecting the UN's tenure in New York. The lack of adequate schools for diplomats' children was another. While the problem was eased during Wagner's final days in office when the United Nations International School signed a long-term lease on property for a new facility, the project would need continuing attention. And other problems persisted: housing difficulties for diplomats, both for rental and owned property, exacerbated by concerns over diplomatic immunity as well as race discrimination; confusion over taxes, from which foreign governments may be exempt under international law; and a plethora of questions from foreign governments regarding zoning, building codes, and city services, issues often bewildering to even lifelong New Yorkers, but far more so to diplomats from other countries.

Before she departed, French wrote to the incoming mayor, John V. Lindsay. She knew the forty-four-year-old Yale-educated lawyer well. In the summer of 1964, she had taken a leave from her UN liaison post to wage an unsuccessful campaign as the Democratic-Liberal candidate in a bid to unseat Lindsay, a moderate Republican then running for his fourth term as the U.S. Congressman from Manhattan's East Side. Now, she told the mayor-elect that while she was proud of her steps to improve the city's partnership with the UN, more work needed to be done. "I recommend strongly that this Commission remain a part of the Mayor's office," she wrote her former political foe.[42]

The Commission Tradition

Indeed, French's role during the Wagner administration would serve as a model for the commissioner's office and it would become a permanent fixture of the UN-city relationship, although some observed that its goals and priorities would be uneven over the years.

Lindsay appointed Frances Lehman Loeb to the job and expanded it to include the city's Consular Corps committee, liaison with the scores of Consulates General in New York. A wealthy and well-traveled philanthropist whose father and husband both were prominent bankers, she would stay on in the role during the administration of the next mayor, Abraham Beame.

When Ed Koch was elected mayor in 1978, he appointed Gillian Sorensen to the office, and for the first time made the job a salaried position. A Smith College graduate who had also studied at the Sorbonne and was a former television producer, Sorensen had worked for Koch's election campaign, and she said later the commissioner's post was one she eagerly sought. "I believed I could make a real difference in addressing not only the challenges, but the tremendous opportunities, of the complex city-UN partnership."[43]

Sorensen, who oversaw a full-time paid staff of fourteen and forty-five trained volunteers, would gain a reputation, both within city circles and the diplomatic corps, as a very effective and respected commissioner, and she was associated with the city and the UN for years to come. She stayed with Koch during his twelve years in office, and then was recruited by UN Secretary General Boutros Boutros-Ghali to serve as his Special Advisor for Public Policy. Under the next UN chief, Kofi Annan, she served as Assistant Secretary General for External Relations, and later was National Advocate and Senior Advisor to the UN Foundation, a Washington-based group that advocates for the UN's work around the world.[44]

When Mayor David Dinkins came to office in 1990, he named Paul O'Dwyer commissioner. The eighty-two-year-old labor and civil rights lawyer and former city council president was the younger brother of William O'Dwyer, the mayor who had secured UN headquarters for the city back in the 1940s. Dinkins credited Paul O'Dwyer with helping him get his start in politics, and when O'Dwyer said he wanted the commissioner's job, he got it. "Uncle Paul could have whatever he wanted," Dinkins said years later.[45] But O'Dwyer resigned within two years, saying the diplomacy required for the job conflicted with his desire to speak out about human rights abuses around the world.[46] He was replaced by Nadine Hack, head of the city's Sister City program, which coordinated relationships with other major world cities, an effort that had been a part of the commissioner's office since Koch asked Sorensen to take it on in 1983.

In 1994, Mayor Rudolph Giuliani appointed Livia Sylva, a Romanian-born head of a beeswax cosmetics company and a major Republican campaign contributor, to the office, and then Bruce Gelb, former director of the U.S. Information Agency and ambassador to Belgium under President George H. W. Bush. Later, Giuliani added the city's protocol duties to the job and appointed Irene Halligan, a former public relations executive active in Republican politics, as City Commissioner for the United Nations, Consular Corps, and Protocol.

After Michael Bloomberg was elected mayor in 2002, he named his younger sister, Marjorie Tiven, a former social worker, to the post. She was paid no salary.[47] During her time, the Sister City program was merged into a broadened effort, New York City Global Partners, and the commissioner's office got a new, lofty designation: the "Mayor's Office for International Affairs."[48]

While Tiven's twelve-year tenure came to be known for its focus on the operational aspects of the city-UN relationship,[49] the next commissioner, Penny Abeywardena—appointed by Mayor Bill de Blasio in the fall of 2014—promised to bring a "new narrative" to the job that would strengthen the link between the city and its global partner.

Born in Sri Lanka and raised in Los Angeles, Abeywardena earned a Master of International Affairs degree from Columbia University and was working for the Clinton Global Initiative when she was tapped for the job. She said the mayor made it clear from the start what her goals should be. "We want to 'demystify' how New Yorkers think about the UN," she said. "We want our citizens to understand that having the UN located here is not just about traffic jams and parking tickets, but about the cultural and educational resources it represents, and the financial boost it brings to our city.

"And just as important," she said, "we want New Yorkers to have a greater appreciation of what the UN stands for and how its goals mirror our own in so many ways."

Shortly after she moved into her new role, her office was collecting financial information to show how the UN community benefits the city economically, a report that had not been compiled and widely distributed since 1989, when Sorensen was commissioner.

And Abeywardena developed a number of initiatives to capitalize on the interaction between the city and the UN, introducing a "NYC Junior Ambassadors" program to give seventh-graders throughout the city's five boroughs the opportunity to interact with the UN and its diplomats.

A "Global Vision/Urban Action" initiative was set up to highlight the synergies of the city's goals for environmental and economic sustainability with the UN's "Sustainable Development Goals," adopted by UN member states in the fall of 2015.

And, in a symbolic move to make UN employees and delegates feel more a part of New York, she sponsored a two-week "pop up" booth in the UN Secretariat to register UN staff for the city's municipal ID card, a photo identification card introduced by the de Blasio administration and available to New Yorkers regardless of immigration status.

Even Secretary General Ban Ki-moon signed up. "After more than eight years of calling New York home, I will finally be able to say that I am a New Yorker," he said.[50]

7

Learning to Live Side by Side

When Frances Lehman Loeb was named the city's commissioner to the United Nations in early 1966, she knew her job was going to be tough. She came to the role with a strong belief in the organization's work and a healthy dose of realism. Now twenty years since the UN first settled in New York, the fifty-nine-year-old Loeb—known to everyone in the city by her childhood nickname, "Peter"—recalled the enthusiastic welcome the UN had initially received. "Our city was proud—even thrilled at the thought of becoming a world capital," she said shortly after taking office. "Now—somehow the bloom is off the rose."[1]

Indeed, for many New Yorkers, the "bloom" was a fading memory. The UN member countries now numbered 117, and Peter Loeb's boss, the city's new mayor, John V. Lindsay, faced innumerable problems that many believed were only aggravated by the UN's presence. "Traffic congestion, overcrowding of schools, housing shortages, increasing air pollution and ethnic agitation—combined with the staggering growth of the United Nations itself—have resulted in a certain amount of disenchantment," Loeb said of New Yorkers' attitudes toward the UN at the time.[2]

At the UN, meanwhile, Arthur Goldberg recently had been appointed U.S. ambassador after Adlai Stevenson's sudden death of a heart attack in mid-summer 1965. Goldberg was a U.S. Supreme Court Justice when President Lyndon Johnson asked him to move into the UN mission job. Like Stevenson, Goldberg was disheartened by city residents' lack of enthusiasm for the world organization, as well as foreign delegates' growing discontent with their environs. He spearheaded formation of a "good neighbor" group of fifteen UN nations, structured along the lines of the Security Council. Initially, its goals were unclear to some, one West European member explaining that it was aimed simply at "halting annoyances."[3]

Then soon, after Goldberg saw results of a Louis Harris poll of UN delegates and their attitudes toward life in New York, he realized more needed to be done. The survey showed delegates increasingly dissatisfied with the city, particularly by the discourtesies to nonwhite diplomats and discrimination on the part of New York landlords. Coordinating with Lindsay, Goldberg formed the "Host Country Advisory Committee to the United Nations." Under the auspices of the State Department, it worked out of the U.S. Mission and was intended to supplement the efforts of Loeb's city commission.[4] Like the commission, it would become a long-standing permanent office, in later years renamed the "Office of Host Country Affairs." Meanwhile, the UN's "good neighbor" group was later formalized to become the "United Nations Committee on Relations with the Host Country."*

While friction between the city and the UN troubled Goldberg, he was just as concerned about the anti–UN fervor that was taking hold throughout the United States, fueled, in part, by rhetoric coming out of the previous year's presidential race. Conservative Republican Barry Goldwater, running against Democrat incumbent Lyndon Johnson, had repeatedly used the campaign stump to call for a drastic cut in U.S. support of the UN, which he viewed as a propaganda tool of the Soviet Union. The conservative's charges, in the midst of the Cold War, were bolstered by a growing sentiment at the UN to replace the U.S.-backed Republic of China (Taiwan), a member of the world body since its founding, with the Soviet-backed People's Republic of China.

And paranoia over Soviet spying was increasingly widespread, as reports of undercover agents associated with the Soviets' UN presence continually trickled out. Many recalled a heated and widely reported debate in the UN Security Council in 1960, after an American U-2 spy plane piloted by Francis Gary Powers was shot down over Soviet territory. During the impassioned discourse, U.S. Ambassador Stevenson read off a list of eleven Soviets who had been caught spying in the United States in recent

*The UN Committee was established by a 1971 General Assembly resolution. Its traditional chair is the Cypriot UN ambassador, and it meets regularly with the U.S. UN Mission's "Office of Host Country Affairs." As of 2017, nineteen member states were represented on the committee.

years and quietly expelled from the country. Five were workers for the UN or the Soviets' UN mission.

Throughout the country, it was becoming accepted wisdom among editorialists, politicians, and ordinary Americans that Communists had infiltrated the ranks of UN workers at an alarming rate; that the organization's seemingly anti-U.S. positions, such as its Taiwan stance, made it unworthy of the country's hefty membership dues; and that the world body was simply a magnet for spies.

The disenchantment Commissioner Loeb's office faced at the city level, on the other hand, was of a more parochial nature—parking hassles, traffic congestion, and unpaid bills by foreigners claiming diplomatic immunity. Long before, New Yorkers, representing a broader spectrum of ethnic backgrounds than even the UN member nations, had become accustomed to living side by side with the big world organization—with workers and diplomats from countries whose ideologies might be at odds with their own; with UN policies many found offensive and that were likely to spark an outburst, usually awkward, from their mayor; and with networks of spies, generally known to be circulating in the city under cover of the world body.

New York's First UN Spy

For decades, the city's hundreds of hotels and restaurants, public parks, miles of subway and bus lines, diversity of its people, and simply its round-the-clock bustle had provided an ideal haven for spies. But when the UN came to town, a new and especially convenient cover was added to the list. Agents were said to be crawling all over the UN complex—in Secretariat offices, the cafeteria, in the crowded Delegates Lounge, and in the UN library, a favored spot for a spy's "dead drop" message, placed within pages of a book, easily identified for retrieval later. By the 1960s, New Yorkers had become reconciled to the fact that undercover intrigue was playing out all around the UN. But in 1949, when the story of the man who became known as the "first UN spy" came to light, almost everyone had been taken by surprise. The tale of Valentin Gubitschev and his New York girlfriend would become one of the biggest spy stories in city history.

Gubitschev had been known to many New Yorkers in the UN's early days, including architect Wallace Harrison and city officials such as Robert Moses, who remembered him as the gentle-mannered translator for

Nikolai Bassov, the Soviet member of the group that designed the UN headquarters buildings.

He had first come to New York in 1946, part of the Soviet delegation to the UN. Later, the thirty-year-old Gubitschev became a Secretariat employee, and when Bassov needed help communicating with his fellow designers, he was one of two interpreters assigned to work with him. He spent long days with the design team, attending the architects' meetings in the RKO Building at Rockefeller Center, and joining them at social get-togethers and weekend outings. Short and stocky, he was particularly quiet, once bringing a smile to their faces when he shyly told the architects to call him by his anglicized first name, "Valentine." Moses later claimed to have been suspicious of his activities all along, observing that Gubitschev continually "watched [Bassov's] every move."[5]

When the design work was complete, Gubitschev went to work in the office coordinating construction of the UN buildings. He and his wife, Lydia, settled into an apartment on the Upper West Side. It was then that Gubitschev began an occasional evening rendezvous with a pretty, petite Brooklynite named Judith Coplon. She was twenty-seven years old and a cum laude graduate of Barnard College where she majored in history and had joined the Young Communist League. Now she was employed as an analyst at the U.S. Justice Department's Internal Security Section in Washington. But she often came to New York to visit her ailing parents, who lived on Ocean Parkway in Flatbush, *and*, it turned out, to see Valentin Gubitschev, with whom she would say she was in love.

Soon, on reports from Washington that some of Coplon's Justice Department analyses seemed slanted toward the Soviets, the FBI was monitoring her movements. And before long, three FBI men were watching Gubitschev at his UN job and two were monitoring his apartment. Daily, he was followed as he entered and left the UN construction site, and at his apartment on West 108th Street, unsuspecting neighbors offered the agents details about his family life.

Then on the evening of March 4, 1949—in an undercover operation involving some twenty FBI agents and a fleet of radio cars—agents tailed Coplon and Gubitschev as they met on Upper Broadway, where they passed each other, at around 191st Street, without speaking. The FBI then followed as Coplon alone took the subway to Forty-second Street and Eighth Avenue and walked slowly, and seemingly aimlessly, through Times Square, where she met up with Gubitschev again. The two took the Ninth Avenue bus to Fourteenth Street and then caught a Brooklyn-bound subway to Manhattan's East Side where the FBI lost sight of them near Union Square. Moments later, they were spotted again as they strolled along the east side of Third Avenue to a shadowy spot under the El between Fifteenth and Sixteenth streets. There, they were arrested. Coplon was carrying a handbag full of papers that included sensitive FBI reports on Soviet affairs, as well as fictitious material the FBI had planted on her desk at the Justice Department.[6]

It was the first big spy story in the city since the end of World War II, and it captivated New Yorkers and the entire country. "For a time between 1949 and 1950, Americans couldn't get enough of Judith Coplon," said intelligence historian H. Keith Melton, who likened the lover spies to a "1950s version of a reality TV show."[7]

Coplon was tried and found guilty of espionage and, along with Gubitschev, of conspiracy. He was expelled. Her convictions were eventually overturned on technicalities involving illegal wiretaps and lack of a warrant.*[8]

With the Gubitschev-Coplon affair, New Yorkers had come to recognize that life going forward would include a new kind of spy, the "UN spy." As home to the United Nations, the city was "central to the world of espionage," said Melton, "with probably more spies walking the streets of New York than any other city in the world."[9]

Then within just a few years, in the early 1950s, the growing fear of Communism throughout the United States would bring another quandary for the city and the UN, one that strained the relationship as never before, and touched average New Yorkers in personal, often tragic ways.

City's UN Workers Face the Country's "Red Scare"

On Thursday, November 13, 1952, less than a month after the UN opened its first session in the new General Assembly Hall on the East River, the Secretariat staff received some shocking news. The UN's top lawyer, Brooklyn-born Abraham Feller, had jumped to his death from his twelfth-floor apartment on Central Park West.[10]

The forty-seven-year-old Feller had been employed by the UN since its early formative days in London, and he had the distinction of being the UN's first employee in New York City. In early 1946, Secretary General

---

*Coplon continued to live quietly in New York, mostly in Brooklyn, until her death in 2011. She married one of her appellate lawyers, Albert Socolov, and they had four children.

Lie had asked Feller, a graduate of Columbia College with a law degree from Harvard, to set up a UN office in the Waldorf Astoria to begin hiring Secretariat staff. The young lawyer had gone on to become one of Lie's most trusted advisors. He was in charge of working with the city on transfer of the riverside site to the UN, and he had provided counsel to Lie on some critical international issues, including the Palestinian question and the Korean conflict.[11]

Recently Feller, now the UN's General Counsel, had been advising Lie on a particularly troubling matter—charges that some of the approximately two thousand Americans working for the UN Secretariat were Communists or Communist sympathizers. It was a problematic issue for the UN, an international entity in the midst of the largest city in a nation that was increasingly gripped by the fear of Communism. And New York City found itself in the uncomfortable position of being capitalist host city to an organization of nations of many ideologies, Communist and non-Communist alike.

By the fall of 1952, the "Red Scare" was reaching a fever pitch throughout the country, and nowhere was it more apparent than in New York. Public school teachers and college professors were being investigated under the so-called Feinberg Law. Congressional hearings were targeting some of the city's most talented actors, writers, and musicians, leaving them "blacklisted" and out of work. Municipal and social workers were being investigated as a prerequisite to employment. And two high-profile investigations were looking into suspected U.S. Communists working for the UN Secretariat.[12] A federal grand jury was hearing evidence from a young, ambitious assistant U.S. attorney, Roy Cohn, who was doing his utmost to keep his UN probe in the spotlight. And the Senate Judiciary Committee's Internal Security Subcommittee investigating suspected Communist subversion in the United States had moved its hearings from Capitol Hill to Manhattan's Federal Court House. The subcommittee's head, Senator Pat McCarran, a Democrat from Nevada, said he wanted to be closer to his latest target—the UN. "A vantage ground for the infiltration of the United States," he said of the world organization.[13]

As American UN employees were called to testify before the two panels, some refused to answer questions about possible Communist activity and invoked the Fifth Amendment to protect themselves against self-incrimination. It left UN Secretary General Lie in a difficult spot. He deplored what he called the "hysteria" taking hold in the United States over the fear of "Reds," but he also felt that with the UN permanently headquartered in the United States, it was "plain common sense not to want any American Communists in the Secretariat." He fired or put on compulsory leave employees who took the Fifth. It was Feller who was given the stressful job of asking his colleagues to clear out their desks, while at the same time defending the UN's position in the press.[14]

On Tuesday, November 11, the session of the McCarran hearings was particularly stormy. The senators heard from a Midtown Manhattan woman who worked as a UN translator, a Bronx man who was a UN library clerk, and the wife of a UN documents editor who lived with her husband in Peter Cooper Village. Asked if they had ever been members of the Communist party, each pleaded the Fifth. When the session ended, McCarran and a fellow senator, Democrat Willis Smith of North Carolina, emerged onto Foley Square to angrily tell reporters that if the UN couldn't rid itself of "spies and saboteurs," then it "ought not to be allowed to sit in America."[15] The harsh language was splashed across newspapers throughout the country.

Two days later, Feller jumped to his death, landing in the courtyard behind his apartment building at Central Park West and Sixty-fifth Street. Lie was having lunch at the Metropolitan Club when he got the news. He rushed to the Feller home, and told reporters gathered outside that the New Yorker's suicide was the result of the strain in defending his American colleagues against "indiscriminate smears and exaggerated charges." Feller was, Lie said, the victim of the "witch hunt." While Feller had not been called to testify before the grand jury or the Senate subcommittee, and there was never any indication he was suspected of Communist leanings, Lie said the "awful pressure of the hysterical assault upon the United Nations" brought on by the Red Scare "finally grew too strong, and he broke."[16]

Soon, the assault would move directly inside the walls of the Secretariat.

The early recruiting of UN staff had been hasty, as the newly formed organization needed to ramp up quickly. In 1946 and 1947 alone, more than 27,000 people applied for jobs at the UN, and some 2,500 were hired. The vast majority were New Yorkers, who filled virtually all of the lower-level jobs such as guards, filing clerks, machine operators, and typists. Despite Lie's requests, the United States had refused to recommend or provide background on applicants for UN jobs. It wanted to avoid the appearance of influencing the UN's selections.[17]

Then finally in January 1953, outgoing President Truman issued an executive order that gave the UN more leverage in filtering out suspected Communists among the Americans. It allowed for Federal Bureau of Investigation checks of U.S. staff in higher level UN positions and applicants for those jobs, and Civil Service Commission checks of lower-level employees.[18]

Lie agreed to let FBI agents move into the UN's Secretariat offices, where U.S. citizens on the staff were fingerprinted and interrogated. He said he did so for the convenience of the employees. But the unorthodox on-site "loyalty" investigations by a U.S. agency within international territory were criticized from all sides—by the staff being questioned, by many of Lie's key aides who thought it was a mistake to allow such U.S. infringement on UN soil, and by the UN's member nations, who took up the matter in a stormy General Assembly debate. It was a "grave crisis," claimed the French representative, who said U.S. workers' careers now depended on "blind docility." Delegates from the Soviet bloc claimed the UN had been turned into a "police station."[19]

It would be months before a semblance of normality returned to the offices of the Secretariat. By then, Cohn's grand jury had concluded its proceedings without a single indictment, the Senate subcommittee hearings had moved back to Washington, and the UN had a new Secretary General, Dag Hammarskjold. Lie had resigned in the face of a break with the Soviet Union over his siding with South Korea after it was invaded by the Communist North in 1950. But aides made it clear he also had been deeply disturbed by the ordeal emanating from the attacks on alleged American Communists at the UN.[20] When Hammarskjold came on board in April 1953, he began to take a firmer stand with the Americans and their investigatory procedures, and asserted a style of leadership that the disheartened UN staff greeted warmly.[21]

Still, the complex and uncomfortable episode had tainted the hosts' relationship with the UN for years to come. And it would foreshadow what was to follow, as the UN's diverse membership took positions with which many New Yorkers disagreed and even found offensive, and which the city's leadership often felt compelled to challenge.

Local Politics Meets Global Policies

Balancing the concerns of an urban constituency as diverse as any in the world with the desire to be a gracious host to the United Nations would forever prove challenging for New York's mayors. While no city leader has failed to appreciate the financial and symbolic benefit of having the world organization in New York, most have found it difficult—some might say politically impossible—to stay out of the foreign affairs arena when UN member states' policies bump up against New Yorkers' views. The interference, most often met with a knowing smile by New Yorkers, has caused more than a little political angst in Washington, and some serious irritation on the part of UN leaders.

As far back as 1950, when the world organization was still a newcomer in town, the acting mayor, Vincent Impellitteri, hosted a dinner for UN delegates at the Waldorf Astoria during which the governor of the state, Thomas Dewey, took to the stage to lecture the diplomats about the Soviet Union's "slave labor" and "torture" practices. As the Soviet delegates stalked out of the ballroom, Impellitteri—a Democrat, then facing his first election for mayor—proceeded to tell the press he thought the Republican governor's remarks were "splendid."[22]

In 1957, Mayor Wagner refused to acknowledge Saudi Arabia's King Saud when he visited New York after a meeting with President Eisenhower in Washington. But Wagner didn't stop at that. Facing an upcoming re-election campaign in a city heavily Jewish and Catholic, Wagner made it quite clear how he felt about the king. "He is not the kind of person we want to recognize in New York City," the mayor told reporters. "He is a fellow who says slavery is legal, and in his country our air force cannot use Jewish men and cannot permit any Roman Catholic chaplain to say mass."[23]

Wagner won re-election. But Washington cringed. "These uninhibited outbursts make it very difficult to conduct foreign policy," one Washington official complained at the time.[24]

Nine years later, Washington again winced when another mayor snubbed another Saudi king. This time it was Mayor Lindsay and Saud's younger brother, King Faisal. It was a sensitive time in Middle East affairs, and the king was in the country to meet with President Johnson, who was honoring him with a formal state dinner at the White House. Afterward, the king's plans called for a New York visit, where he would meet with UN officials. At the urging of the White House, Lindsay had agreed to host a dinner party for the king in an elegant Spanish Renaissance patio at the Metropolitan Museum of Art. But as Faisal left Washington, he held a press conference, and when asked about the Arab boycott of those doing business with Israel, responded, "Jews support Israel and we consider those who provide assistance to our enemies as our own enemies."[25]

Within hours, Lindsay's office received more than four hundred constituent calls, all but six of them insisting the mayor call off the dinner.[26]

But Lindsay also got calls from Washington, from Secretary of State Dean Rusk, who pleaded with him to go ahead with the event. Rusk even came up with dinner remarks the mayor could use to diplomatically express dissent from the king's position.[27]

By early afternoon on the day of the banquet, it appeared Rusk had gotten his wish. The dining tables were set, the museum's patio was decked out with fresh flowers and shrubs, and chefs from New York's high-society caterer, Robert Day-Dean, were hard at work in their kitchens.

Then suddenly, the pressure from constituents took hold. "The dinner is canceled," read a curt, hastily worded statement from the mayor's office. The last-minute decision left City Hall staffers scrambling to get word to the guests before they headed to the Met for dinner, the White House hastily telephoning the king to apologize for the city's last-minute snub, and the king dining alone in his presidential suite at the Waldorf Towers.[28]

The next day, Faisal crossed First Avenue into United Nations territory, where he received a gracious welcome at a lunch hosted by Secretary General U Thant and attended by U.S. UN Ambassador Goldberg, himself a Jew.[29]

In the years following, mayors and their forays into foreign policy would continue to disturb Washington. But it was probably Mayor Ed Koch, who came into office in 1978 and whose three terms were peppered with seemingly endless, ever-quotable, barbs against the UN, who caused the greatest turmoil. Koch's press secretary in the early 1980s, Evan Cornog, remembered that the calls from his boss he dreaded most were the ones that "came at 7 o'clock Sunday morning after he had read the papers and found some matter of international import he wished to comment upon . . . usually on the latest UN muddle."[30]

Koch had been elected to office after serving three terms in the U.S. Congress, where he represented the Manhattan East Side district surrounding the UN. As mayor, his criticism of the UN was at its most vitriolic in 1982 in the months after the UN Security Council condemned Israel for its annexation of the Golan Heights. Seven years earlier, the General Assembly's vote declaring "Zionism is a form of racism and racial discrimination" had created a furor among New York's heavily Jewish population.* Now, Koch—who liked to describe himself as a "proud Jew" governing a city with more Jews than live in Tel Aviv—notoriously called the UN a "cesspool" of anti-Semitism and a "den of iniquity," and he

---

*In 1991, the General Assembly voted to repeal the Zionism resolution.

once told the press, "The UN is hypocritical and cowardly, and I would not be concerned if, in fact, it moved from the city."[31]

"Henry Kissinger I'm not," he once conceded in remarks to the Overseas Press Club. "But I *am* mayor of a city that comprises over 175 ethnic, racial and religious groups which . . . represent the nations and cultures of the entire world. My constituents have an interest in world affairs, and therefore so do I."[32]

In 1982, he announced he wanted to change a verse that had been chiseled into a city retaining wall on First Avenue facing the United Nations back in 1950. The words, the backdrop for the small Ralph Bunche Park, referenced the Bible's Book of Isaiah: "They shall beat their swords into plowshares." Koch said he wanted to add some other words from the Bible: "hypocrisy, immorality and cowardice." While the mayor backed down before the stone-cutters were hired—taking the advice of his staff, who told him he really must move on to other matters—the newly elected Secretary General, Javier Pérez de Cuéllar, decided it was wise to cancel a "get acquainted" lunch scheduled with the mayor. "It could be difficult at this moment," conceded Koch's ever-diplomatic commissioner to the UN, Gillian Sorensen.[33]

Still, Koch readily acknowledged the UN's hefty economic contribution to New York. And as the first mayor to fully fund the UN Commissioner's office and to staff it with a professional leader with strong diplomatic skills, many believed he showed a far higher regard for the organization than his rhetoric indicated. But Koch never could resist letting it be known he thought the world body gained more from being in the spotlight of New York, a media mecca, than his city benefited from hosting it. "If the UN would leave New York, nobody would ever hear of it again," he once quipped.[34]

Over time, the UN member states grew accustomed to the mayor's slights, and both the city and the UN came to rely on Sorensen to make amends. "Sorensen proved to be a discreet diplomatic counterpoint to the brashness of Koch's pronouncements," said Jonathan Soffer, a Koch biographer.[35]

Some referred to her as "New York City's foreign minister,"[36] and speculated that her adroit manner of dealing with the diplomats left Koch more at ease to snub the city's international guests. "Well, he certainly never said as much," Sorensen recalled years later, "but I did try to smooth the waters."[37]

Occasionally, she even managed to get Koch himself to soften his tone regarding the UN. "You always hurt the one you love," he said in a conciliatory moment.[38]

Still, in 1985, when the mayor sent a specially etched Tiffany paperweight to each UN mission in celebration of the organization's fortieth anniversary, some delegates were skeptical. The police received a number of calls from delegations who suspected a bomb might be in the signature blue box wrapped up with its pretty white bow.[39]

8
Autumn in New York

Apprehension about the contents of Mayor Koch's blue box seemed to have dissipated by the time another mayor, Rudolph Giuliani, presented another memento from New York's legendary Tiffany & Company—this one a porcelain box painted with the city's landmarks—to guests at an elegant candlelit dinner celebrating the United Nations' fiftieth anniversary.[1]

It was October 1995, and some five hundred kings, prime ministers, presidents, and top UN leaders dined on wild mushroom risotto cakes, herb-crusted rack of lamb, and breast of chicken in the glass-enclosed Winter Garden of the World Financial Center in lower Manhattan. Just a few weeks earlier, Giuliani—a Republican now in his second year in office—had addressed the General Assembly, the first mayor to do so since 1952. Now, his remarks at the dinner mirrored his amiable talk before the Assembly: "I am happy to confer on you citizenship as New Yorkers. You are all New Yorkers tonight," the mayor told them, "and you'll be New Yorkers for as long as you want to be."[2]

UN Secretary General Boutros Boutros-Ghali was even more effusive. "The UN and New York have had a love affair," he said of the fifty-year relationship, calling it a "romance."[3]

Most at the dinner party probably agreed that "love affair" was an overstatement, but the anniversary did come at a particularly peaceful interlude in the rocky relationship. By some estimates, 180 world leaders were in town—the largest gathering of heads of state in history—and city officials were eager to celebrate the milestone with style. Each of the high-level visitors received a handsome blue and gold souvenir booklet offering Giuliani's ebullient thanks for making the city the "Capital of the World" and citing the ways in which the city showed the UN member countries its appreciation each and every day.[4] Then two nights after the sumptuous Winter Garden gala, Giuliani hosted the dignitaries at a New York Philharmonic concert at Lincoln Center's Avery Fisher Hall, an affair for some two-thousand that was sponsored by a private group organized by the mayor.

It was at the concert that the city's stylish welcome got side-tracked.

Gillian Sorensen, who had gone on to work for the UN as an advisor to Boutros-Ghali after Koch left office and had a key role in the fiftieth anniversary commemoration, recalled the awkward incident vividly. The Secretary General had been scheduled to join Giuliani in welcoming the global guests to the concert, but when he canceled at the last moment, he asked Sorensen to speak in his place. It was a formidable assignment, she remembered thinking at the time. "Representatives of all the member and observer nations were invited, and I thought, 'What? The entire world's leaders, and I am to speak on behalf of the Secretary General?'

"But with no time to dwell on that, I rushed home, pulled on my best black dress and high heels, and headed to Lincoln Center."

She was backstage preparing for her remarks when Giuliani arrived. "He was in a fit, he was in a fury," she said.

"'Is it true? Is Yasir Arafat out there?' he asked me, and when I answered 'yes, he was invited like all the others' he replied, 'Well, I want him out.' And he started having a temper tantrum, he was red in the face, stomping his feet and raising his arms. I thought he might hit me."

Arafat—leader of the Palestinian Authority, which held observer status at the UN—recently had shared the Nobel Peace Prize with Israel's Shimon Peres and Yitzhak Rabin for his Middle East peace efforts that led to the so-called Oslo Accords. Viewed as a turning point in Arab-Israeli relations, Arafat and Rabin had signed the agreement at the White House, President Clinton by their side. Now, with talks between Israel and the Palestinian Authority set to continue, Washington was investing considerable time and effort in diplomacy that might lead to a permanent peace settlement.

"Giuliani turned to an aide and ordered him to tell Arafat to leave," Sorensen remembered. "So I watched, and I saw the aide go out into the audience and deliver the mayor's message to Arafat, who seemed startled, sort of shocked," she recalled.

As the Philharmonic opened with Beethoven's Ninth Symphony,

Arafat left. "And Giuliani went off to the tabloids to brag about what he had just done," Sorensen said.[5]

"I would not invite Yasir Arafat to anything, anywhere, anytime, any-place," Giuliani told news reporters, reminding them—and his constituency—of past terrorist acts by the Palestine Liberation Organization. "I don't forget," he said.[6]

"Rudy's One Rude Dude," shouted a headline in the *Daily News* the next day, a sentiment echoed by the State Department.[7]

Indeed, the Clinton administration was not pleased with Giuliani. "An embarrassment to everyone associated with diplomacy," said a White House official.[8]

"Arafat should be treated with respect and dignity," said the State Department. "He is the leader of the Palestinian people and he is negotiating with Israel."[9]

And soon, Ed Koch—the mayor who had more scrapes with the United Nations over Mideast policies than any mayor before or since—went public with a scathing critique of Giuliani. "Crazy," he called Giuliani's snub of Arafat. It was evidence the current mayor had a "behavioral problem"[10] and a "schoolyard bully persona,"[11] claimed Koch, who at the time was having a personal political feud with the mayor.

Giuliani struck back. "I think that if we're going to take lessons in diplomacy . . . the last person you should take it from is Ed Koch."[12]

Meanwhile, the Palestinian Authority, which confirmed that, indeed, Arafat had been given a ticket to the concert, called the whole incident sad. "It only indicates that the office of the Mayor has been hijacked by some fanatics in this city," said a Palestinian official. "It is also sad that while boasting about New York as the capital of the world, as a great city—and it's true—he has misbehaved in such sensitive political issues."[13]

Still, at least according to a *Daily News* call-in poll, most of Giuliani's constituency stood by him. More than 60 percent of New Yorkers said the mayor was right to boot Arafat from the Philharmonic concert. Some New Yorkers chose not to take sides, instead suggesting that the whole episode was just another reason why the United Nations should not be located in New York City.[14]

Sorensen saw the incident as regrettable and counterproductive. "The concert was to be a unifying concept. For at least two hours, we were to set politics aside, and let music bring us together."[15]

The Annual Pilgrimage

Apart from the mayor's bad manners, the UN's symbolic half-century anniversary would be remembered for the record number of state leaders who came together to celebrate. And while the high-level attendance would be repeated during special UN commemorations in the decades to follow, even a typical opening General Assembly session and General Debate draws up to one hundred leaders. From the president of the United States to representatives of the tiny island nations of Tuvalu and Palau, each takes a turn at the podium—the Assembly Hall's familiar green marble rostrum behind them—to express to the world their countries' particular concerns.

Security is tight for the annual pilgrimage. Thousands of city police are posted in the area around the UN, and Manhattan's far East Side literally shuts down to automobile traffic and even to pedestrian traffic on some blocks. At times, entire buildings become "frozen" zones, with residents and office workers prevented from leaving or entering. Checkpoints, manned by the police, the U.S. State Department security detail, Secret Service, and UN Security, are set up throughout the neighborhood. A Coast Guard flotilla patrols from the East River. Police helicopters fly overhead. Bomb-sniffing dogs check cars entering the UN parking garage, sand trucks barricade critical intersections, and nearby high-rise apartment and office towers open up their roof space to security patrols and sniper teams.[16]

All the while, broadcast news trucks, anchormen, and reporters are camped out on a so-called press island, a stretch of land in front of the UN, its backdrop of member flags long familiar to television viewers around the world.

The New York police direct a steady stream of black sedans with presidents and prime ministers dropped off at the UN delegates' tented entrance, to be picked up later and returned by speeding motorcades to their missions or hotels. And at spots all over the city, government leaders hold private side sessions, usually shrouded in secrecy, and creating a security nightmare.

The Waldorf Astoria on Park Avenue and One UN New York Hotel on East Forty-fourth Street traditionally each have had some thirty heads of state in residence during the opening session.[17] Handling so many high-level officials can be an exercise in diplomacy equal to negotiations at the UN itself. One UN New York has considered itself fortunate that its building is designed with rooms in two towers. The hotel management can discreetly separate countries that may be at odds with one another. And at the Waldorf Astoria, the job of rotating the national flags flown over the Park Avenue entrance has been delegated to an employee well-attuned to international sensitivities.

A panoply of color fills East Side sidewalks, as UN delegates in their distinctive national dress spill out into the neighborhood. Area restaurants fill up fast, and have learned to set aside a few tables for last-minute reservations for visiting dignitaries. Local shops, from grocery stores to shoe repairmen, ready themselves for a rush. "Welcome General Assembly," reads a "sandwich-board" sign on the sidewalk outside a tiny hardware store on Second Avenue. A small framing shop nearby sees its business triple in the days leading up to the General Assembly opening, as delegations assure portraits of their new leaders, the result of coups or elections, are properly framed for display in their missions.[18] And at "UN Diplomat Outfitters," with a window display touting "Italian-cut suits for $99," business jumps 50 percent during the General Assembly session, mostly with customers from the Gulf States and Africa. "The delegates wear their national dress to UN sessions," explained the store's manager, "but they want a Western business suit for evening receptions."[19]

Directly across the street from the UN, at the narrow block-long park named Dag Hammarskjold Plaza, the annual debate attracts scores of demonstrations and rallies. It is one of only two locations near the UN where protests, with sound, are permitted.* The New York City police precinct covering the UN neighborhood, the 17th, orchestrates what are akin to theater performances, and issues protestors a "Guide to Planning a Demonstration" that explains the United States' First Amendment rights—"Congress shall make no law prohibiting freedom of speech, or the right of the people peaceably to assemble," but advises in large print: "Notification to the local Police Precinct of occurrence is requested." And in a congenial gesture, the police help the protestors get maximum exposure. Detective Frank Bogucki, for years the precinct's coordinator of the rallies, prearranges the protestors' positions on his computer screen. "If a group wants to have a vigil, or has a visual display, then I try to put them in the center of the Plaza," said Bogucki. "Or if they are aiming their protest at a particular mission, then I stage them as close to that mission as possible."

---

*The other is the smaller Ralphe Bunche Park, on First Avenue. But because it is directly across from the UN entrance, for security reasons it is off limits during the General Assembly opening session.

The year 2000, when the UN held a special summit in conjunction with its annual Assembly session, broke a record for the number of protests. Bogucki handled ninety-two rallies in the little plaza in just three days. Then in 2008, the Assembly opening attracted almost as many protests, from twenty-five Bangladeshis, to three hundred Tibetans, to ten thousand protestors rallying against President Mahmoud Ahmadinejad of Iran, an event organized by a Jewish coalition that spilled out into midtown blocks far beyond the Plaza.[20]

While it is customary for neighborhood residents to complain about the annual autumn disruption—the stalled traffic, continual "gridlock alerts," shrieking sirens, unruly protests, and overbooked restaurants—others find it exhilarating. For at least two weeks each year, they can rightly claim to live at the very core of the "center of the world."

Khrushchev and the Anniversary to Remember

Looking back over the UN's special sessions and anniversary celebrations, an early one—the fifteenth, in 1960—provided a month of drama and chaos that New Yorkers would talk about for years. The city, then led by Robert Wagner, found itself playing host to some thirty world leaders, including Premier Nikita Khrushchev of the Soviet Union and the young Cuban revolutionary leader Fidel Castro, at a time when the Cold War was at its most frigid. Just a few months earlier, Khrushchev and the United States had dueled over the downing of a U.S. spy plane over Soviet territory, a dispute played out largely at the UN Security Council. And now a new player, thirty-four-year-old Castro, was coming to the UN for the first time since leading a revolution that had ousted his country's dictator.

Of all the visiting leaders, New Yorkers generally agreed that Khrushchev, for one, overstayed his welcome. He arrived in mid-September and remained in the city for twenty-five days. But the Soviets probably argued that Khrushchev never got much of a welcome in the first place. Even before his arrival, the city, citing an insurance requirement, balked at issuing a docking permit for his ship, the *Baltika*, until the Soviets got Washington involved and Mayor Wagner was urged to hurry things up.[21] Then when his ship, a converted 1939 military transport vessel, approached New York Harbor, a group of International Longshoremen's Association activists met Khrushchev—and the leaders of several Soviet satellite countries traveling with him—in a chartered Hudson River Day Line boat covered with giant anti-Soviet placards. "Roses are red; Violets are blue; Stalin droped [sic] dead; How about you?" was a typical sentiment.[22]

Soon, as the *Baltika* neared its berth, Pier 73—an old dilapidated dock near Twenty-fifth Street on Manhattan's East Side—the Soviet contingent learned that the longshoremen were refusing to service the ship, and it had to be moored by the Soviets themselves. It was a clumsy effort at best, as even the Soviets acknowledged.[23] And beyond that, Khrushchev was none too happy with the outdated pier the Soviets had been given.[24]

Once settled into the Soviet mission and residence, then at Park Avenue and Sixty-eighth Street,[25] the Soviet leader complained bitterly about the one hundred New York police officers—including twenty-two on horseback—who guarded over him. The police countered that the heavy protection was necessary for the man they dubbed "Krooshy," in light of the serious death threats repeatedly being made against him.[26]

Then when the UN's anniversary session got under way in the General Assembly Hall, Khrushchev kept the world on edge. Not only was he boisterous—interrupting speakers with insulting shouts and pounding his fists on his desk—but he took to removing his sturdy Soviet-made shoe and banging it on the desk—even waving it in the air—when he didn't like the proceedings. One tirade was in the course of a speech by Secretary General Hammarskjold. Another interrupted the reserved British prime minister, Harold Macmillan. Delegates were not amused. But Khrushchev laughed and told his comrades back at the Soviet mission that it had served to "inject a little life into the stuffy atmosphere of the UN," recalled Arkady Shevchenko, then a young Soviet advisor who traveled with the Khrushchev party.[27]

Finally, the Kremlin chief got irritated when he realized that a constraint set by the U.S. State Department because of security concerns restricted his travels to Manhattan Island. He had thought he was going to spend his weekends at the Soviet's Glen Cove compound on Long Island. It was a wish he finally got after he complained to Washington. But then he found his entourage tagged by a string of New York City and Nassau County police cars, and a State Department motorcade and hovering helicopters. And once at the compound, county and State Department security officers were posted at the front gate for the entire duration of his stay.[28]

All the while, Khrushchev repeatedly called for the UN to move its headquarters from New York City. Perhaps Switzerland or Austria, he suggested. Still, his intelligence service, the KGB, was more than content with

New York and its convenient cover for the Soviets' growing UN spy net-work. "The slightest rumor that UN headquarters might move was cause for panic" among the KGB agents, Shevchenko remembered.*[29]

Castro up in Harlem

The Cuban leader, Fidel Castro, stayed in New York only half as long as Khrushchev, but caused just as much of a stir. After he had trouble finding a hotel that would accept him and his entourage of eighty, the U.S. State Department interceded. The Shelburne, a sedate hotel located in Murray Hill, in the East Midtown area of Manhattan, finally agreed to accept him. "I was the patsy," the owner of the hotel, Edward Spatz, later said.[30] Within twenty-four hours, Castro had stalked out of the Shelburne, and headed to the UN Secretariat to complain to Secretary General Hammarskjold that the hotel was "anti-Cuban." He was under heavy surveillance, he said, and had been asked to put down a $10,000 deposit on his rooms. The hotel's story was that the Cubans were caught cooking chickens in their rooms, leaving behind chicken bones and moldy meat, and therefore, at the very least, a hefty deposit—typically required for any large group—was in order.[31]

Castro hastily decamped from his Murray Hill post, and checked into the early-twentieth-century Hotel Theresa on 125th Street and Sev-enth Avenue. Often called the "Waldorf of Harlem," the hotel was well known for its celebrity guests over the years, from Louis Armstrong to Lena Horne to Sugar Ray Robinson. Now, from his two-room suite on the ninth floor, Castro held court, thriving on well-publicized, much-photographed visits from Nation of Islam leader Malcolm X; Egypt's Gamal Abdel Nasser, president of the United Arab Republic; and Khru-shchev, whose personal security team let it be known it was none too pleased with their leader taking them up to Harlem. But Khrushchev in-sisted, eager to show the young Cuban leader that he, too, was a man of the people.[32]

When it was Castro's turn to address the UN General Assembly, he outdid even Khrushchev, who had spoken for a long two hours and twenty minutes. Castro held the podium for four hours and twenty-six minutes, a record for UN speeches.[33]

---

*Shevchenko, who became a high-ranking Soviet official, defected to the United States in 1978 and subsequently wrote a memoir.

Quiet, but Costly, Twenty-fifth

After the raucous fifteenth, New York was well prepared for the UN's twenty-fifth anniversary in 1970. The member states now numbered 127, and at least seventy presidents and heads of state were expected to show up to celebrate the silver anniversary. At the time, Mayor Lindsay's administration and New York State were engaged in delicate and contro-versial planning to provide more office space for the growing UN, amidst recurring calls from some UN delegates to move the organization out of New York altogether. Now, the mayor was primed to show the UN celebrants the city's appreciation for their presence in its midst. Arriving dignitaries would be met at the airport with flower bouquets and a per-sonal letter from the mayor, and Lindsay's staff planned parties and gala musical evenings, and ordered an enormous birthday cake to be personally delivered to the UN Delegates Lounge by the mayor himself, the icing on the cake to read: "UN is New York's Most Important Hope." Meanwhile, the police department, recalling the rowdy anniversary ten years earlier, prepared the most comprehensive, and costly, security plan in the city's history.[34]

But the turnout of leaders was far less than expected. In the weeks im-mediately preceding the October anniversary, world tensions rose. Mid-east peace talks broke down; Palestinian guerrillas hijacked four airliners, blowing up three; civil war broke out in Jordan; and—just days before the UN General Assembly celebration was to begin—President Nasser of Egypt died suddenly of a heart attack.

Only some forty-five national leaders—and some of the lesser-known names at that—made the trip to New York. Premier Alexei Kosygin of the Soviet Union stayed home, as did the leaders of most of the Soviet satellite countries, including Poland and Hungary. Castro remained in Havana; Prime Minister Emilio Colombo, in Rome; and Prime Minis-ter Jacques Chaban-Delmas, in Paris. Lindsay and city officials were dis-appointed. In fact, some said only the New York police—who breathed a sigh of relief that their tough new security plan had not been fully tested—were happy with the meager attendance.[35]

Still, the security precautions had been pricey, especially for a city that was feeling the early signs of an oncoming fiscal crisis. Lindsay turned to Washington for help. He wrote President Nixon: "We think it only fair that the taxpayers of our City not be forced to single-handedly bear the expense of this national and international event," he wrote, pointing out that money recently had been granted to the police department of San Clemente, California, home to Nixon's western White House.[36]

It wasn't the first time Lindsay had tried to get federal help for UN protection. Ten years earlier, at the time of the UN's fifteenth anniversary in 1960, when Lindsay was a second-term congressman from the Manhattan district surrounding the UN, he and the rest of the New York delegation had supported legislation sought by then-Mayor Wagner to provide financial aid for the city's costs of securing the UN festivities. At the time, Lindsay said he believed federal money should be forthcoming not only for the fifteenth anniversary celebration, but on an ongoing basis.[37] But his New York colleagues recognized that a permanent fix was asking too much. Congresswoman Edna Kelly, a Brooklyn Democrat, introduced legislation asking for reimbursement for only the 1960 celebration.[38]

Conservative Republicans fought back. "New York City asked for this Tower of Babel and got it," Iowa's Howard Royce "H. R." Gross told colleagues on the House floor, referring to the city's pursuit of the UN headquarters back in the 1940s. "Now," he turned to Congressman Lindsay, "you want the taxpayers of the Third District of Iowa . . . to bail you out.

"I do not think we ought to give them a dime," Gross concluded.[39]

And that is what New York City got in 1960: not one dime. While the bill passed the Democrat-controlled House, it died before it was taken up by the Senate.[40]

Now, ten years later, Lindsay was mayor and the cost of security precautions, particularly for special UN sessions, had risen dramatically. The city said the security price tag for the twenty-fifth anniversary alone was $2.6 million. "Providing adequate security for this major world event should be the responsibility of our national government," Lindsay wrote in his letter to Nixon.[41]

At the same time, City Comptroller Abraham Beame was exchanging letters with the acting director of the White House Office of Management and Budget, Caspar Weinberger. Weinberger argued against the city's request, maintaining that the presence of the United Nations benefited the city, both in tangible and intangible ways. The very presence of the United Nations, he told Beame, "has made New York City the 'capital of the world.'"[42] Beame snapped back that the city was the capital of the world long before the UN ever came to the United States. "In fact, the UN settled here in New York City precisely because it was (and still *is*) the capital of the world," he wrote Weinberger.[43]

In the end, the Nixon administration agreed to support legislation to provide the city with half the cost of police coverage for the anniversary, while Brooklyn Congressman Emanuel Celler introduced a bill to reimburse the city for the full amount.[44] But the bills got nowhere, and by the time Beame succeeded Lindsay as mayor in 1974—the city's financial situation now precarious—no federal relief for UN security had been forthcoming. Beame wrote to President Ford: "For years, I have sought federal reimbursement," he said. "While we have heard sympathetic responses, we have received no action on this matter—and certainly no money."[45]

Then in late 1975, two New York legislators at opposing ends of the political spectrum—Conservative Republican Senator James Buckley and Liberal Democratic Congresswoman Bella Abzug—rallied behind a bill that ultimately provided the city with some relief. It reimbursed six U.S. cities, including New York, with up to $3.5 million annually for protecting foreign diplomats.

And finally, during the administration of Ed Koch, who took office in 1978, the city was able to secure aid specifically for protection of diplomats assigned to the United Nations missions. It came in the form of new Treasury Department regulations issued in 1980 that allowed reimbursement not only for extraordinary coverage for UN-related events, but for "fixed post" coverage, such as round-the-clock security for high-risk UN missions.[46] Federal support was set at an annual limit of $3.5 million, and then two years later, under intense lobbying from the Koch administration, was raised to $7 million a year.[47]

The topic of security reimbursement, the appropriation for which was transferred to the State Department in 1984, remained high on Koch's agenda during the rest of his three terms in office, and he and his staff, including Commissioner Sorensen and Deputy Commissioner and General Counsel to the police department Ken Conboy, met frequently with committees of Congress to make the case.[48]

"I am very proud of what we accomplished," Sorensen said years later. "The mayor asked us to take it on. But I had always felt our New York police were functioning on behalf of the nation, and therefore support from Washington, which had been talked about for so many years, was in order."[49]

By the time Koch left office at year-end 1989, the city had received more than $70 million in federal money for police costs associated with protection of dignitaries visiting the UN and other UN-related security.[50]

Over the years, the city continued to be eligible for reimbursement of security costs related to foreign affairs activities, under the State Department's Foreign Missions and Officials program, while routine police work around the UN community was paid for by the city. For the federal fiscal year ended September 2014, the city was reimbursed approximately $22 million of a total of $31 million it estimated was spent on police protection of events involving high-level foreign guests, or 73 percent. For the fifteen-year period beginning in 2000, the average reimbursement was 77 percent.[51]

Recurring UN Summitry

By the year 2000, New Yorkers had become reconciled to the fact that UN anniversary sessions and high-level conferences were sure to disrupt their daily lives to some extent. But for one planned that autumn, even the UN felt compelled to prepare the city. A special three-day Millennium Summit—an assemblage to set the organization's agenda for the new century—brought an estimated two hundred heads of state and high-ranking officials to New York, a record at the time. Secretary General Kofi Annan's staff diplomatically forewarned New Yorkers: "Let [us] thank in advance the good people of New York, our neighbors in New York, for their patience," said a deputy to Annan. "We know their patience will be tried in the course of the summit week, but we would like to . . . reassure them that this is really for a good cause."[52]

Indeed, it was a summit that would test the citizenry's patience. Speeding motorcades and traffic gridlock; more than six thousand police officers diverted from normal duty to deal with the chaos; the East River cleared of all boats aside from Coast Guard and the police; Fidel Castro back in town for the first time in several years; and Detective Bogucki orchestrating the record-setting ninety-two rallies in tiny Dag Hammarskjold Plaza in just three days—protestors shouting with bullhorns, beating drums, and meditating in silence all at the same time.

Just "one big foreign party," said one New Yorker, expressing surprise that the UN was reaching out to the community to thank them for the inconvenience. A UN spokesman said the world body was simply trying to get across to city residents the importance of the millennium meeting. "Hopefully New Yorkers will realize what is going on at the summit will affect their lives, too," he said.[53]

And for the first time, the UN used the Secretariat's curtain wall of

"Walk Right In"

Well, not exactly—you must go through security screening—but a day inside the headquarters of the United Nations is not as "off limits" as many might think. For starters, the Delegates Dining Room serves a weekday prix fixe buffet lunch that's open to the public (reservations required, 24 hours in advance). Located on the fourth floor with floor-to-ceiling windows overlooking the East River, it offers classics from around the world, as well as lesser-known dishes from smaller nations. After Mayor David Dinkins left office in 1993, he frequently lunched at the Delegates Dining Room, once remarking that it was "the best kept secret in New York City."

Also, the UN's highly regarded one-hour tours are offered each weekday. The guides, from some fifteen countries and conducting tours in twelve languages, are not only knowledgeable about the architecture and art in the distinguished halls and council chambers, but—with a briefing each morning on events and issues being taken up that day—add a newsworthy immediacy to the walk around the UN buildings.

The UN Bookshop, located on the lower level of the General Assembly Hall, offers an international selection of books, including titles published by the United Nations, many children's books, and official UN emblem merchandise, often sustainably sourced. The UN Gift Shop, across the hall, is stocked with creative and high-quality ceramics, handicrafts, and jewelry from UN member states. Identified by country of origin, the selection offers a kind of "tour" of the world's artisans.

For further information, and to be advised of holiday and other closings, check the UN Visitor Centre website, at www.visit.un.org.

more than five thousand windows to thank New Yorkers for their endurance. Office lights were turned on in the evening in an arrangement that spelled "Thank You NY," an enormous thirty-nine-story display shining out over the city.[54]

Fifteen years later, with scores of foreign leaders in town as the UN marked its seventieth anniversary in the fall of 2015, it was New York's turn to use illumination to celebrate its international neighbor. On the eve of UN Day, October 24, New York's Commissioner for International Affairs Penny Abeywardena accompanied Secretary General Ban Ki-moon to the top of the Empire State Building, where he symbolically turned on a switch to light the city's iconic skyscraper a brilliant "UN blue." Thus, the city's legendary office tower joined some three hundred locations around the world—from the pyramids in Egypt to the Great Wall of China—in a celebration orchestrated by the UN to mark its milestone with the radiant glow of blue.[55]

9
Tussle over Tickets

Mayor Giuliani came into office in January 1994 pledging to confront "quality of life" challenges facing New Yorkers. A crackdown on perpetrators of petty crimes—from peddlers to subway turnstile jumpers to "squeegee guys" who wiped car windshields at stoplights and then demanded money for their work—became the centerpiece of his commitment. So it was perhaps inevitable that sooner or later the mayor, a Republican who had been U.S. attorney for the Southern District of New York, would take on UN diplomats for ignoring tens of thousands of parking tickets under the protection of diplomatic immunity.

The spat over diplomatic parking and immunity was as old as the UN-city relationship itself, from Robert Moses' early clash with Dag Hammarskjold over the UN parking garage, to Eleanor French's "diplo-parking" battles in the 1960s, to Mayor Lindsay's gingerly approach a decade later, when he was in the midst of negotiations to keep the UN from abandoning the city and setting up headquarters elsewhere. Lindsay was frustrated by the growing number of parking tickets being ignored by foreign delegations. In 1970, he was riding in his car near Gracie Mansion when the police officer traveling with him picked a traffic summons out of the gutter. It had been served on a member of the delegation from the United Arab Republic. For Lindsay, it represented the last straw. But his response was muted. He vented his frustration with a letter, which he requested remain private, to the U.S. Ambassador to the UN, Charles Yost. The automobile had been parked in the middle of a bus stop, he wrote, making "life unbearable for pedestrians, Sanitation Department curb sweepers and the police . . . and . . . God knows what it did to the morale of the bus driver." He told Yost to expect a city crackdown on the UN offenders.[1]

But little was done, and as the years went by, confusion over diplomatic immunity and scofflaws lingered on, occasionally simmering to the top in the late 1970s and 1980s, during the administrations of Abraham Beame and Ed Koch. Shortly before Koch left office in 1989, Sorensen, his UN commissioner, said that "no single issue concerning the diplomatic community is of greater concern to most New Yorkers than the perception that diplomats abuse their parking privileges."[2] Yet, with the diplomatic community's annual contribution to the city economy totaling some $1 billion by the 1980s, it was easy for mayors to be forgiving of what was estimated to be a few million dollars in unpaid parking fines each year.[3]

In 1993, as the next mayor, David Dinkins, was about to leave office, the city and the State Department worked out a deal that promised to put an end to the diplo-plate controversy. But the program got lost somewhere in the transition to the Giuliani administration, and there it rested for the next several years.[4]

Controversy Revived

Then, in late December 1996—Giuliani now mayor—two UN envoys got into a midday scuffle with two police officers at the corner of West Eighty-first Street and Amsterdam Avenue on Manhattan's Upper West Side. The story got the attention of New Yorkers—and their mayor—and within days, the diplo-plate debate was catapulted into the headlines, where it would remain for months to come.

The police claimed the men, a Russian and the other from Belarus, were drunk and abusive when their car was ticketed for being too close to a fire hydrant. But the diplomats said the driver, the Russian, had drunk only one glass of white wine with a meal of chicken and cashews before the confrontation, which, they said, had left him with broken eyeglasses, a dislocated shoulder, and torn clothes. The police department, meanwhile, was quick to point out that the Russian mission had more parking tickets for the previous year than any other mission.[5]

Giuliani announced a get-tough campaign. Starting April 1, 1997—in essentially the same deal that had been worked out in the latter days of the Dinkins administration but never implemented—the city would remove license plates of cars that were towed for safety violations, and would take away the diplomatic license plates of cars whose parking fines were left unpaid for more than a year. In order to start off on a level playing field, Giuliani promised to provide diplomats 111 new parking spots on city streets, bringing each UN member up to the maximum of two guaranteed spots for their mission and one for the ambassador's residence, or a total of 555. In addition, each country's Consulate would have two.[6]

Within days of the announcement, the city found itself embroiled in a skirmish with the UN that was, literally, of international proportions.

The UN's top lawyer declared the mayor's plan violated diplomatic immunity and U.S. obligations as host country, part of the treaty signed with the UN in the late 1940s. The main point of contention was the provision calling for removal of license plates and non-renewal of registration until a fine is paid, provisions that "appear not to be in full compliance with international law," the UN legal counsel wrote to Giuliani's office.[7] The dispute moved to the UN's Committee on Relations with the Host Country, which voted to take the matter to the full General Assembly for debate. (The United States was the only dissenter.) Some delegates even suggested the parking ticket question should go to the World Court in The Hague.[8]

A miffed Giuliani countered that this might be just more proof that the UN didn't belong in New York. "If they'd like to leave New York over parking tickets, then we can find another use for that area of town," he said of the UN's eighteen acres overlooking the East River. "It happens to be just about the most valuable real estate in the world."[9]

Soon, ordinary New Yorkers, who initially cheered their mayor's efforts, started to take another look at the deal and thought maybe Giuliani was being too easy on the UN. Giving them an extra 111 parking places seemed excessive. "Why do diplomats need all these parking spots?" asked Melvyn Kaufman, a prominent real estate developer whose organization had four office towers in the UN area, some with UN-reserved parking spots out front. He complained that access to his buildings was being impeded. "Why do they need free parking at all? They're not priests giving last rites, or doctors saving dying people. What's wrong with the subway?" he asked.[10]

What's wrong with the subway, answered the French UN delegate, Hubert Legal, was that it was "a blot" on the city. And, he said, "most taxis are a wreck," and buses are fine "if you have three hours to waste!"[11]

Meanwhile, UN delegates began to sense that the police, now emboldened by the mayor's declaration of war to back them up, were becoming overzealous in enforcing parking regulations. And they claimed the mayor's almost daily pronouncements on the subject were riling up his constituents, resulting in UN missions being vandalized and diplomatic cars left with threatening notes on their windshields. Some envoys said they suspected the mayor had cooked up the whole crackdown simply as a political ploy pandering to voters.[12] Indeed, Giuliani faced re-election in the fall.

In Washington, the State Department soon announced that it had taken a second look, and maybe the UN's legal department had a point. It seemed the plan did indeed violate the principles of diplomatic immunity. Washington soon backed down, promising to work on a compromise solution, a U.S. representative expressing the opinion that perhaps the General Assembly should spend less time worrying about parking tickets, and more time dealing with the world's problems like the civil war then raging in the central African country of Zaire.*[13]

Now it was Zaire's turn to enter the fray. Lukabu Khabouji, the country's UN representative, countered that the city should worry more about the safety of New Yorkers taking public transportation. Considering "all the incidents that take place daily in the subways and the buses, I myself would not take the risk," he said of the city's public transit system. His charge was particularly annoying to the mayor since the system's safety record had shown significant improvement in recent years.[14]

During the early spring, the State Department's compromise planning sputtered along. Giuliani continued to deride Washington for not having the "resolve" to match its "bluster" on the parking pact.[15] And his office reported the total number of parking summonses issued to UN missions during the full year 1996: a record 125,000.[16]

Meanwhile, there were reports of retaliation overseas. Russia, Belarus, and Brazil were among those countries adding parking restrictions for American diplomats working in their countries.[17]

By April 17, the city-UN row had grown so hot that the U.S. Ambassador to the UN, Bill Richardson, said he needed to try to "cool the temperature." Recently appointed to succeed Madeleine Albright, Richardson was a former New Mexico Congressman who had undertaken some critical foreign policy missions for the White House, including to Iraq, North Korea, and Serbia. Now, he was dealing with weighty Mideast

*Later in 1997, Zaire's name was changed to the Democratic Republic of the Congo.

issues in the Security Council, but he took the time to pay a midday call on Giuliani at City Hall.[18] Neither the mayor nor Richardson immediately reported on their one-hour meeting, but Richardson later remarked, "Over the years, I've negotiated with the toughest characters abroad . . . But I want to tell you, the toughest guy I've ever had to negotiate with is Rudy Giuliani."[19]

Giuliani may have been tough, but Richardson clearly won the debate: The day after their meeting, the mayor announced that he had agreed to a compromise version of the parking plan, an interim fix under which diplomats' license plates could not be removed. "The State Department caved in," Giuliani told the press. "We disagree . . . but the fact is that I don't run the State Department."[20]

Then on April 28, 1997, Giuliani's office issued a curt three-paragraph statement that caught many UN watchers by surprise: The city's Commissioner for the United Nations and Consular Corps, Livia Sylva, was stepping down.[21]

Sylva—the Romanian-born head of a cosmetic company, a meat-packing heiress, and a big Republican campaign contributor—had been appointed to the UN liaison job shortly after Giuliani took office. She had played a key role in producing the attractive souvenir booklet that Giuliani presented to UN delegates on the occasion of the UN's fiftieth anniversary two years earlier. Now, someone on the mayor's staff pointed out that amidst the booklet's many words of gratitude to the UN for having made the city the "capital of the world" and the list of ways the city, in turn, showed its appreciation, was this statement: "Diplomats are not required to pay for parking tickets."[22]

While City Hall never publicly made the connection to her resignation, aides said Giuliani was furious when he realized that the highly visible commemorative booklet included a clear contradiction to his vocal, months-long campaign to persuade UN diplomats to honor their tickets.

With Sylva's abrupt departure, her UN responsibilities were turned over to Bruce Gelb, Commissioner for International Business, and shortly thereafter, to Irene Halligan, Giuliani's Commissioner of Protocol.[23]

While the diplo-parking dilemma would continue to fester during the remainder of Giuliani's time in office, the problem did improve significantly. Either the UN delegations had gotten the message, or were simply weary of fighting City Hall. Within three years, the number of parking summonses slapped on diplomats' cars was reported to be down by one-third, and the money owed for parking tickets fell from $15.8 million in 1996 to $4.8 million in 1999.[24]

Finding a Fix

Still, the next mayor, Michael Bloomberg, was determined to come up with a permanent resolution. Within a year of his taking office, the city and the State Department announced a deal that finally seemed to put the matter to rest. The agreement, for which Bloomberg gave his predecessor much of the credit, was, in fact, similar to the program that had been attempted during Giuliani's administration. But under Bloomberg's approach, the city could not remove license plates of any diplomatic cars, the main sticking point in the previous plan. Bloomberg announced his deal, which had the agreement of the UN Legal Affairs chief, in late August 2002.[25] The program provided 530 dedicated parking spaces on city streets, including two for each UN Mission, a maximum of two for each Consulate, as well as thirty-five shared spaces for delivery vehicles. To identify the cars, special decals would be issued. The program then set in place penalties on countries and individual diplomats who ignored three or more parking tickets for one hundred days, and countries with forty or more past-due tickets would have their parking spaces taken away.[26]

While the new parking program called for some adjusting on the part of both the city and the diplomats, it eventually worked. Time may have been a factor. As UN diplomats, initially unhappy over limited parking spaces assigned by the city, moved on to other assignments, new ambassadors coming to the city simply had no recollection of the "way it was."

By the end of Bloomberg's term at year-end 2013, the city reported that since the new program took effect in 2002, the number of tickets incurred by diplomats had decreased 84 percent, and 90 percent of tickets issued were answered within one hundred days.[27]

As for New Yorkers, long accustomed to complaining about diplo-tickets, some simply refused to believe the parking puzzle had been solved. Indeed, shortly before Bloomberg left office, and as his staff was polishing up his record for the history books, the mayor's website was updated with a review of the parking situation: "Contrary to popular perception," the staff felt compelled to point out, "the city has successfully addressed the diplomatic parking problem."[28] It was a point reaffirmed by the next administration, when it publicly reported that in all of fiscal 2014, only .04 percent of summonses issued in the city were for vehicles that were part of the diplomatic parking program or had diplomatic license plates.[29]

Unlike some of his predecessors, Bloomberg was rarely, if ever, drawn into public spats with the UN, whether over local irritants like parking, its member nations' politics, or the organization's sometimes controversial foreign guests. The wealthy businessman once said, "As the host city for the UN, we have to—even when it is painful and disgraceful and disgusting, any term you want to use—we have to be willing to let anybody that the UN wants to credit, or visit them, come here.

"I don't have to give them the keys to the city, or a proclamation," he said, but "the bottom line is, either you are going to be the host city or you're not."[30]

For Bloomberg, resolution to the ticket tussle was an early, and satisfying, success. But another long-standing UN-city dilemma would have his attention during much of his three-term mayoralty. With the UN membership standing at 189 countries when he came into office, and with related agencies expanding as well, his administration would face the same conundrum as his predecessors, dating back to the 1970s and the administrations of John Lindsay and Abraham Beame: Where would adequate space be found for the UN on the crowded island of Manhattan?

During his weekly radio broadcasts in 1945, Mayor Fiorello La Guardia repeatedly assured New Yorkers that the UN, then looking for a countryside site for its permanent headquarters, would instead select New York, because, he said of his city, "There is nothing like it." (*The La Guardia and Wagner Archives, La Guardia Community College, The City University of New York*)

Rendering of the site first proposed by New York for the UN's permanent home, the former 1939 World's Fair grounds in Queens. The city later enhanced the plan, but the organization was not interested and instead chose to use the site as temporary space. (*The La Guardia and Wagner Archives, La Guardia Community College, The City University of New York*)

As part of the temporary arrangements, the Hunter College Bronx campus (*above, top*) housed the UN Security Council, while the City Building on the old World's Fair grounds in Queens (*above, bottom*) served as General Assembly Hall. Secretariat offices were in a former factory on Long Island. (*United Nations Photos*)

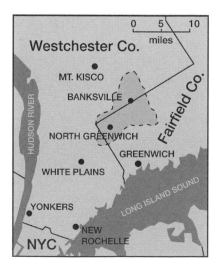

In early 1946, the UN announced its choice for a permanent site, a forty-two-square-mile swath of land (*shaded on map*) in Connecticut's Fairfield County and New York's Westchester County, where it planned a self-contained international community. Residents vigorously fought the plan. (*Map by Orin Buck*)

With the UN discontented with life in New York in mid-1946, the city launched a "charm offensive" and asked members of high society to help. Here, Mrs. Cornelius Vanderbilt (*right side, sixth from bottom*) hosts a candlelight dinner for UN delegates at her Fifth Avenue mansion. Seated to her right is Sir Alexander Cardogan, Britain's UN ambassador. The dinner party was featured in *Life* magazine. (*Bert Morgan / Getty Images*)

Before the General Assembly opened its first session at its temporary quarters in Queens on October 23, 1946, the city arranged a motorcade to deliver delegates to the steps of City Hall for an official welcoming ceremony, and a ticker-tape parade along lower Broadway. (*United Nations Photo*)

In late 1946, with a donation from John D. Rockefeller Jr., the UN finally settled on its permanent site—six blocks of mainly stockyards and tenements in Midtown Manhattan, seen here looking northeast from Forty-second Street. (*United Nations Photo*)

UN Secretary General Trygve Lie (*left*) receives a check for $8.5 million from John D. Rockefeller III, on behalf of Rockefeller's father, for purchase of the Manhattan site. (*United Nations Photo*)

A team of international architects led by New Yorker Wallace Harrison (*tall, smiling, at center in rear*) designed the UN buildings. Brazilian Oscar Niemeyer (*in front of Harrison*) and French-Swiss architect Le Corbusier (*second from left*) are generally credited with the principal design. (*United Nations Photo*)

Oscar Niemeyer's plan was considered a breakthrough. It is shown here from the southwest looking north. The large building at the far north was never built. (*Avery Architectural and Fine Arts Library, Columbia University*)

Niemeyer's design was later modified to orient the General Assembly building to face north. (*Avery Architectural and Fine Arts Library, Columbia University*)

Mayor William O'Dwyer (*front*) and Manhattan Borough President Hugo Rogers hack at bricks of a tenement on Forty-second Street in July 1947, the first of fifty buildings demolished to make way for the UN. (*United Nations Photo*)

From her apartment's fire escape on First Avenue, a neighbor views progress of the UN Secretariat's construction in September 1949. (*Bettman / Getty Images*)

A window washer at work outside the Secretariat, shortly after the building was completed in 1950. In the background, the General Assembly Building, under construction, would be completed in time for the Assembly's 1952 fall session. (*United Nations Photo*)

The UN's Ralph Bunche (*in rear at right, holding child*) at the United Nations International School (UNIS) in 1950, shortly after being awarded the Nobel Peace Prize. At the time, UNIS, where Bunche's son was a student, was holding classes in Parkway Village, a Queens housing complex. Today the main UNIS campus is in Manhattan. (*United Nations Photo*)

Mayor Vincent Impellitteri presents retiring UN Secretary General Trygve Lie with the city's Medal of Honor on the steps of City Hall in April 1953. Lie's daughter Guri is at left, and incoming Secretary General Dag Hammarskjold, at right, looks on. (*United Nations Photo*)

Each year, the UN General Assembly session brings world leaders to New York, along with gridlock and protests. In 1960, Soviet Premier Nikita Khrushchev visited Cuban leader Fidel Castro at Harlem's Hotel Theresa, requiring heavy police protection that led, in part, to the city's request for federal reimbursement for certain UN-related security. (*AP Images*)

A typical autumn traffic jam (*below*), this one on Second Avenue during the General Assembly opening session in 2005. (*Mariela Lombard Photography*)

A pro-Tibetan demonstration at Dag Hammarskjold Plaza (*above*) in the fall of 1996, one of scores of protests near the UN during the General Assembly opening session. (*AP Images/Todd Plitt*)

After the UN's Millennium Summit in 2000, when almost two hundred heads of state came to town, the organization thanked New Yorkers for their patience with a light display from its headquarters. (*United Nations Photo / Eskinder Debebe*)

New York Mayor Ed Koch and the city's UN Commissioner, Gillian Sorensen, at a temple in Japan in 1985, the twenty-fifth anniversary of the New York–Tokyo "Sister City" relationship. Sorensen's office oversaw the program, an effort to cultivate ties between international cities. (*Private Collection*)

In the days after the 9/11 World Trade Center attacks, UN Secretary General Kofi Annan (*back to camera*) and Mayor Rudolph Giuliani embrace at Ground Zero. At right, New York Governor George Pataki looks on. (*United Nations Photo / Eskinder Debebe*)

The UN buildings, shown here in the 1950s, were state-of-the-art when first completed but needed serious upgrades by the 2000s. (*United Nations Photo*)

After the UN announced a renovation plan, New York developer Donald Trump testified before a U.S. Senate subcommittee in 2005 claiming he could handle the job for half the UN's projected cost. "If that is the case . . . then I would encourage him to bid," responded Secretary General Kofi Annan. The project was eventually completed in line with the UN's projections and without Trump's help. (*AP Images / Dennis Cook*)

As UN renovation got under way in 2008, sculptures standing on the UN's North Lawn were moved to make way for a temporary building where staff would work during the project. Here, a prominent equestrian statue is lifted from its pedestal. (*United Nations Photo / Paulo Filgueiras*)

During the UN renovation, the Secretariat was gutted and its 5,040 window panes were removed and replaced with an entirely new window system matching the original 1950s look. (*United Nations Photo / Devra Berkowitz*)

Secretary General Ban Ki-moon and Mayor Michael Bloomberg at a June 2009 press conference, announcing plans for the first Climate Week NYC. After Bloomberg left office, he was appointed the Secretary General's Special Envoy for Cities and Climate Change. (*AP Images / Seth Wenig*)

In the fall of 2016, the city sponsored bus shelter posters around New York, touting the city's pride in hosting the UN. "5 boroughs, 8.6 million residents, 200 languages spoken, 1 United Nations," the posters read. They were part of the de Blasio administration's push to strengthen bonds with the UN.

A small space in Midtown Manhattan, Trygve Lie Plaza, was re-dedicated at a gathering of city and UN officials in late 2016. Named for the first Secretary General, a strong supporter of locating the UN in New York, the plaza took on added significance as the city and UN entered their eighth decade together. The clock on the wall forms the international peace symbol twice a day. (*New York City Department of Parks and Recreation / Daniel Avila*)

Joining revelers in Times Square at midnight on December 31, 2016, New York Mayor Bill de Blasio and his wife, Chirlane McCray, and UN Secretary General Ban Ki-moon and his wife, Yoo Soon-taek, are poised to push the crystal button starting the countdown to 2017 and marking the end of Ban's ten years as UN chief. (*AP Images / Invision / Greg Allen*)

Ban Ki-moon's successor, António Guterres, heads up the steps to UN headquarters on his first day on the job as the ninth Secretary General. (*UN Photo / Mark Garten*)

10
Trio Created

Times were grim in New York City in the fall of 1975. The city's financial health had been precarious for years, but now the unthinkable was a real possibility. New York was teetering on the brink of bankruptcy. To cut costs, municipal services had been reduced, with close to 30,000 city workers dismissed—from school and library staff, to hospital, fire, and sanitation workers, and the police force. Others had their wages frozen and overtime limited. City streets turned dirty and dangerous. The subway was deemed unsafe. And popular spots like Times Square and Central Park were now places that many avoided.

When New York turned to Washington for help, it was rebuffed. In late October, President Ford declared that under the circumstances, he would veto any federal bailout of the city, an announcement forever remembered by a front page headline in the *New York Daily News*: "Ford to City: Drop Dead."[1]

Abraham Beame was mayor, having succeeded John Lindsay in January 1973. City comptroller during Lindsay's time, Beame had run for the mayoralty largely on his financial expertise. Now, two years into his term, the sixty-nine-year-old Democrat was shuttling between Washington and the state capital in Albany in a hectic attempt to find monetary relief for his city. On Wednesday, November 19, 1975, he and New York's Governor Hugh Carey flew to Washington for a morning meeting with the chairman of the House Banking Committee, and then directly on to Albany, where he met with state legislators in a late-night session over tax increases that were now the key to changing the president's mind about helping New York.[2]

The next day, the mayor was back in Manhattan, at Forty-fourth Street and First Avenue, standing proudly with UN Secretary General Kurt Waldheim to mark the formal opening of what was one of the few bright spots in the city's otherwise dismal picture.[3] A striking tower of reflective blue-green glass rising tall into the air—505 feet, slightly shorter than the UN Secretariat—would house offices for UN staff and a hotel. Called One United Nations Plaza, the building was highly acclaimed by architectural critics. But it came to be built only after some ten years of painstaking planning, controversy, and compromise that began during the Lindsay administration.

Squeezed for Space

When Lindsay had taken office in January 1966, the number of UN member nations was more than double the original fifty-one. By the end of his first year in office, another five countries had joined the UN roster, bringing the total to 122. At the same time, the organizations related to the UN were growing rapidly as well. Already, two agencies—the United Nations Children's Fund (Unicef) and the UN Development Program—had been squeezed out of office space on the UN campus and had moved their workers to leased space in a building nearby.

Besides offices, the diplomatic community needed more hotel rooms within easy reach of the UN complex, and more restaurants, housing, and recreation facilities. Some UN leaders started to renew calls for moving the headquarters out of the crowded city, a threat that troubled Lindsay, already besieged with the city's mounting fiscal problems, as well as labor and racial unrest.[4]

From his days in Congress representing the district surrounding the UN's territory, Lindsay had a good understanding of the UN's space needs, as well as New Yorkers' growing concerns about UN infringement on their city.

Now, as mayor, he recognized the financial contribution the UN made to New York, and he believed strongly the city should help the organization with its office and housing needs. He soon met with a group called the East River–Turtle Bay Fund. With financial backing from the Ford Foundation and the Rockefeller Brothers Fund, East River–Turtle Bay was exploring options that would provide more space for the UN.[5]

The Fund's preliminary focus was on land south of the UN's Forty-second Street border, including developing an office complex between Fortieth and Forty-first streets on land that then was the site of a seven-story Con Edison service building. The location was just south of a block housing the Queens-Midtown Tunnel ventilating building, a block that had been purchased by the city when the tunnel project was started in the 1930s.[6] Land to the east and west of the diagonally situated brown brick ventilating structure was designated public parkland, and later studies looked at the possibility of building on its western section, a flat asphalt playground space that was rarely used.[7]

Absent from the planning was Robert Moses, whose once-influential voice in UN matters had been sharply curtailed during the Wagner administration and whose relationship with Lindsay was strained. But that didn't stop Moses from writing to Lindsay in late 1966 with his thoughts on the subject. Moses called building on land south of the UN property "wholly impractical."[8]

"The most workable ultimate expansion—if they stay and don't move to Geneva—would be across the River to the twenty-two-acre Pepsi-Cola plant," he wrote.[9]

Until recently, both Pepsi-Cola's bottling plant and corporate headquarters were on a large site in Long Island City, on the Queens side of the East River. But the company had now moved its headquarters to Manhattan, and Pepsi's president, Herbert Barnet, told Moses the company was considering relocating its bottling operations as well.[10]

So Moses suggested Barnet and UN-city planners get together to work out a deal.[11] "With improved tunnel and perhaps ferry access . . . this would provide living and recreation facilities, as well as additional office space," Moses told Lindsay.[12] Moses also thought it would be an expedient way to eliminate what he called "the big, obtrusive sign" atop the bottling plant, the 120-foot red neon Pepsi-Cola light that had provoked complaints from UN executives years earlier. But neither Barnet nor the UN-city planners pursued the idea with any enthusiasm. And another Moses suggestion, using the south end of Welfare Island (renamed Roosevelt Island in 1971) for UN facilities, got no traction either.[13]

The Expansion Expands

Soon, the East River–Turtle Bay group was formalized under the name Fund for Area Planning and Development. One of the premier architects in the country, Kevin Roche, joined the team. In the late 1940s, the young Roche, once a student of Mies van der Rohe, had worked on construction planning for the original UN buildings. Most recently, he had designed the handsome Ford Foundation headquarters on East Forty-second Street, distinguished by its vast glass–enclosed atrium.[14]

In early 1968, the Fund released a brochure outlining its plan for UN facilities, the sheer magnitude of which surprised many New Yorkers. The properties south of Forty-second Street were no longer the focus. Instead, at the heart of the proposal was a "super block," to be created by closing and eliminating Forty-fourth Street between First and Second avenues. Two forty-four-story towers and four lower-rise buildings would provide office, hotel, and luxury residential space, all amid a setting of green parkland. First Avenue between Forty-second and Forty-seventh streets would be closed to through automobile traffic, and would become a visitors' observation area surrounded by trees and shrubs. Finally, a five-block walkway above street level would connect the super block with Dag Hammarskjold Plaza, the narrow strip of parkland at Forty-seventh Street that was slated for improvements.[15]

Many in the nearby community saw the design as an enhancement to the neighborhood and supported the plan, including the activist Turtle Bay leader, Peter Detmold.[16] Others were opposed. To accommodate the super block, land had to be cleared between First and Second avenues. It included some small apartment buildings and two large and much-admired Beaux Arts apartments at 307 and 310 East Forty-fourth Street, built in 1930 and designed by Raymond Hood and Kenneth Murchison. More than six hundred households would be displaced. Also to be torn down were some First Avenue office buildings, including the recently completed Church Peace Center,* designed by the highly regarded architect William Lescaze.[17] And Tudor City residents, living south of the proposed super block, feared their buildings, too, might be swept up in the expansion.

Still, the plan moved forward. By June 1968, Nelson Rockefeller, now in his third term as governor of New York State, had signed legislation creating a state entity called the United Nations Development Corporation (UNDC), a public benefit corporation with authority to implement the expansion. It was indeed the same Rockefeller whose enthusiasm more than twenty years earlier had convinced New York City to woo UN headquarters to the city, and whose father had donated the money to purchase the site. Now, Rockefeller would play a key role in keeping the UN satisfied with Manhattan. Under its charter, UNDC would finance,

*Later named the Church Center for the United Nations.

build, and operate the buildings using private financing through the issuance of bonds. UNDC also took over the planning activities, continuing to work with architect Kevin Roche. John McCloy, a well-respected lawyer and diplomat who had once served as president of the World Bank, was named UNDC chairman.

About the same time, the United Nations General Assembly began to consider an expansion plan of its own, renewing an interest in the area immediately south of Forty-second Street. A seven-story office building would wrap around the tunnel ventilating shaft and an esplanade would extend from the Secretariat southward. While separate from the UNDC proposal for a super block west of First Avenue, the $80 million project was meant to complement those plans.[18]

Funding for the UN's separate plan depended on congressional approval of a $20 million contribution from the United States, which Lindsay said he would seek to match with city funds. Lindsay also intended that the city would contribute the land.[19] But in Congress, strong anti-UN sentiment had taken hold, spurred in part by the world body's nearing vote to replace the U.S.-supported UN member, the Republic of China (Taiwan), with the Soviet-backed People's Republic of China. And New York lawmakers grumbled about Lindsay's commitment to match the funding at a time when the city was already struggling financially. Soon, Secretary General U Thant was advised that the UN should not hold out hope for U.S. funding. The proposal was "beclouded," the U.S. ambassador to the UN, George H. W. Bush, diplomatically informed Thant. In effect, the UN's plan was dead.[20]

But the UNDC project progressed, its design and scope changing again.

A "Beautiful Monster"

A new UNDC proposal, made public in the fall of 1969, was larger still. The super block with its two tall buildings and landscaped green space had given way to a complex of four forty-story towers, all enclosed by reflecting glass panels. "Radical," the *New York Times* called it.

The park-like feel of the earlier plan was missing. Missing also was the visitor observation space covering First Avenue. Though the Church Peace Center would now be saved, the rest of the plan was nothing short of colossal. Still a super block that would eliminate Forty-fourth Street between First and Second avenues, the new concept called for more than four million square feet of space in the four lofty towers stretching from

Forty-third to Forty-fifth streets. The towers would be enclosed in a glass structure, a kind of reflective glass bubble, that itself would be forty stories high. Architectural critic Ada Louise Huxtable pointed out that St. Peter's dome in Rome could fit comfortably inside.[21]

At the base of the complex of offices, hotel rooms, apartments, and businesses would be a park, enclosed within the glass bubble. "This will provide the neighborhood with much needed public open space," read the UNDC's new project brochure.[22] But to most in the Midtown neighborhood, including leader Detmold, the interior public space was no substitute for the outdoor grassy areas of the previous plan.

The proposal required relaxation of city zoning regulations to accommodate its bulk, a variance that would have been the highest in the city to date. Residents were concerned about congestion, both vehicular and pedestrian, created by such huge buildings rising on such a small area.[23]

Ed Koch, then a first-term Congressman representing the East Midtown area of Manhattan—Lindsay's former district—was among the staunchest critics. He called the new plan nothing but "a bonanza for commercial speculative landlords."[24]

At the City Planning Commission's first hearing on the matter in late 1969, Detmold took on the proponents. "Not since Manhattan Island was stolen from the Indians for twenty-four dollars in junk jewelry has such a barefaced real estate swindle been attempted in New York City," he shouted.[25]

And Pete Hamill, a popular local newspaper columnist, wrote a scathing commentary. "Somehow these free-loading diplomats assigned to the UN have some blessed right to live across the street from their job, while the rest of us have to come screaming into Manhattan on subway cages."[26]

Andrew Stein, the area's assemblyman in Albany, wanted the whole project moved to Welfare Island, one of Moses' suggestions. "You can read the UN charter from end to end, and you will find nothing in that charter that guarantees to its personnel and officials the privilege of rolling out of bed directly into their offices," Stein said.[27]

Huxtable, initially complimentary, turned skeptical over time, referring to the project as a "beautiful monster, created by monstrous economics that can both damage the city and set damaging precedents."[28]

In the end, the "monster" was never built. While the proposal was narrowly approved by the City Planning Commission and later by the Board of Estimate, ultimately the UNDC failed to obtain federal loan guarantees, and in June 1971, a compromise plan was announced. One building, thirty-nine stories—the same number of floors as the UN Secretariat, but several feet shorter—would rise at the corner of Forty-fourth Street and First Avenue. It would house offices for the UN and a hotel. No neighborhood residents would be displaced, since it would be built on the site of two small office buildings. Local residents were pleased.[29]

One, Two, Three

Now, all that was needed was UN General Assembly approval of a rental agreement with the UNDC, considered by many a formality. But as the plan had been moving slowly through the halls of city government, resistance among UN member countries had been building. The deal had the support of Kurt Waldheim, the former Austrian ambassador to the UN who replaced U Thant as Secretary General in January 1972. But a growing number of member nations now were calling for the UN to move out of New York City altogether. At the core of the discontent was a recent, hotly debated, vote to lower the ceiling on UN member assessment rates, which are calculated using a formula to determine an individual country's capacity to pay. The United States, whose contribution was by far the largest, had initiated the move to adjust the ceiling downward. It reduced the U.S. share from slightly over 31 percent to 25 percent.* Now, opponents contended that to pay rent to the UNDC for New York City offices was, in effect, just a device to reduce the U.S. contribution still further.

The vote on the UNDC rental deal, in late 1972, was a cliffhanger. Cuba led the opposition, with strong support from France, the Soviet bloc of countries, plus a number of Arab and African countries. "We are chained to the city," objected Jamil Baroody, the Saudi Arabian delegate.

Now, after the city's long struggle with the UNDC plan, the General Assembly approved the deal by a mere two votes, and Waldheim's people were sent off to negotiate for twenty-six floors in the new UNDC building.[30] It would house offices for some one thousand UN staff currently working in leased space at locations scattered around the city. Once again, the UN had committed to staying in New York.

And so it was that in the fall of 1975, after almost ten years of planning, Mayor Beame joined Secretary General Waldheim to mark the opening of One United Nations Plaza. In addition to office space, it housed a 292-room hotel, initially operated by Hyatt Hotels. The building had

*The ceiling was lowered again in 2000, bringing the U.S. assessment for the regular budget to 22 percent.

been financed with bonds issued by UNDC. The state had helped secure the $55.2 million offering with a reserve fund that could be used if
needed. But in the end, it was not, and UNDC would go on to finance
two other buildings nearby. Two United Nations Plaza, a forty-story sister building directly next door on Forty-fourth Street, was completed in
1983, and also housed offices for UN and UN-related agencies, as well as
hotel space. And across the street, Three United Nations Plaza—thirteen
stories above a two-story base—was opened in 1987 as the world headquarters for Unicef, with some residential apartments on the top floors.[31]

Architecturally, the three buildings—all designed by Kevin Roche—
received high praise. Critic Paul Goldberger called Nos. One and Two,
with their glass towers of sloping setbacks, nothing less than "exquisite
minimalist sculpture."[32] The last of the trio, with alternating bands of light
and dark brown granite, was different in style from One and Two. Roche
designed it to complement the glass and brick bands of the two 1930s
Beaux-Arts apartment buildings down the street. Ironically, they were the
same buildings that had been slated to be demolished in Roche's earlier
"super block" plan. Now they took on renewed prominence.*

At the same time, and independent of the UNDC project, the UN
itself expanded its campus buildings in the late 1970s. It added a forty-
foot extension to the north end of the Conference Building, an annex at
the southeast corner of the UN grounds, and a 60,000-square-foot space
underneath the UN North Lawn to house the organization's printing
operation.[33]

While the UNDC and UN expansion would meet the need for more
office and hotel space for some years to come, there were other requirements as well. The number of UN member nations stood at some 150
by the late 1970s, and many were looking for new or expanded space for
their missions, homes for their families, and schools for their children.
Some thirty years since the UN first moved to New York, the countries
of the world would continue to make a mark on the landscape of New
York.[34]

---

*In 1989, the two Beaux Arts apartment buildings were designated city landmarks
by the New York Landmarks Preservation Commission.

11
Making a Mark

Flush with cash from soaring oil prices in the late 1970s, the government of Libya announced that it had bought a vacant lot on East Forty-eighth Street near the UN. There, the regime of the controversial leader Muammar el Qaddafi planned a twenty three story building that would include the country's UN mission, offices and apartments for its diplomatic staff, and a school for the diplomats' children. It would be called Libya House.[1]

While some Midtown neighbors voiced concerns about living next door to Libya House—two large residential buildings adjoined the site—work permits were granted and excavation began in 1980. But by the time the building neared completion in mid-1984, the United States had broken off all diplomatic ties with Libya and declared the country a "state sponsor of terrorism." In April that year, machine gun fire from the Libyan embassy in London killed a British policewoman and wounded ten student demonstrators. Now, the U.S. State Department joined wary New Yorkers in wondering just what was going to take place within the walls of Libya House.[2] Washington insisted that until the Libyans clarified their intentions, they could not move into the building, and the State Department asked Mayor Koch to hold up the city's "certificate of occupancy" until it got an answer. Still, Koch should allow construction to continue, he was told.

The mayor complied, but was admittedly confused: "We don't know who's a workman and who's a diplomat," he responded, as he ordered a squad of New York City police to surround the building.[3]

The miffed Libyans replied that everything in their new home would be "perfectly legitimate."[4] Still, Washington held out for a fuller explanation. When an acceptable response finally came, the State Department gave Mayor Koch and the city police much of the credit: "Only after the New York police ringed the building" did we get a reply, a State Department lawyer told the press.[5]

When the Libyans finally moved in, they were proud of their new gray concrete building, and the country's UN ambassador, Ali Treiki, took a *New York Times* reporter on a tour, showing off his top-floor triplex apartment with a terrace for which he had commissioned Italian designers to create a traditional Bedouin tent in tones of aqua and peach. There, Treiki said he and his family—restricted by the U.S. government to travel only within the city's five boroughs—could retreat from what he said were less-than-hospitable neighbors.[6]

Eclectic Transformation

While Libya House may have been among the more controversial, it was hardly alone in changing the landscape of East Midtown. Starting in the early 1960s, several UN and UN-related entities and independent global organizations built new quarters on First Avenue across from the UN. Small apartment buildings and warehouses were demolished to make way for, among others, the headquarters of the Carnegie Endowment for International Peace, the Church Peace Center, the Institute of International Education, the IBM World Trade Corporation building (later the Turkish Consulate and Mission to the UN), and, at the southwest corner of First and Forty-fifth Street, directly across from the General Assembly Building, the United States Mission to the UN. Designed by Kelly & Gruzen and Kahn & Jacobs, the twelve-story U.S. mission opened in 1961, replacing rented quarters at 2 Park Avenue. Its look was unusual, with a glass curtain wall covered by somber molded stone grill siding.[7]

Then some twenty years later, as a wave of new construction swept across a city recovering from its 1970s fiscal crisis, a number of new diplomatic buildings rose throughout the Turtle Bay neighborhood. They were an eclectic mix. Even before the Libyans broke ground, Uganda House had opened. A fourteen-story structure on Forty-fifth Street between First and Second avenues, directly next door to the U.S. UN Mission, it would prove to be as much a monument to a tyrannical leader of the African nation of Uganda, Idi Amin, as a space for the country's tiny UN mission staff. Uganda moved into its new quarters in 1978, just a year before Amin was overthrown. At the time, the mission had fewer than a dozen employees, but the building incorporated a ballroom, space for an art gallery, offices, and five apartments, including a terraced penthouse on the top floor, reserved for Amin should he come to New York. When a new regime arrived after Amin's ouster, it found the building filled with elaborate surveillance and listening devices, and construction so cheap that the building insulation on one side of Uganda House had been attached directly to the wall of the building next door.[8]

In 1986, Kuwait opened a fourteen-story mission on Forty-fourth Street between First and Second avenues, adorned with intricate Muslim motifs on a granite base. And India commissioned one of its leading architects, Charles Correa, to design a distinctive-looking mission on Forty-third Street between First and Second avenues. Its red polished granite façade had been quarried in south India, and its intricately carved wood-and-brass doors handmade by Rajasthani craftsmen.[9]

In the late 1990s, Germany built a twenty-three-story tower of reddish-brown granite along First Avenue for its UN mission, consulate, and information center. Korea hired the firm of architect I. M. Pei to design an eleven-story building featuring a giant diamond-shaped skylight for its top-floor conference room.[10] And soon the government of Singapore bought an old parking garage on East Forty-eighth Street and tore it down to build a six-story structure, fronted by delicately etched glass, for mission and consulate offices.

Over the years, many governments purchased condominium space for their missions in modern Second Avenue buildings. In the late 1950s, the demand for mission space was so great that the design of a large building planned as an apartment house at 800 Second Avenue, between Forty-second and Forty-third streets, was converted to offices. Since then, it has continually been among buildings housing the most missions in the city.[11]

Some smaller countries bought historic, often elegant, Midtown townhouses and brownstones for missions and consulates, sometimes to be combined with living space, and mostly in the area near UN headquarters. In 1990, Luxembourg purchased a distinguished house on Beekman Place, in a tiny two-block residential enclave hugging the East River just north of the UN. The 1930s house had been the longtime home of songwriter Irving Berlin. Also moving to some of the Beekman Place houses were the missions of Tunisia, Niger, Swaziland, Mozambique, and Yemen. And in 2013, the prime minister of Qatar bought probably the most prestigious Beekman Place property, a Georgian-style house that dated back to the 1800s.[12]

This takeover of old Manhattan homes throughout the East Midtown area was welcomed by some city neighbors, who believed it brought good security and proper upkeep. But others felt it was part of a continuing infringement on a historic and peaceful residential neighborhood. William Curtis, a longtime local resident who succeeded Peter Detmold as president of the Turtle Bay Association (TBA) in the early 1970s, expressed concern. "We can appreciate what the UN stands for and its important work, but that doesn't mean we have to like its physical expansion beyond its original tract of land," he said.

Curtis and his TBA group—representing residents working to improve quality of life in the Turtle Bay neighborhood, which abuts the UN property—had long been troubled by new high-rise construction in the area, much of it UN-related. But in the 2000s, Curtis became especially disturbed by the many missions and UN-related organizations that were buying the area's coveted brownstone buildings and converting them to offices. Most of the houses had been built in the mid-1800s and were the pride of the local community. "Our neighborhood is becoming more institutional, less and less residential," he lamented.[13]

At the start of the new century, Curtis and his neighbors watched as a second cycle of diplomatic construction began, when the United States demolished its 1961 mission to make way for a larger twenty-two-story structure designed by the American architect Charles Gwathmey. The original mission building had never won over architectural critics, and the new structure was equally controversial. Terrorism concerns led to a design with one overriding feature in mind—security. Built to be blast-resistant, the building had thirty-inch-thick walls of pale beige concrete, and was designed without windows up to the seventh floor. Then, tiny windows grew progressively wider as they neared the top. The architect himself said the building was designed "to withstand the failure of itself and everything around it."[14] A far more damning critique came from a legendary voice. When Oscar Niemeyer—the Brazilian architect credited with much of the UN's original design—was shown a rendering of the mission in 2006, he observed that the design was just the opposite of the transparency and openness of the UN buildings. "Bad imagination makes bad solutions and here is another example that there is no limit on bad ideas," he opined.[15]

In late 2016, just a block north of the U.S. mission on First Avenue, Turkey prepared to tear down its 1960s mission and consulate offices to build a new thirty-two-story tower, called Turkevi Center, inspired by a Turkish crescent and adorned with filigree-like metal paneling.[16]

Family Life

While the need for office space was critical for the UN and related organizations over the years, the more personal—finding homes for UN families and schools for their children—was a continuing concern. First addressed by Robert Moses in 1946 with development of Parkway Village in Queens, housing was a complicated matter, hampered by discrimination during the UN's early years, and later by landlords' questions about diplomatic immunity and the possibility occupants would "walk away" from their leases or maintenance obligations. Still, in a city where residents pride themselves in their diversity, UN families generally found New York to be a comfortable place to live, even a place with sizable local populations of their countrymen, from Koreans in Queens, to Haitians in Brooklyn, to Albanians in the Bronx.

Over the years, some UN workers and diplomats have settled in Midtown, close to the organization's headquarters, but most have moved farther away—to other parts of Manhattan and other boroughs, some to the suburbs, and many to two communities just across the East River from the UN, Roosevelt Island and Long Island City in Queens. In fact, when the first of many residential complexes opened on Roosevelt Island in 1975, they were heavily marketed to UN families, for both their convenience and affordability. Reached by river-spanning tram from Midtown Manhattan, and by subway since the 1990s, Roosevelt Island would continue to attract diplomats, including Kofi Annan, who lived there prior to his appointment as Secretary General in 1997.[17]

And when a development known as Queens West in Long Island City opened in the mid-1990s, many in the UN community were attracted to its cluster of high-rise condominium and rental buildings hugging the East River. Not only were they affordable and convenient—one subway stop from Grand Central Terminal—but they were located directly across the river from the UN complex, fronting Gantry Plaza State Park, twelve acres of greenery that offered arguably the city's best views of the UN's iconic buildings.

Some crossed the Hudson River to live in towns in New Jersey, while still others chose New York's northern suburban Westchester County. In particular, New Rochelle—a community of 80,000 residents known for its diversity, good schools, and attractively priced housing—became home to a large contingent of diplomatic families, many from West African and other less developed countries. Some bought the town's historically significant homes, including the coveted 1850s Chateau Sans Souci, a

Secretary General at Home

Since the 1970s, the permanent residence of the UN Secretary General has been a town house on Sutton Place in Midtown Manhattan. But the first official home for the UN's leader was a Tudor Revival house in Forest Hills, in the borough of Queens near the UN's temporary quarters in Flushing Meadow. In early 1946, as the city worked feverishly to attract the UN to settle in New York permanently, a group of wealthy New Yorkers, led by banker Winthrop Aldrich, purchased the fourteen-room 1920s turreted house and rented it to the UN for then-Secretary General Trygve Lie and his family.

By the time Dag Hammarskjold was elected to the top UN post in 1953, the UN headquarters was on its permanent site in Midtown Manhattan, and Hammarskjold preferred a home nearer to his office. He chose a two-story duplex rental apartment on East Seventy-third Street in Manhattan, which Hammaskjold, a bachelor, tastefully decorated with modern Scandinavian furniture and some family antiques.

Hammarskjold's successor, U Thant, lived farther from the headquarters, moving with his family to a large house in Riverdale in the Bronx.

Then when the fourth Secretary General, Kurt Waldheim, came into office in 1972, he preferred something closer to work, and about the same time, a distinguished house was available on a quiet residential avenue overlooking the East River, just a few blocks from the UN headquarters. The four-story, 14,000-square-foot neo-Georgian house, 3 Sutton Place, just north of Fifty-seventh Street, had been built by the financier J. P. Morgan for his daughter Anne in the early 1920s. After she died in 1952, it was sold to Arthur Houghton Jr., president of Steuben Glass. Now Houghton was leaving New York, and he was persuaded by his friend, Paul Hoffman, the first head of the United Nations Development Program and a longtime United Nations Association supporter, to donate the house to the UNA. In turn, UNA sold the house to the United Nations, with the proceeds going to UN-related causes.

Every Secretary General since Waldheim has lived at 3 Sutton Place, although when Ban Ki-moon came into office in January 2007, he and his wife temporarily resided at the Waldorf Astoria Hotel while the UN embarked on a $4.5 million renovation of the aging house, including security upgrades.

ten-bedroom house with eight fireplaces and a ballroom, purchased by the government of Chad in the early 2000s.[18]

Still, the preferred address for families associated with the UN remained New York City. A survey conducted by the city in 2014 found that more than three-quarters of the nearly 16,000 households directly employed by the UN community—the UN, affiliates and agencies, and missions—were living within the five boroughs.[19]

Like housing, the need for schools for children of UN families dated back to the arrival of the first UN workers. In 1947, a small private school offering a globally oriented curriculum was opened in a guest house at the temporary UN complex at Lake Success on Long Island. Called the United Nations International School (UNIS), its facilities were far from adequate, and soon it was moved to Queens, to four converted apartments in Parkway Village. By 1960, with the UN member states almost double the original number, and with diplomats settling into New York life and more likely to bring their families with them, the Queens school had expanded to nine apartments, but was still inadequate, with no labs, no gym, no arts and crafts room, no cafeteria. Soon, a second campus opened in leased space on Manhattan's Upper East Side in the city's P.S. 82, after that school's shrinking student body had been transferred to other facilities—and then to two temporary sites in the East Fifties. All the while, numerous proposals for a permanent UNIS site were floated, ranging from the southern tip of Roosevelt Island, to the north end of the UN's own North Lawn, to two properties in the East Thirties.[20]

Then, in the waning days of the three-term administration of Mayor Wagner, who had worked diligently to improve city-UN ties, a permanent solution was announced. Wagner and Under Secretary General David Vaughn signed a lease—a ninety-nine-year lease for a dollar a year—on property at Twenty-fifth Street and the East River, where a new UNIS facility would be built. The site was an old city dock, Pier 73, just south of the then-planned Waterside apartment complex.[21] The Ford Foundation agreed to contribute to the school's construction, the Rockefeller family paid for the necessary landfill at the site, and the building was designed by the firm of Wallace Harrison, director of the UN's original architecture team.[22]

The new school—for children of both UN families and the general public, pre-kindergarten through the twelfth grade—opened in 1973. A smaller branch for kindergarten through eighth grade was located in Jamaica Estates in Queens. Together, the highly regarded pair served approximately 1,500 students, about 80 percent of them affiliated with the international community, and 20 percent other city residents.[23] Many other UN families enrolled their children in New York's public school system.

So Near and Yet So Far

Over the years, some New Yorkers expressed regret that city residents and the UN community did not interact to a greater extent. The UN often seemed isolated and its staff uninvolved with the city, they believed. In particular, the diplomatic corps—ambassadors who are generally assigned to represent their countries at the UN for short stretches of time, typically three or four years—aren't residents of New York long enough to assimilate into the local community. And even if they stayed longer, their work, for the most part, was unrelated to the local environment around them. "They live in a separate world," said Stephen Schlesinger, who authored a book on the founding of the United Nations, *Act of Creation*.

"Unlike an ambassador to a country, the UN diplomats are representatives to an *organization*," Schlesinger pointed out, noting that envoys to the United States living in Washington feel a responsibility to become involved with the local community and its residents. It is a part of their job. "By contrast," he said, "emissaries to the UN are for the most part detached from their immediate surroundings."[24]

Schlesinger referred to an observation made by his father, historian Arthur Schlesinger Jr., in his Pulitzer Prize–winning book, *A Thousand Days*, published in 1965. As a frequent visitor to the UN while serving as an aide to President John F. Kennedy, the elder Schlesinger wrote that the UN was an "all-enveloping environment," and "a world of its own, separate, self-contained and in chronic crisis, where a dozen unrelated emergencies might explode at once, demanding immediate reactions across the government and decisions [or at least speeches] in New York."[25]

Decades later, it seemed to many that nothing had changed. As the number of member states grew rapidly in the years after Schlesinger wrote of a "separate" and "self-contained" existence, his words still held true.

As a result, said a report published by the New York City Bar Association's UN Committee in the early 2000s, the city appeared "unappreciative of the benefits of the UN's presence, unable to take better advantage of the UN's presence, and mired in petty disputes over parking tickets and local taxes."[26]

Jonathan Bing, a lawyer and former New York State Assemblyman representing the area surrounding the UN territory, agreed. The interaction between the UN community and local residents could be improved, he said. He pointed out that his young daughter, a student at P.S. 59 near the UN, was friends with children of diplomats from India, Japan, and several other countries. "She has access to kids from all over the world," he said, with some envy. "When the families of diplomats are involved in our schools and community, it benefits all of us by increasing our understanding of each other's cultures. The more diplomatic missions are engaged in all aspects of our neighborhoods, the better it is for them, and for their neighbors."[27]

Meanwhile, Curtis, whose TBA membership totaled some 1,500 by the early 2000s, could not recall a single UN-related employee being directly involved with the organization during its decades-long history. Though he described the Turtle Bay area as the city's "neighborhood host" to the UN, it seemed that no UN worker had ever taken an active role in the group's efforts to enhance life in the area: They hadn't been asked, nor had they stepped up to do so. And leaders of the area's Community Board 6—one of the city's formalized residents' groups that advocate for local neighborhoods—could not remember having had a member of the UN community involved in its work.[28]

Curtis acknowledged a long-standing "strain" between some of his members and the UN, mostly over residents' unease with UN-related physical infringement on the neighborhood. He said those concerns also were often tainted by TBA members' apprehension over policy positions of the UN General Assembly, principally regarding Israel. "Unfortunately, that has tarnished their attitude about having the UN as a neighbor," he said.[29]

The Bar Association report, meanwhile, pointed to numerous advantages of a closer bond between the city and the world organization, from cultural and educational opportunities, to even the more important questions of state. Diplomats' perceptions of the entire country "can be colored by what they experience with New Yorkers and with the City of New York," the report said, and suggested that a delegate's response to a U.S. position at the UN may be affected by whether they have been treated "fairly, kindly and helpfully by the City."[30]

So many in New York City applauded when, in 2014, the incoming administration of Mayor de Blasio appeared to make a concerted effort to embrace the world body as a vital part of the city. Shortly after the mayor appointed Penny Abeywardena to head the city's UN liaison office—giving her a mandate to "demystify" how New Yorkers think about the organization—she designed an initiative called "The New Yorkness of

UN Economic Contribution to New York

Over the years, the city has analyzed the economic benefits and costs of hosting the UN, the most recent such study issued by the de Blasio administration in late 2016. The report found that the UN community—defined as the UN, its agencies and affiliates, and the missions—contributed some $3.7 billion in total output, a measure of sales, to the city's economy for the fiscal year ended June 30, 2014.

The study reported that the UN community directly or indirectly supported some 25,000 full- and part-time jobs in New York. It directly employed some 16,000 employees, of whom 12,000 lived within New York's five boroughs. Their earnings helped create and sustain an additional 8,000 jobs in the city. Further, the report estimated that the spending of more than 30,000 visitors attending meetings and conferences associated with the UN during the year helped support at least another 1,200 jobs.

Total earnings paid to local workers who were either employed by or associated with operations of the UN were estimated to be $1.98 billion for the year. And the study found that the UN community contributed $110 million in revenue to the city in the form of taxes.

Major costs of hosting the UN included some $45 million for public school education for children of UN families and some $8 million for police protection of high-profile UN events that was not otherwise reimbursed by the federal government (see Chapter 8).

In addition, the report said the city forgoes an estimated $99 million in tax revenue in hosting the UN community, including $72 million because of the tax-exempt status of buildings owned by the UN and missions that are owned by government entities, $26 million due to the fact that some three-quarters of employees of the UN community are not U.S. nationals and therefore are exempt from paying local personal income tax, and $1 million because some diplomats are exempt from paying sales and use tax on personal purchases. Further information on the report released in 2016 is at www.nyc.gov/international and www.edc.nyc/UNImpactReport2016.

Studies of the international community's economic contribution to New York had been conducted in the past, although results are not comparable because the analyses used different methodologies. The first came in 1977 during the Beame administration; two reports were issued by Mayor Koch, in 1981 and 1989; and another was prepared in 1995 during the Giuliani administration, but not widely distributed.

the UN." Its goal was to find better ways to integrate the UN community into the fabric of the city. She highlighted educational and cultural
links, and stressed the economic benefits of having the UN in NewYork.
In late 2016, for the first time in almost thirty years, the city released a
detailed analysis of the UN community's financial contribution to the
city, estimating that its annual boost to the city's economy was some
$3.7 billion.[31]

"The city of United Nations" became Abeywardena's mantra, perhaps
most vividly displayed at bus shelters throughout the five boroughs, touting the bond with bold blue-and-white ads reading: "We are the city of
United Nations. . . . Together we are greater."[32]

"Great bus stop advertisement!" tweeted the Netherlands' UN ambassador Karel van Oosterom, a few days after the first of the series were
installed. Like most of his fellow diplomats, Van Oosterom liked living in
NewYork, although he said he didn't find much time for day-to-day local
community life. Assigned to his post in 2013, he described his weekdays
at the UN as "an ocean of work," and his weekends consumed with the
city's museums, theaters, and concert halls, which he compared to his UN
work: "without end!"

For Van Oosterom, the new ads celebrating the UN in NewYork were
a smart step for the city. He had long believed New York should not become too complacent about its relationship with the organization. While
it was clear that the UN headquarters weren't going to be moving from
NewYork any time soon, he cautioned that many cities around the world
would be only too happy to step in to host various agencies and other
bodies of the organization.[33]

It was a word of warning de Blasio and his predecessors had heard
before. From Wagner's administration in the 1950s, to Lindsay's and
Beame's years later, mayors had grappled with how to accommodate the
UN's office needs. More recently, in the 1990s, Mayor David Dinkins
had fought to prevent several UN agencies from defecting to other cities.

Flirting with Others

In 1990, having defeated three-term Mayor Ed Koch in the Democratic
primary, Dinkins went on to beat the Republican candidate, Rudolph
Giuiliani. A former Manhattan borough president who earlier served as
a State Assemblyman and city clerk, Dinkins became New York's first
African-American mayor. He had a great appreciation of the UN's
contribution to the city, and he didn't hesitate to criticize Koch for his

anti–UN rhetoric over the years. "I believe New York is eminently better off because of the UN," he said.[34]

By the time Dinkins took office, the organization's membership had leaped to 159 states, and once again the UN community was outgrowing its office space. But this time the recent fall of the Berlin Wall and a scrappy New York suburban community would add new obstacles to the Dinkins administration's efforts to make room for the world body.

By mid–1991, the parliament of the reunified Germany had voted to move the seat of government from Bonn—the city on the Rhine River where it had been located since the end of World War II—back to the traditional German capital, Berlin. This would leave Bonn with empty government buildings, houses, and apartments, and the prospect of a serious economic downturn. Bonn was quick to seize on reports that UN agencies were increasingly unhappy with their tight quarters in New York. For the Germans, the discontent presented an opportunity.

Indeed, four UN agencies soon announced they were considering leaving New York and would look for a new home base—the Development Program, the United Nations Population Fund, the Development Fund for Women, and the fastest-growing of them all, Unicef. If they all left, it would mean the loss of some 2,300 jobs, a third of the UN-related workforce in the city at the time, and representing a fifth of the local UN economic contribution.[35]

Dinkins was concerned not only about the direct financial impact to New York, but also the impact on the city's growing reputation as a place from which major employers were fleeing. Just recently, two oil giants had moved their headquarters out of the city—Mobil to Fairfax, Virginia; Exxon to Plano, Texas. Retailer J.C. Penney had left for Dallas, and the city's Wall Street firms were increasingly discovering that modern technology allowed them to move their "back office" staff—such as computer and communications workers—to cheaper quarters in the suburbs and beyond. And by 1992, the large financial institution Morgan Stanley was threatening to move its entire headquarters from Midtown Manhattan to Stamford, Connecticut.[36]

The German government's offers for the UN agencies were enticing, from rent-free accommodations in Bonn, to substantial help with relocation costs, and even free German-language lessons for agency staff. And as an added incentive, the Germans promised to increase the country's financial contribution to the world organization if the agencies settled in Bonn.[37]

But competition for the most visible of the four—Unicef headquar-

ters—turned more local. Not only was Germany wooing Unicef, but
the financially battered Westchester County suburb of New Rochelle—
just eighteen miles north of the city—was bidding for the organization
as well. A diverse community that over the years would become home
to many UN delegates and their families, now embarked on a vigorous
public relations campaign to lure Unicef to its midst. Its efforts recalled
some of the ill-fated spectacles put on by U.S. communities back in the
1940s when they had tried to win the UN headquarters site. "I've never
seen a city or its people as united or excited as they are," said the chairman
of the town's "New Rochelle for Unicef" committee.

New Rochelle offered a "designed-to-order" twenty-story headquarters tower that would reduce Unicef's annual rent by nearly 80 percent, and promised the organization reduced parking fees and utility rates,
and low-cost housing. Signs of "Welcome to New Rochelle, Home of
Unicef" would greet drivers on the New York Thruway access. The
town's central traffic circle would be renamed "U.N. Circle." And one
of the town's landmark buildings would be turned over to Unicef for an
international children's library.[38]

As competition narrowed to Manhattan and New Rochelle, the Westchester suburb appeared to have the superior proposal. "New York City
must do a lot to match it," said Unicef's chief, James Grant.[39]

To counter the suburban offer, New York City once again worked
through the UNDC. And it got help from some high-level Unicef staffers
who let it be known they worried the organization might lose prestige
in an outlying area, and preferred to stay near the UN's Manhattan headquarters. That didn't surprise the mayor. "The city is, after all, the place
to be," Dinkins remarked.[40]

But it irked New Rochelle's mayor, Tim Idoni. "They are not moving
to Kansas!" he exclaimed to reporters, "They are twenty-three minutes
away by car."[41]

Twenty-three minutes may not have been much, but in the end, the
city and UNDC came up with an offer too good to reject. "Little New
Rochelle has to be a remarkable community to have stimulated New York
City to offer this massive response," said a Unicef official in announcing,
in October 1993, that the UN had finally decided to stay in Manhattan. "It took the city a good deal of time to come up with an offer we
couldn't refuse."[42]

The offer—contingent on Unicef maintaining its world headquarters
in the city—called for a long-term lease of Three United Nations Plaza at
reduced rent, with the payments being used to purchase the building over

the long term. By 2026, Unicef would own Three UN Plaza. The deal also called for UNDC to buy additional space, in a nearby office building at 633 Third Avenue, for additional offices for Unicef staff.*[43]

In the end, not only Unicef, but all four agencies kept their headquarters in New York City.[44] It was considered a major victory for the Dinkins administration, although not all New Yorkers were happy with the outcome. Some in the surrounding Turtle Bay community voiced their concern about the increasing concentration of UN offices in their midst. "This neighborhood is becoming a residential theme park," said Perry Luntz, a local leader in East Midtown. "We are here just for the benefit of the tourists, demonstrators and UN workers."[45]

Still, the Playground

Once again, the UN space problems appeared to have been resolved. But UN expansion needs would be a recurring and controversial issue for years to come. The ideas that Moses expressed to Mayor Lindsay back in the 1960s—his preference for the Pepsi-Cola site in Long Island City or the southern tip of Roosevelt Island, just 400 yards from the UN headquarters campus—were never given much consideration. Instead, the residential Queens West development was built on the spot where the old Pepsi-Cola bottling plant once stood (the company's neon sign, which now had the eye of preservationists, remained).[†] And in 2010 construction began on the Franklin D. Roosevelt Four Freedoms Park at the southern tip of Roosevelt Island, a memorial dedicated to the former president, conceived in the early 1970s and designed by the architect Louis Kahn.

Nor was there ever much stock put in Moses' belief that taking over the small playground surrounding the Midtown Tunnel ventilating shaft wasn't workable. The space, just across Forty-second Street from the UN campus, continued to be seen as a prime option for UN offices. And ironically, in 1982, a year after Moses' death, the two-section parkland, until then unnamed, was designated "Robert Moses Playground." The City Council had moved swiftly to approve the name after the real estate de-

---

*UNDC later sold its interest in 633 Third Avenue, with Unicef continuing to lease space from the new owner.

†In 1988, the Pepsi-Cola sign was proposed for New York City landmark status, and in 2016, it was designated a landmark by the New York Landmarks Preservation Commission.

veloper Harry Helmsley proposed to swap two private parks in his Tudor
City development for the city's land next to the ventilating shaft. There
he planned a fifty-story office and apartment tower.[46]

While the city thwarted the Helmsley scheme, in the process the small
nondescript parcel of land was given new life—now with a real, and
recognizable, name. The City Parks Department resurfaced the asphalt
plot, and roller hockey players began gravitating there from around the
city for weekend games. But the bare, unadorned space most often remained unused. For years to come, Robert Moses Playground would be
the center of recurring debate over UN expansion.[47]

12
Quandary over Age

On an early September evening in 2004, Eva Moskowitz faced a hostile group of constituents. The bright, forty-year-old city councilwoman represented Manhattan's East Side, including the neighborhood surrounding the United Nations. A Democrat who had first been elected to the Council five years earlier, Moskowitz was known to be ambitious, with aspirations of running for mayor one day. So she was visibly upset at having to defend herself against harsh criticism from a core group of voters. "I resent your saying I have 'callously abrogated' my obligations to the community," she began. "I find these accusations unfair." When some in the audience interrupted her, she shot back in a shaky, but strong, voice, "Let me talk!"[1]

The group she was up against, the Turtle Bay Association, had circulated a newsletter with scathing criticism of their councilwoman. "Eva Moskowitz . . . has betrayed those who elected her to represent them," the TBA charged. "Her job . . . is to represent her district in the City Council, an obligation she has now callously abrogated" by "abandonment of both the park and her constituency."[2]

The "park" was Robert Moses Playground. Now, some forty years since it was first eyed as land for UN offices, and more than twenty years since it was graced with a name, the two-section city park, located just south of the UN on either side of the Queens Midtown Tunnel ventilating building, still provoked controversy. The eastern part was home to basketball and handball courts and a dog run. But the west side, a spare asphalt section, two-thirds of an acre between the ventilating building and First Avenue, stood vacant most of the time, awaiting the roller hockey players and their weekend games. Now, the little space was about to become the centerpiece of one of the most contentious issues the city and United Nations had ever faced.

With the growing UN once again looking for more office space—and with the original, aging UN buildings in serious need of repair—Moses Playground had been catapulted back into the news. Mayor Bloomberg's administration and the UNDC, which had financed and built the trio of buildings for the UN and UN-related agencies in the 1970s and 1980s and since 1994 was chaired by developer George Klein, had put together a plan for a new office tower to be built on the asphalt half of the playground. It was a "lease to own" arrangement, giving the UN the option to purchase the building at no cost at the end of an approximately thirty-year rental term. Replacement park space would be provided on an esplanade to be built out over the East River.[3]

While many viewed the stretch of asphalt as subpar, seldom-used park space, for some nearby neighbors it represented one of the few playgrounds in the area. Indeed, Moskowitz's council district was among those with the least park acreage in Manhattan. So, community leaders reasoned, if half of Robert Moses Playground was to be taken over by the United Nations, then the neighborhood deserved to have a replacement park. And it shouldn't be an esplanade, which the TBA took to calling just a "facelifted walkway and bicycle path."[4]

Residents of Tudor City, just south of Turtle Bay, were critics, too. Not only would they lose park space, but a high-rise building across First Avenue from their huge complex of some three thousand apartments would result in serious loss of sunlight and, for some, views of the East River.

The playground is "under siege," the TBA told neighbors, alerting them to be ready to "take up the cudgels" to fight. And the organization was counting on the support from the area's local elected officials, including Eva Moskowitz.[5]

So when Moskowitz let it be known that she was warming to the city's UN–Moses Playground plan, the TBA had fiercely criticized her and she asked to meet the group. "I firmly believe that we need to keep this symbol of international cooperation in New York City," she told them, and she said she saw Moses Playground as the most workable site for UN expansion. Still, she agreed to continue to pursue options for substitute park space beyond the "facelifted walkway."[6]

Showing Its Age

Four years earlier, in 2000, the iconic thirty-nine-story Secretariat—the first building completed in the UN complex—had marked its fiftieth birthday. Its gleaming walls of windows, the "glass curtain" that had captivated New Yorkers in the 1950s, still impressed passersby with their shimmer in the morning sunlight and glow in the evening. But window washers at the UN knew another side of the story. During the warm summer months, they could feel the chill of air conditioning seeping out through the closed windows.[7] The mid-century window structures were corroded and deteriorating, the effect of years of air and water infiltration and condensation.

Yet the energy-inefficient windows were only a small part of the problem. The UN buildings were contaminated with asbestos and the walls covered in lead paint, commonly used at the time of construction but long since banned as health hazards. Roofs and pipes leaked. It was not unusual to see a bucket placed in the hallways to catch water dripping from overhead, and plastic sheeting protected desks and computers from not only water, but chunks of falling ceiling as well. Steam valves exploded on occasion. The buildings had virtually no sprinkler systems, their fire alarms were outdated, and the whole complex was in need of an enhanced security system. One visible sign of the aging Secretariat Building was a notice tacked outside a padlocked room housing electrical transformers on the 28th floor. "High Voltage," it warned, "In case of necessity, call MUrray Hill 2-4477," a neighborhood-named telephone exchange that hadn't been used in decades.[8]

The buildings themselves were state-of-the-art when first constructed, their plumbing and electrical systems "real Rolls-Royce, top shelf for their time," said a longtime foreman at the UN. But the mechanisms of the buildings were meant to last some thirty years, and the complex had been designed to handle up to seventy member states and seven hundred meetings a year, while by 2000, UN members numbered 189 and conferences were up to almost eight thousand annually.[9]

In the late 1990s, the UN hired the Arup Group, a prominent international engineering firm, to assess the necessary repairs. Based on their report, the UN soon unveiled a renovation plan, which it called the "Capital Master Plan." Its budget was just under $1 billion.[10] The UN acknowledged it would be difficult to get the member states to sign off on such a pricey project. But the repairs were essential, not only to correct the obvious cosmetic effects of age, but to bring the complex into com-

pliance with the city's current building, fire, and safety codes, and accessibility requirements.[11] And the alternative, completing the work gradu-
ally over twenty-five years or so, was neither economically feasible nor
practical.[12]

Logistics also played a role. Where were employees who worked on
the UN campus—numbering approximately five thousand—going to be
housed during such extensive repair work? Renting space in nearby office
buildings was an option, but rents were high, particularly for short-term
leases. Some thought the entire UN headquarters should be moved off-
site for the duration of the project, to Geneva perhaps, already home to
a number of UN entities. And others suggested the UN just leave New
York for good. Bonn, it was pointed out, still had considerable vacant
space since the relocation of the German capital to Berlin.[13]

By 2002, the question of money was still up in the air, but the logistics question—where to locate the UN staff during renovation—seemed
resolved. The UNDC's proposed high-rise office tower on the western
half of Robert Moses Playground would serve as "swing" space where
staff would work while the old UN buildings were being restored. Once
the renovation was complete, employees would be moved back to their
updated offices and the new tower would become permanent space for
other UN staff, including those currently housed in rented offices around
the city, and in UNDC Buildings One and Two, which the city would
then be able to sell at current market rates.[14]

Now, the renovation appeared feasible. The UNDC's plan "has drasti-
cally changed the situation," a UN report to the General Assembly stated,
calling it "indeed a welcome development."[15] And it was anticipated that
the United States would offer an interest-free loan for the renovation
work, similar to the interest-free loan granted by the host country for
construction of the original UN buildings back in the late 1940s.[16]

The UNDC moved forward with a competition to select an architect
for the new tower, a contest among some of the world's greatest designers, in keeping with the celebrated team that originally conceived the
UN complex. Only winners of architecture's most prestigious honor, the
Pritzker Prize, were considered. In early 2004, the Japanese modernist
Fumihiko Maki was selected. He designed a thirty-five-story tower of
more than 900,000 square feet, complementing the existing UN buildings
and connected to them via a tunnel under Forty-second Street. It was
projected to be completed by 2008.[17]

But, in fact, construction of the tower was far from certain. For a structure to be built on Robert Moses Playground, the New York State Legis-

lature needed to weigh in. By law, conversion of any parkland in the state to another use, an action called alienation, must be approved by the State Legislature. So now lawmakers in Albany found themselves holding virtually all the cards.

Legislative Limbo

The timing could hardly have been worse for convincing the Legislature to help the United Nations with just about anything. In addition to the long-held sentiment among some state lawmakers that the UN was anti-Israel and anti-American, and the old complaint that diplomats are interloping scofflaws who don't pay their parking tickets, a high-level scandal involving a huge UN humanitarian effort was finding its way to the top of the news. In early 2004, it was alleged that the UN's Oil-for-Food Program—set up in the 1990s to help ordinary Iraqi citizens in the face of their country's UN-imposed economic sanctions—was corrupt, with charges that some of the organization's officials had accepted kickbacks and bribes in conjunction with the program. Soon, not only was a high-level UN investigation, headed by former U.S. Federal Reserve Chairman Paul Volcker, under way, but in Washington some five U.S. Congressional investigations were ongoing as well. The chairman of one, Minnesota Republican Senator Norm Coleman of the Senate Permanent Subcommittee on Investigations, a longtime critic of the UN, was soon calling on Secretary General Kofi Annan to resign over the corruption charges,* a sentiment reflected by many in the State Legislature.

Further complicating the Albany vote was the prominent New York real estate developer Sheldon Solow. Known for building one of the city's most desirable office buildings, 9 West Fifty-seventh Street, back in the 1970s, Solow recently had purchased nine acres of prime East River frontage just south of Moses Playground, land that formerly was the site of an old Con Edison generating plant. There he planned a complex of residential high rises and an office tower, where he hoped to persuade the UN to expand, rather than to the UNDC building on the playground site. Now he was lobbying to stymie the bill that would pave the way for the UNDC tower, the legislation to eliminate the playground. It was "a full-

---

*The final Volcker report, issued October 27, 2005, cleared Annan of any corruption charges, but accused nearly half of the companies involved in the program of kickbacks and illegal payments.

out lobbying and campaign-contribution press," the political watchdog group Common Cause later said of Solow's effort.[18]

As the Bloomberg administration continued to push hard for the bill's passage, the city's UN detractors took the opportunity to argue against just about anything that would benefit the world organization. "We had a lot of colleagues not even close to the neighborhood telling us what to do," remembered Democrat Jonathan Bing, who at the time was the assemblyman representing the Midtown district that would lose the playground space. "For me, it was all about being assured of adequate replacement recreation area for my constituents."[19]

When the city pointed to the UN's economic contributions to New York and the fact that the building's construction alone would add thousands of jobs in the metropolitan area, Vito Fossella, a conservative Republican Congressman from Staten Island, shot back: "When they created the UN fifty years ago, it wasn't for the economic benefit to New York City. I don't think the economic argument trumped anything else then, and it shouldn't trump anything else now."[20]

Republican Senator Martin Golden of Brooklyn argued against the plan on the basis of security, contending a building shouldn't be built over the Queens Midtown Tunnel, a potential terrorist target.[21] And the majority leader of the State Senate, Republican Joseph Bruno of upstate New York, asked, "How can we trust the UN nations to pay the fees to pay off this debt [for the UNDC building] when they don't even pay their parking fines?"[22]

Anthony Weiner, a young Democratic congressman from Brooklyn, chimed in: "The UN barely goes a week without doing something that infuriates me," he said. "Its members run up parking tickets, fritter away oil-for-food money, and pass resolutions that are virulently anti-Israel."[23]

City council members, considering two dueling resolutions on the matter, were split. While the Council's vote was non-binding, since authority to alienate parkland rested with the State Legislature, the council members' positions still got plenty of attention. "We don't want the UN here, and if they are here, we're not going to do anything to make them more comfortable," said Simcha Felder, Democrat of Brooklyn.[24] But other council members, such as Eva Moskowitz, agreed with their speaker, Democrat Gifford Miller, who tried to steer the Council away from UN policy issues. Miller saw the Moses Playground plan as a city economic and real estate matter. "I don't think that we should be turning this into a referendum on the policies and views of the member nations," Miller reasoned.[25]

The *New York Daily News*, a frequent critic of UN positions, agreed with Miller. Despite the world organization's "good for nothing reputation," the newspaper wrote in late 2004, "the UN is good for something. And that something is New York City. Like it or not, the United Nations pours billions into the economy and supports tens of thousands of jobs, while adding a fillip to New York's image as global capital. Let that not be forgotten as city and state politicians elevate the sport of UN-bashing to a fever pitch."[26]

A *New York Times* editorial concurred. "The failings of the United Nations, large and small, don't make a case for threatening action tantamount to an eviction notice," the *Times* wrote. "The obstructionists need to get out of the way."[27]

Still, despite the newspapers' backing and Bloomberg's best efforts—including a last-minute trip to Albany by his sister, the city's UN commissioner, Marjorie Tiven—the legislation got nowhere. "It doesn't matter if it's the mayor's sister, uncle, aunt, or anyone else," said Assemblyman Dov Hikind, conservative Democrat from Brooklyn. "My sentiment of the United Nations is that I don't trust them."[28]

In the end, the legislature neither approved the little park's alienation and UNDC's plans nor disapproved them. Instead, Republican Majority Leader Bruno refused to allow the proposal to go to the floor for a vote before the 2005 legislative session ended in the early summer, and the plan to build on Moses Playground simply died. The UN would not have a new tower to turn to during its renovation. State Senator Liz Krueger, a Democrat representing the area surrounding the UN and who supported building on the playground, issued some advice for the UN: "They need to go to Plan B."[29]

One Step Forward, Two Steps Back

Unfortunately, there was no Plan B. But the city's Economic Development Corporation and boosters around the metropolitan area moved quickly to propose alternative temporary space, from spots in Downtown Brooklyn, to Willets Point in Queens, Seven World Trade Center in downtown Manhattan, the Bronx, and even Governors Island.[30] At one point, the UN reported it had considered over one hundred properties, and found that because of either size or rent, none would work. The conservative *New York Sun* newspaper had its own proposal. The best Plan B, read an editorial, was for the UN to "set about packing up and getting out of town." Only then, the newspaper said, would the land on which the UN stood be put to productive use.[31]

In July 2005, with no temporary home yet in sight, the UN Secretary General appointed an experienced New York architect to oversee the renovation project, Louis F. Reuter IV, or "Fritz." Reuter had recently overseen a $1 billion rebuilding of the Weill Cornell Campus of New York Presbyterian Hospital. Now, he looked forward to handling a project of the size and prestige of the United Nations.[32]

Instead, Reuter soon found himself confronting obstacles both practical and political. First came the search for Plan B swing space. Shortly after he arrived, he told the press he was "scrambling" to find a spot for dislocated employees, with every option on the table, including "boats, barges, islands, and tents."[33] Or, his assistant added, even New Jersey.[34]

And before long, the architect faced another complication. The New York developer Donald Trump had entered the fray, with plenty of advice for both Reuter and the UN. It started with a general observation: "The United Nations is a mess."[35]

A few years earlier, Trump had built what was then the world's tallest residential building almost directly across First Avenue from the UN. The height of the 861 foot Trump World Tower was controversial. It was more than 300 feet taller than the Secretariat Building, made possible under city zoning regulations when Trump quietly bought up air rights from nearby buildings. Among the many high-profile critics who had spoken out against the outsized tower was Secretary General Annan, who joined neighbors—including retired television news anchor Walter Cronkite—in pleading that the building not soar higher than the UN's Secretariat. Their position reflected an "unwritten rule" along Midtown's First Avenue—that no nearby building should dwarf the Secretariat. But when the rule was tested in the courts, Trump could not be stopped, and before long his condominium skyscraper loomed over the Turtle Bay neighborhood and the UN.[36]

Soon, Trump turned his attention to the UN's proposed renovation. A letter from a UN ambassador, Sweden's Pierre Schori, seemed to have spurred him on. Schori had written to Trump in 2000—"a long letter and a very beautifully written letter," Trump later said—with admiring words about Trump's new residential tower and wondering if he might be able to help the UN with its costly renovation plans. The New York billionaire soon was making headlines with claims that the UN's projected budget, on a per-square-foot basis, was almost twice the cost of his brand-new ninety-story apartment tower. Trump got the attention of conservatives in Washington, and in the summer of 2005, he was called to testify before the Senate Homeland Security and Governmental Affairs Subcommittee looking into the U.S. share of the renovation costs, and chaired by a leading UN critic, Republican Oklahoma Senator Tom Coburn. "Anybody that says that a building renovation is more expensive than building a new building does not know the business," Trump testified. "It only costs a fool more money."[37]

He likened the UN project to his renovation of a New York City skating rink years earlier. "This is a bigger version of the Wollman Skating Rink, that is all it is," he told the Senators, waving a picture of New York's East River skyline above his head.[38]

Twenty years earlier, Trump had persuaded a skeptical Mayor Koch to let him take over renovation of Central Park's Wollman Rink. The popular skating venue had been closed for six years, as the city faced one construction glitch after another. Trump wrote to Mayor Koch: "The incompetence displayed on this simple construction project must be considered one of the greatest embarrassments of your administration."[39] Koch, faced with further delays and cost overruns, finally agreed to a deal in which the city would pay for the project, up to $3 million, with Trump responsible for anything over. Within five months the job was done, Trump boasting that not only had he come in under budget, but with money left over to renovate some adjacent buildings.[40]

So now, he argued, why not let him take on the UN job, which he said he could handle for less than half the UN's estimate, by year-end 2005 projected at $1.6 billion.[41] As U.S. Congressional support for the UN project waned and with the real estate developer's claims getting in the way, Reuter asked to meet with Trump. In late November 2005, Reuter, with his boss, Under Secretary General for Management Christopher Burnham, called on Trump at his Trump Tower office on Fifth Avenue. Facing the same claims in person that he had read in the media, Reuter invited him to come to the UN to see for himself the extent of repairs involved in the work.[42]

Trump didn't take Reuter up on his offer. But a short time later, after Reuter met with Senator Coburn in Washington and the suggestion was made that a team of outside construction experts review the UN's Capital Master Plan documents and pricing, one of Trump's contractors was sent to the UN to conduct the review.[43]

During early February 2006, HRH Construction—a New York firm that had handled several Trump projects—was provided a conference

room at UN headquarters and given the full set of renovation plan documents for the contractor's independent review. Within ten days, an HRH
representative approached the UN architect, telling him, "Fritz, this is
getting very complicated, because we are pretty much in agreement with
your numbers," Reuter later recalled.[44]

It was no surprise to Reuter, but of little comfort either. The Trump
contractor team never made its internal analysis public,[45] and resistance
in Washington only continued. But for a while, at least, Trump's public
boasting stopped.[46]

By now, the United States had a new UN ambassador, John Bolton.
The blunt-spoken conservative, who took office in August 2005, came
to the job when President George W. Bush used the presidential device
of recess appointment after congressional confirmation appeared unlikely.
A harsh critic of the way the UN functioned, he once commented, "The
Secretariat building has 38 stories. If you lost ten stories today, it wouldn't
make a bit of difference." Joe Biden, then Democratic Senator from Dela-
ware and on the Senate Foreign Relations committee, compared posting
Bolton to the UN to sending a "bull into the china shop."[47]

Now Bolton would be keeping a close eye on the Capital Master Plan
financial projections.

Dirty Tours

As Reuter and his staff continued to lobby member states, particularly
the United States, to get the renovation under way, they had begun a
kind of "show and tell" exercise of the UN's infrastructure problems.
Unlike the popular UN sightseeing tour that had been conducted since
the 1950s and highlighted the best of the UN, Reuter's tour was designed
to accentuate the worst. It quickly became dubbed the "dirty tour" and
was intended to give influential congressmen, state and local officials, and
news reporters a close-up look at the UN's deficiencies, from exfoliating
asbestos-clad pipes, to old motors showing their 1951 manufacture date,
to the "High Voltage" warning sign with directions to call the outdated
"Murray Hill" emergency number.

During one of his "dirty tours" for elected officials in the early spring
of 2006, with funding for the project still up in the air, Reuter assessed
four options for swing space: renting space in nearby buildings, too pricey;
postponing some of the renovation, cost inefficient; building a UN-
financed permanent tower on the UN's North Lawn, an idea now being
floated, too challenging for the UN to finance;[48] and lastly, a scenario now

nearing final approval: renovating the buildings in stages, the Secretariat Building ten floors at a time, with displaced staff moving to nearby rental space and to a temporary building on the North Lawn. That building also would house conferences and meetings, including the General Assembly, while the permanent facilities were gutted and refurbished. Once the project was complete, the temporary building would come down and the land would return to its use as the UN's landscaped park.

But then he added a fifth possibility: "There is still talk of moving the entire UN out of New York," he said.[49]

Adding to the architect's concerns about the project was yet another hurdle, the hold-up by the United States of an important intermediate step in getting the project off the ground. The UN budgetary arm needed to approve $100 million of funding for further pre-construction planning. But the United States, whose support was needed for the customary consensus approval, was holding up the expenditure. "We're not trying to slow this down, but we want to proceed in a careful and prudent fashion," Bolton told the *New York Times*.[50]

In May 2006, Reuter resigned, his statement to the media citing the "lack of support from many stakeholders and the difficulties of working within the UN practice as it applies to a large building project." But in fact, he later said, "I was simply frustrated that even my own government was not backing the project."[51]

Then in early December 2006, Bolton resigned, when it became clear he would not have the Senate votes to be confirmed beyond his recess appointment, which lapsed at year-end. Later that month, the Capital Master Plan moved ahead. The General Assembly approved the project and a budget of $1.9 billion. In lieu of a U.S. government loan offer, the funding would come from assessments on each member state, based on the formula used for its annual dues.[52]

Now, as the search began for a new architect to head the renovation, word started to circulate that the Bloomberg administration and the UNDC hadn't given up on building on the small asphalt patch of land across Forty-second Street from the UN. Within weeks, Robert Moses Playground would be back in the headlines.

13

Renewal of a Cityscape Icon

Back in 1948, after the international team of architects completed designing the UN headquarters buildings, the group's director, Wallace Harrison, and George Dudley, the young designer who had been at his side keeping notes of the work, were ready to move on to other endeavors. At the time, Nelson Rockefeller was starting a new venture, the International Basic Economy Corporation, with a subsidiary, IBEC Housing, that would produce low-cost housing in less-developed countries. He asked Harrison to chair the housing company and Dudley to serve in the more hands-on role as president. For the next twelve years Dudley oversaw Rockefeller's IBEC projects around the world, from a complex of concrete cube-like houses in Puerto Rico, to jobs in Central and South America, and Iraq, Iran, and Kuwait.

Then in 1960, Dudley again got a call from Rockefeller, who had just been elected to the first of what would be four terms as governor of New York State. Rockefeller had decided the capital of Albany should have a grander, more fitting government complex to surround the late-nineteenth-century Capitol building, and Dudley soon found himself in upstate New York working on preliminary designs for the "South Mall," an ambitious ten-building project that would be named the Nelson A. Rockefeller Empire State Plaza.

When his work on the Mall ended, Dudley stayed in the Albany area, and was named Dean of Architecture at Rensselaer Polytechnic Institute (RPI), an engineering school with a highly rated architectural program in the nearby city of Troy. From his student days at Yale, Dudley remembered the camaraderie between faculty and classmates, and the lasting impression it had made. Now, at RPI, he took the same approach, spending time with his students after class and sharing stories of his accomplished career.[1]

One of his students was an aspiring young architect from Brooklyn, Michael Adlerstein. "Dean Dudley particularly liked to talk about his time with the UN design team in the late 1940s," Adlerstein remembered years later.

Adlerstein would go on to Harvard University's Graduate School of Design as a Loeb Fellow, and then to a long career with the U.S. Park Service, overseeing such high-profile restoration projects as Ellis Island and the Statue of Liberty. But he never forgot Dudley's stories about the UN. "They were a powerful influence," he said.

And so when he was offered the job leading the team to update and renew the aging UN buildings, it was like a "dream," he said. "I started my architectural learnings hearing from George Dudley about the original UN design, and now, at this point in my life, to be involved in the restoration of such a highly acclaimed project was a real thrill."[2]

Ban Ki-moon, who became UN Secretary General in January 2007, announced Adlerstein's appointment as Executive Director and Assistant Secretary General of the Capital Master Plan in early July. It was the position Reuter had held prior to his resignation the year before. Now, for the next eight years, Adlerstein would oversee the UN architectural staff and, at the project's peak, more than one thousand contractor and sub-contractor employees. The $2.15 billion project would be completed substantially on time and on budget.[3]

Adlerstein believed being a New Yorker helped a lot. "New York City is a complex place, and it would have been much more difficult for a non–New Yorker to do the job." The "insider" language of the mayor's office, the commissioner's office, the Buildings Department, and other city agencies would have been difficult for a non–New Yorker to decipher, he said.[4]

One of Adlerstein's first decisions was to change course on the project's employee relocation plan. Rather than emptying ten floors of the Secretariat at a time, virtually the entire staff, more than three thousand employees, would be relocated at one time. "Noise carries in high-rise buildings," said Adlerstein, "and the kind of work we would be doing was going to be very loud and disruptive."

Fortuitously, the cost of renting office space in Manhattan, thought to be prohibitively high for a short-term rental, was eased when several floors of 380 Madison Avenue, a Midtown building owned by developer

Sheldon Solow with a land lease expiring in just a few years, became available on reasonable terms. Along with offices in a 1920s building on Forty-sixth Street, the Madison Avenue building was outfitted for the temporary use of some 1,800 staff. Other employees would move to the United Nations Federal Credit Union building at Court Square Place in Long Island City, in Queens.[5]

Still, the most visible swing space would be a temporary, low-rise structure to be built on the landscaped North Lawn. Over the course of the renovation, it would be used at various times for offices for Secretariat staff, including the Secretary General; for conference space; and then late in the project, in 2013, for the General Assembly session. Likened by some to a "Walmart-style box," the white corrugated metal structure featured unfinished concrete floors and stark plaster walls designed to ensure it would never become a permanent fixture of the UN complex.

With staff relocation and swing space dilemmas behind him, Adlerstein and his team soon walked into an unexpected hurdle from the city. Like spats in the past—from Robert Moses' clash with Dag Hammarskjold over garage space, to Mayor Giuliani's tirade over UN diplomats' parking tickets—the city and the UN would find themselves uncomfortably at odds with one another.

The "Cultural Gulf"

For years it had been well known that the UN headquarters buildings were in violation of New York City's fire and safety regulations. They had been completed in 1952 under the city's 1938 building code in effect at the time. While the law had been updated in 1968, buildings constructed prior to that year were exempt from the regulation, under a "grandfather" clause, until such time as they would be renovated. Now, the UN viewed the breaches as a key reason for the massive renewal. When it first unveiled the Capital Master Plan in 2000, the organization emphasized that one of the goals of the renovation was to make the complex "compliant with host city building, fire and safety codes."[6] And then as it began lobbying member states, including the United States, for financial support for the multimillion-dollar project, the UN pointed to the need to correct the code violations—conducting its "dirty tours," holding press conferences, and supplying facts and figures to those in a position to influence the outcome.

At the same time, New York City, too, was zeroing in on the UN's fire and safety code violations as never before. The post-9/11 environment had heightened sensitivity to the need for stringent precautions in high-profile buildings. "Given the [UN] organization's iconic status, its attractiveness as a terrorist target, and its exceptionally high tourist traffic, facility-wide safety is a significant ongoing concern," the city's Commission for International Affairs stated on its website.[7]

In early 2006, city officials informed the UN that they wanted to send inspectors onto UN property to check for violations. That would be unprecedented for the inviolable site, and the request had lawyers poring over terms of the original 1947 United Nations–United States Headquarters Agreement before the UN agreed. Within a year, the city's Fire and Buildings departments had identified 866 violations, some more serious than others, from the lack of sprinkler systems to unlighted exit signs.[8]

At the UN, the inspection results were generally viewed as reinforcing the need for the renovation, and supporting its call for member states to approve the big expenditure. Indeed, by year-end 2006, the General Assembly had okayed the Capital Master Plan budget and its funding. Now, the outdated safety and fire standards were on track to be brought up to date.[9]

But the city, it seemed, saw it differently. Mayor Bloomberg called on Ban Ki-moon in April 2007, just four months after the former South Korean foreign minister took office. Accompanying the mayor were his sister, the city's UN Commissioner Marjorie Tiven, and Fire Commissioner Nicholas Scoppetta. Bloomberg told Ban there was strong local media interest in the UN compound's safety issues, and he cautioned him that if the issue wasn't addressed soon, while Ban was still in what Bloomberg referred to as his "honeymoon" period, the matter could harm perceptions of the Secretary General's office. Ban replied confidently that correction of the violations was on track with the recently approved Capital Master Plan. But Bloomberg said the length of the job—at the time estimated to take seven years—was too long for the violations to go unfixed. The two left the meeting agreeing that the city and UN staff would continue to discuss the matter.[10]

A few months later, Tiven sent a tersely worded letter to the UN. "The city cannot allow this situation to continue," she wrote. "You are putting at risk the lives of the people who work and visit the United Nations, as well as the public safety personnel who would respond to an emergency. We implore you to act now."[11]

The UN responded that while some of the work to address the violations had begun, it wasn't sensible to make too many fixes when the problems would be comprehensively corrected by the big renovation. If, for instance, the UN installed a full fire sprinkler system before the renovation, it would have to be torn out and replaced later. "We don't have a pot of money," a perplexed UN Department of Management official responded to a news reporter.[12]

In the fall of 2007, another letter arrived at the UN, this one signed by Mayor Bloomberg but drafted by his sister's office. "The New York City Fire Department estimates that less than twenty percent of the 866 previously issued violations have been cured," the letter stated, and the city demanded that the remainder be resolved by early 2008, including a "separation and compartmentation" project that required erecting fire walls, a major expense. If the UN didn't adhere to the deadlines, the letter said the city would be forced to, among other things, stop all public school tours of the UN.[13]

The school visits had been a feature of the New York City public school system since the 1950s, when Mayor Wagner organized them as a way to "smooth the wrinkles" in the city-UN relationship. Over the years, the tours had become a kind of "sentimental link" between New York and the UN, and by 2007, some 100,000 school children, ages five to twelve, visited the UN each year.

Now, Adlerstein, just a few months into his role as renovator-in-chief, found himself involved in what he later called an "awkward" situation with the city.[14]

In early May 2008, the UN—which maintained that 40 percent of the directives had been addressed, not 20, as the city estimated—informed the city that it didn't plan to implement all of its demands. The organization had installed some of the fire walls the city demanded, but had determined it was too expensive to implement the full plan when the renovation project, now about to begin, would correct the deficiencies permanently.[15] "We had a plan to do all the things the commissioner's office was asking, but she seemed to think we could do it all by *tomorrow morning!*" said Adlerstein.[16]

When the school year began in the fall, the city made good on its threat. All public school visits to the UN were canceled. And in a stern letter released to the press, Tiven called into question the safety of others visiting and working at the UN. "It is not within the United Nations' discretion (or the City's) to assign different values to the lives of tourists in the Headquarters public areas, versus the lives of United Nations employees and business visitors," she wrote.[17]

But the tours for the general public continued, and employees and diplomats still walked the UN halls. So Tiven's staff produced large red and white metal signs with cautionary language about the compound's fire and safety conditions. They were placed throughout the UN grounds.[18]

The signs may have made the city feel more comfortable, but the whole situation rankled the UN community. "I half-expected to see Marjorie Tiven at the corner of Forty-fifth Street and First Avenue personally waving people away from the buildings!" said the head of a non-governmental organization who frequently attended meetings at the UN.[19]

The city's actions were "upsetting" to the UN, said Adlerstein. "Whatever we were, we had been for decades, and now we had a plan to comprehensively fix all the issues. The city's reaction was overkill, not necessary."[20]

But Tiven appeared unconvinced. On meeting with U.S. ambassador to the UN Susan Rice in 2009, she assessed the problem: "The UN doesn't seem to have the capacity to cross the 'cultural gulf'" to meet safety codes, she told Rice.[21]

Work Under Way

On a sunny Saturday morning in the spring of 2008, trucks rolled onto the UN's North Lawn, and crews chopped down some two dozen of its lush flowering Japanese cherry trees. A gift from New Yorker Mary Lasker back in the 1950s, the trees were being removed to make way for the temporary North Lawn Conference Building, the swing space to be used during the UN's renovation. While a New York City regulation that restricted destruction of healthy trees didn't apply to the UN property, the organization was sensitive to the trees' demise. In a press release, it announced that not only would the trees be replaced when the North Lawn structure came down, but additional trees would be planted in and around the UN complex—a "greening" effort that it said was aimed at transforming the complex into a model of sustainability.[22]

Soon, sculptures that stood on the Lawn—gifts from member states over the years—were towed away. Among the first to go was a forty-two-foot-tall "Peace" monument, an equestrian statue that stood on a pedestal at the garden's center. The stately statue, by Croatian sculptor Antun Augustincic, had been a gift from Yugoslavia in 1954 and was the first member-donated sculpture gift to the UN.[23] Now, like the others, it would be covered with tarpaulin, out of the way of construction for the next eight years.

Ground was broken for the "box-like" two-and-a-half-story building in early May 2008 and by the end of the next year, Ban and some three hundred UN staff had moved from their Secretariat offices to the completed temporary structure. The rest of the Secretariat workers went to rental offices nearby, and the Security Council and other councils relocated to interim space within the General Assembly Building.[24] After some ten years of scrutiny, second-guessing, and cajoling, the UN's Capital Master Plan was finally under way.

The project would be both a restoration to preserve the architectural significance of the 1950s buildings and a renovation to remove asbestos and other hazardous materials, upgrade systems to meet stringent sustainability goals and current security needs, ensure accessibility standards, and, of course, bring the buildings into compliance with the city's building, fire, and safety codes.[25] The council chambers housed in the Conference Building and the General Assembly would retain virtually all of their historic characteristics, while the thirty-nine-story Secretariat would maintain its highly recognizable Le Corbusier-inspired exterior glass curtain wall, but its interior would be gutted and renovated into a modern open floor plan of offices.

Kent Barwick, former New York City Landmarks commissioner and longtime president of the Municipal Art Society, an influential organization that promotes quality urban planning, praised the effort to preserve the original design and décor of what he called "a landmark of the highest quality and architecture in the world." While the structures, standing on territory owned by the UN, were not designated city landmarks and not subject to local laws governing their renovation, Barwick, who headed a group of international architects advising the Secretary General on the renovation,* said he believed every modification made during the renovation would easily have received city approval.[26]

Three of the four biggest firms hired for the renovation were based in the New York metropolitan area—construction manager Skanska USA, engineers Syska Hennessy Group, and architects HLW International—and they were joined by the New York office of Chicago-based architects Perkins + Will. In a coincidence that proved helpful, Syska Hennessy, a prominent firm that dated back to the early twentieth century, had worked on the original UN building project, and still had copies of some of the original plans that the UN no longer possessed.[27]

---

*The other architects in the group were Susan Njeri Kibue, Kenya; Stefan Kurylowicz, Poland; K.T. Ravindran, India; Anna Torriani, Switzerland; and Jayme Zettel, Brazil.

Another NewYork firm, R. A. Heintges and Associates, was hired for probably the most visible exterior work, reconstruction of the Secretariat's glass curtain wall. And a smaller job, but arguably the most prestigious of them all, went to a firm in the Greenpoint neighborhood of Brooklyn—Walter P. Sauer, a specialty woodworking company that dated back to the late 1800s. Sauer would restore the olive ash horseshoe table used by the Security Council and the maple wood desks of the General Assembly delegates.[28]

Boost to Local Economy

As with most construction projects, the UN renovation was largely beneficial to the local economy. In all, the UN estimated that 95 percent of the total $2.15 billion budget went back into the NewYork metropolitan area, including $1.3 billion in wages for construction workers and $550 million in rent for the temporary swing space. And the UN pointed out that the economic benefit to the city was reflected at the U.S. national level as well. Since the project was financed by assessments proportionate to each member nations' annual dues, the U.S. share of 22 percent for the renovation was offset several times over by expenditures that flowed back into the U.S. economy.[29]

Separately, the U.S. covered the $100 million cost for security upgrades in and around the complex, after security requirements for the compound were raised in response to attacks on UN facilities overseas. The U.S. expenditure, which included installation of perimeter bollards, was in line with a provision of the original 1947 Headquarters Agreement that called for the host country to provide security from threats emanating outside the UN perimeter.

Several countries donated money for decorative work, most notably the three Scandinavian countries—Norway, Sweden, and Denmark—for restoration of the Conference Buildings' Council chambers. The Netherlands donated the interior for the popular North Delegates Lounge, including a handsome curtain of porcelain balls hanging on the east-facing floor-to-ceiling windows. Donations for other rooms came from Austria, Bangladesh, China, Finland, Germany, New Zealand, Thailand, Turkey, Russia, and Qatar.[30]

The Capital Master Plan won high praise from the design community. Jayme Zettel, a Brazilian who once worked for Oscar Niemeyer and was on the project's Advisory Board, lauded what he called the "excellency" of preserving the characteristics that Niemeyer and the mid-century design team had intended.

New York architecture critic and author Carter Wiseman agreed. "I was really quite moved by the detail and concern that went into keeping to the style of the original," he said. And Barwick called the project a "painstakingly thorough job," and particularly praised the work in the three council chambers and the General Assembly Hall. "Breathtakingly beautiful," he called them. "I can't imagine a more careful job of restoration."[31]

Meanwhile, two buildings at the south end of the campus, both later additions to the original complex, were not included in the renovation. The Dag Hammarskjold Library and the South Annex Building were considered structurally too weak to bring up to current security standards and, as the renovation project ended, their future remained to be determined.[32]

But two new small structures were added to the UN complex, one that serves as a staff entrance at the south end and the other, a visitor's entrance and security screening complex near Forty-sixth Street. Visitors enter the new screening complex via a tiered stairway built on land that is technically outside the UN's border. In a rare move, and after long, protracted negotiations, New York City agreed to allow some 1,500 square feet of city property to be used for the entrance.[33]

Despite a setback in October 2012, when parts of the UN headquarters' basements were flooded during Hurricane Sandy, the project was largely complete by the fall of 2014. The temporary building was used one last time to host the UN's Sustainable Development Goals Summit in September 2015, and then the corrugated metal structure was dismantled and the lawn was re-landscaped.

By early 2016, the UN was able to assess what had been, for Secretary General Ban, a top priority—to make the world body a role model of sustainability. Since taking office nine years earlier, Ban had made fighting global warming a key goal of his tenure, and he was committed to assuring the renewed complex would be a world-standard example of efficient use of energy and resources.[34] Indeed, after a full year of measuring energy consumption in the renewed quarters, the UN estimated it was saving slightly over 50 percent on electrical use on the complex, and consuming over 40 percent less water.[35]

Restoring and Renovating

Most of the $2.15 billion project to update UN headquarters, essentially completed in 2015, centered on the compound's three main buildings:

Secretariat Building. The need for work on the glass curtain wall of the tall Secretariat Building had a long history. Soon after the building opened in 1950, the heat and glare of the sun proved a problem, particularly on the building's east side, not sheltered by the Manhattan skyline. A blue-green tinted reflective film was added to the east façade, and a different treatment on the west. Both created an exterior appearance that was never intended, and led to damage to the glass over time. In addition, the windows' structural supports had deteriorated. The solution was an entirely new updated window system that was blast-resistant and lighter, yet designed to match the original look. From a 1950s sample of the glass found in UN archives, a new double-glazed curtain wall was created that was nearly an exact replica of the original.

By contrast, the interior of the Secretariat was, for the most part, a "gut makeover" that—like the other two UN buildings—included necessary upgrades to bring it up to current standards, but also a total redesign to convert the mid-century maze of private offices into an almost entirely open plan of easily reconfigured workspaces that accommodate more staff and benefit from the east and west sunlight. A few spaces retained their original appearance, notably the Secretary General's thirty-eighth-floor wood-paneled office and the ground-floor lobby, its 1950s green marble walls and black-and-white speckled terrazzo tile floors polished and sparkling once again.

Conference Building. Tucked along the East River behind the tall Secretariat and swoop-roofed General Assembly, the Conference Building—home of the fifteen-member Security Council, Economic and Social Council (ECOSOC), and Trusteeship Council—was painstakingly restored. The council chambers originally had been designed by architects from Norway, Sweden, and Denmark, and now the three countries played a major role in their restoration. The three governments made sizeable donations for the work, beyond their required member-state assessment, and chose highly regarded architects from their countries to carry out the projects.

Also renovated were three large meeting rooms and several small meeting spaces in the Conference Building. Enhanced security precautions led to repositioning some of the rooms, which created space for a new lounge overlooking the East River. The Gulf nation of Qatar donated furnishings for the lounge.

General Assembly Building. Last of the UN buildings to get a makeover was the one housing the important Plenary Hall of the General Assembly. The Assembly's 2013 session was relocated to the temporary North Lawn structure, while the entire building was updated and then returned to its original luster—from the delicate ribbon-windowed exterior north façade, to the visitor's lobby, to the Plenary Hall, where years of cigar and cigarette smoking—banned since 2008 in all UN buildings—had long masked its vibrant décor. The Hall's two prominent Fernand Leger orange and blue murals were restored, delegates' desks were inlaid with fresh green leather identical to the original, and the furniture was reupholstered in pastel tones of Naugahyde, an artificial leather popular at mid-century that had been used throughout the UN complex.

For New Yorkers—more likely to walk past than enter the UN—the most notable change was to the building's exterior. Like the Secretariat's end walls of Vermont marble, the General Assembly's English Portland stone was cleaned and its prominent dome brought back to its original state. Shortly after the building opened in 1952, the terne-coated copper-clad dome had begun to leak, and a thick brown coat of water-protective paint was added. Now, the dome was water-proofed and resurfaced to its original state.

Moses Playground: Again in the Spotlight

With completion of the eight-year renovation project, eyes now turned to the UN community's future office needs, the ongoing "growing pains" of an organization that, by 2015, comprised 193 member states and 2 observer states, Palestine and the Holy See, and whose employees—including the UN, its affiliates and agencies, and mission staff—now numbered close to 16,000.

Once again, New York City and the UNDC took the lead in trying to help. And again, plans for a new building would center on the two-thirds of an acre just south of the Secretariat, the western portion of Robert Moses Playground. But this time, having learned from the aborted deal in 2005 when Albany legislators refused to take up a bill to allow construction on the playground, the Bloomberg administration and the

UNDC orchestrated a well-thought-out campaign to win over elected officials, local community leaders, and neighborhood residents to a complex arrangement that promised benefits for both the United Nations and local East Siders.[36]

Likened by some to moves in a Rubik's Cube puzzle, the plan would provide city residents with access to a new twenty-two-block-long landscaped esplanade along the East River—filling a major gap in Manhattan's waterfront greenway, including the six blocks in front of the UN—as well as new parkland in the East Twenties at Asser Levy Place. The new park, formerly a little-used two-block street in front of a city recreation center, would provide replacement space for the Moses Playground land, which would finally—after more than forty years of being eyed for construction—be converted to a site for a new UNDC tower, the thirty-five-story high rise designed by Fumihiko Maki years earlier.

The arrangement worked like this: Upon state legislation authorizing alienation of the Moses Playground land, UNDC would make a payment into a special fund that would be used for the initial phase of the riverside esplanade. Meanwhile, UNDC would offer the UN a thirty-year lease on the new high rise to be built on the playground land, an agreement under which the UN would be able to buy the building for one dollar at the end of the rental term. Once constructed, the new tower would become offices for UN and UN-related staff who had been housed in rental space in One and Two UN Plaza—two of the trio of UNDC buildings constructed in the 1970s and 1980s. The city then would sell One and Two, and use part of what was expected to be a substantial profit to pay for the remaining public waterfront enhancements.[37]

"It's a once-in-a-lifetime opportunity," said State Senator Liz Krueger at the time the deal was set in motion in the fall of 2011, with legislative approval and a subsequent Memorandum of Understanding (MOU) providing the framework for the plan. Krueger said the new arrangement "not only meets the UN's needs for more office facilities, but at the same time provides New Yorkers with desperately needed open space and access to the East River in East Midtown."[38]

State Assemblyman Brian Kavanagh, whose district, like Krueger's, was adjacent to the UN's property, served as lead negotiator in gaining passage of the legislation and approval of the MOU. For Kavanagh, being able to balance constituents' needs with those of the UN was very appealing. "Whenever you are proposing to build in a densely populated space like Manhattan, you must, of course, accommodate the local community," he said. "With this legislation, I believe we have done that, while at the same time demonstrating that we are amenable to meeting the needs of the United Nations."[39]

Kavanagh and Krueger, along with the other elected officials of the neighborhood surrounding the UN, including Congresswoman Carolyn Maloney and City Councilman Dan Garodnick, would serve as members of a board set up to oversee design and implementation of the city projects.

There were critics of the plan. Some in the neighborhood still clung to the idea that Moses Playground could be saved for the hockey players. And the conservative Washington think tank and UN critic, the Heritage Foundation, was skeptical of the UN's need for a new office building and the potential costs to the U.S. taxpayer, although it did call the deal a "win" for New York City and the UN.[40]

When Mayor Bill de Blasio came into office in 2014, he continued his predecessor's enthusiastic support. And two of the first moves of the "Rubik's Cube puzzle"—converting Asser Levy Place to a park, and a three-block waterfront pier to an esplanade space from Thirty-eighth to Forty-first Street—were substantially completed by late 2015.

The next move was the UN's. For the rest of the plan to fall into place, and before work could begin on the remaining nineteen blocks of waterfront walkways and bikeways, the organization needed to approve a deal for the new UNDC tower.[41] While Secretary General Ban recommended the plan to the General Assembly in the fall of 2015, member states had doubts about the organization's future office needs, and as of late 2016—with the UN's workspace requirements under study—the plan appeared stalled.

For the time being at least, Robert Moses Playground would remain an asphalt slab of land awaiting the weekend roller hockey players, and New Yorkers would be left to await their waterside esplanade.

But another nearby open space, a tiny city plaza with historic significance to the UN, was being rejuvenated. The plot of land—just one-tenth of an acre—was at Forty-second Street directly across First Avenue from the Moses Playground space and diagonally across from the UN complex. It had been created in 1948 as part of the city's improvements to approaches to the UN, and was adorned with trees, pavers, and park benches, against the backdrop of a thirty-foot-high retaining wall. Later, it was named for Trygve Lie, the UN's first Secretary General and the man who had been highly influential in persuading his organization to settle in New York.

Over the years, the small plaza fell into disrepair. Then in 2010, the city's Parks Department moved to restore and enhance the little space, with financial support from the government of Lie's home country, Norway; from Lie's two grandsons, New York real estate developers Arthur and William Zeckendorf; and others. Sculpture for the plaza was designed by an award-winning Norwegian artist, Lina Viste Gronli, who created an enormous brass clock, seventeen feet in diameter, that "floats" on the newly refinished retaining wall. Twice a day, its sleek hands form the international peace symbol, at approximately 4:30 each morning and 4:30 in the afternoon.[42]

The renewed space was dedicated in a ceremony in September 2016, just days after the opening of the UN General Assembly's annual fall session. Small as the plot of city land may be, Trygve Lie Plaza stands as a lasting reminder of the bond between New York City and the United Nations. Now more than seventy years old, it was the partnership Mayor La Guardia had once called a "natural" and Lie himself described as a "dream" that became "reality."[43]

Epilogue

As the New York City–United Nations partnership entered its eighth decade in 2017, the new year brought a new leader to the UN and a New Yorker president to the White House. On January 1, António Guterres of Portugal, the UN's former High Commissioner for Refugees, became the ninth Secretary General, succeeding Ban Ki-moon at the end of his two terms in office. And for the first time since the UN was founded, the start of a Secretary General's term coincided with that of a U.S. president, in this case a president who was a lifelong New Yorker. Donald Trump would be the first president from the city since the UN charter was ratified in October 1945. And while his election reflected little support among his fellow New Yorkers—he won just 18 percent of the citywide popular vote, and less than 10 percent in his home borough of Manhattan—concerns about a Trump presidency were even greater within the UN community. He began his term calling for significant cuts in funding of international organizations, including the United Nations.

In contrast to the chill coming from Washington, New York Mayor Bill de Blasio's warm welcome to Guterres included a promise to collaborate closely with the UN on the "many pressing economic, development and environmental challenges ahead." And former Mayor Michael Bloomberg, who had been appointed the UN's Special Envoy for Cities and Climate Change by Ban Ki-moon, committed to continuing his work under the organization's new leadership.

Meanwhile, plans were on hold for the United Nations Development Corporation (UNDC) to build a thirty-five-story office tower to house

UN staff on Robert Moses Playground south of Forty-second Street, as the UN embarked on a comprehensive study of future office needs throughout its worldwide network. In New York, the UN had recently implemented flexible, more efficient workplace arrangements that created space for hundreds of employees to move from leased offices in Midtown to the UN's own Secretariat Building. At the same time, it was undertaking a global study of longer-term reforms, an analysis that could lead to consolidation of administrative jobs, potentially with fewer employees at some locations and more at others. So it remained questionable that the UN would need a new office tower on the playground. Still, the idea—which first surfaced in the 1960s, was studied further in the 1990s, deemed critical to the UN in the early 2000s, and then in its most recent iteration would lead to twenty-two blocks of public waterfront greenway on Manhattan's East Side—remained on the table. It was an option that was viable at least until the end of 2019, a date set by state legislation.

But New York City wasn't waiting for the UN to make a decision. In the spring of 2017, Mayor de Blasio announced that the city would commit $100 million to construct a landscaped pedestrian and bicycling promenade between Fifty-third and Sixty-first streets, the northernmost section of the esplanade that would have been built under the UNDC proposal. Studies conducted for those earlier designs formed the basis of the mayor's plan, and much of the preliminary work was already complete. With the three blocks of waterfront pier recently converted to esplanade space south of Forty-first Street, only twelve blocks—including six directly in front of the UN property—remained to be completed to close the gap in the greenway along the Midtown shore. The mayor emphasized that filling the gap was a priority, part of a push for a contiguous thirty-two-mile waterfront greenway encircling all of Manhattan.

Now, after more than seventy years, New York City and the United Nations continued to show that despite some squabbles and misunderstandings along the way, the great metropolis and the world's central meeting place can indeed coexist on the crowded island of Manhattan. With its freshly renovated and more efficient headquarters, the UN left no doubt it would maintain the partnership for decades to come. And the multicultural city of New York made clear that it was committed to being a congenial host. It was a sentiment perhaps best summed up by a city-sponsored promotional campaign introduced as the pair moved into their eighth decade together: "We are the city of United Nations; Together, we are greater."

Acknowledgments

My thanks for help with this New York–United Nations project are extended to many, from city residents and neighbors of the UN, to the UN community itself.

Representatives and staff of the world organization were very responsive to my inquiries. Early on, I was honored to spend time with one of the first UN employees and a former Under Secretary General, Brian Urquhart, who had vivid memories of the UN's earliest days in New York. Later, Nicholas Emiliou, UN ambassador from Cyprus and chairman of the UN Committee on Relations with the Host Country from 2012 to early 2017, provided me with his perspective on the more recent city-UN partnership. And the UN's Werner Schmidt has my sincere thanks. I first met Werner when he was public information officer for the UN's Capital Master Plan, and throughout my work, no one could have been more responsive in dealing with my many inquiries. And my thanks also go to the UN Department of Public Information's Maher Nasser and his staff.

On the city side of the story, I am indebted to many, from local community leaders, to elected officials, to other close observers of the city-UN relationship. And I am sincerely grateful to Gillian Sorensen, whose many years working as the city's commissioner to the UN under Mayor Ed Koch, and then later as an aide to both Secretaries General Boutros Boutros-Ghali and Kofi Annan, brought a unique and personal perspective to the story.

In my archival research, I thank Douglas Di Carlo and the staff at the

170 **Acknowledgments**

La Guardia and Wagner Archives of the City University of New York, where I spent many days searching the papers of New York's mayors since Fiorello La Guardia. Earlier, when I first started my work, the director of the city's Municipal Archives, the late Leonora Gidlund, kindly took me aside and gave me some valuable tips on researching a New York story such as this. And the staff at the United Nations Archives and Record Management Section were always very accommodating during the time I spent there.

My appreciation also goes to Orin Buck for creating the city-UN map and timeline that appear in the front of the book. And at Fordham University Press, I especially thank Fred Nachbaur, whose guidance and confidence in the project were instrumental in bringing it to fruition, as well as Will Cerbone, Ann-Christine Racette, and Eric Newman.

Notes

Prologue

1. "United Nations Impact Report 2016," a study by the New York City Mayor's Office for International Affairs and the Economic Development Corporation, based generally on fiscal 2014 data, and released on Dec. 6, 2016, www.nyc.gov/international. Also related EDC report, www.edc.nyc/UNImpactReport2016, accessed Dec. 6, 2016.

2. La Guardia and Wagner Archives, La Guardia Community College, City University of New York, La Guardia Collection, Box 26C3, Folder 3, prepared script for WNYC *Talk to the People* broadcast, Dec. 9, 1945; Audio: WNYC Archives ID 71085.

3. Urquhart interview with author, Apr. 29, 2009, and subsequent e-mail, Nov. 10, 2010.

1. City Rebuffed

1. La Guardia and Wagner Archives, La Guardia Community College, City University of New York, (LWA), La Guardia Collection, Box 26C3, Folder 3, prepared script for WNYC *Talk to the People* broadcast, Dec. 9, 1945; Audio: WNYC Archives ID 71085.

2. LWA, La Guardia Collection, Box 26C3, Folder 3, prepared script for WNYC *Talk to the People* broadcast, Dec. 2, 1945; Audio: WNYC Archives ID 71144. (Portions of the audio of this broadcast are missing, including the mayor's UN discussion.)

3. Since 1962, the title has been referred to as "Parks Commissioner,"

reflecting a change in the name of the department. Today the full title of the department is the Parks and Recreation Department.

4. *Why the United Nations Came to New York*, (*City-UN Report*), page 8. The lengthy report was prepared in 1953 for Grover Whalen, who at one point was chairman of the "United Nations Committee of New York," New York City Municipal Library; leather-bound book description, *New York Herald Tribune (NYHT)*, Jan. 9, 1946.

5. Although fifty countries attended the spring 1945 charter conference, Poland signed the charter shortly after, bringing the UN's initial membership to fifty-one.

6. After the Communist victory in China in 1949, the Nationalist government moved to Taiwan and retained the UN membership. In 1971, Taiwan's UN seat was transferred to the People's Republic of China.

7. Verbatim record of Oct. 3, 1945, meeting, UN Preparatory Commission Executive Committee, PC/EX/73, issued on Oct. 16, 1945, UN Dag Hammarskjold Library.

8. LWA, La Guardia Collection, Box 26C3, Folder 3, prepared script for WNYC *Talk to the People* broadcast, Dec. 16, 1945; Audio: WNYC Archives ID 71130.

9. During the "Europe versus America" debate at the Preparatory Commission Executive Committee session in London, U.S. Secretary of State Edward Stettinius, reflecting his country's neutral position, remained silent, but at one point commented that he felt "very much like someone who was being elected to a club and was asked to sit with the membership committee while his character was being discussed." Verbatim record of Oct. 3, 1945, meeting, PC/EX/73, UN Dag Hammarskjold Library.

10. Linda Sue Phipps, in her PhD dissertation, *"Constructing" the United Nations Headquarters* (Harvard University, 1998), includes a list that appeared in the UN Journal of Preparatory Commission (1946) showing invitations from forty-one U.S. locations. And a study conducted for Charlotte Mires's book, *Capital of the World: The Race to Host the United Nations* (New York and London: New York University Press, 2013), concluded that at least 248 localities were involved in the competition to some degree, although not all of the offers were from individuals with direct authority.

11. United Nations Archives and Records Management Section (UNA), UN Preparatory Commission, Hubert Humphrey's letter to the UN: S-0539-0004-16. Cities' bids to become the UN home are well documented in the media, and their offers, letters, and brochures are housed at the UNA, Series S-0539.

12. *Eleanor and Harry: The Correspondence of Eleanor Roosevelt and Harry S. Truman*, ed. Steve Neal (New York: Scribner, 2002), p. 40, Eleanor Roosevelt's letter regarding Hyde Park is dated Sept. 11, 1945.

13. UNA, UN Preparatory Commission, S-539-0004-19.

14. Trygve Lie, *In the Cause of Peace: Seven Years at the United Nations* (New York: The Macmillan Company, 1954), p. 62.

15. *Chicago Tribune*, Dec. 3, 1945.

16. UNA, S-0539-0004-17. A memo from the U.S. deputy delegate to the United Nations Preparatory Commission, Adlai Stevenson, to the Commission's head, Britain's Jebb Gladwyn, urged a forum for "ensuring orderly and dignified presentations" to "make the presence of these gentlemen in London as useful as possible."

17. LWA, La Guardia Collection, Box 26C3, Folder 3, prepared script for WNYC *Talk to the People* broadcast, Dec. 16, 1945; Audio: WNYC Archives ID 71130.

18. *New York Times (NYT)*, Dec. 7, 1945.

19. Ibid., Dec. 12, 1945.

20. UN Preparatory Commission Press Release No. 121, Dec. 15, 1945, United Nations Hammarskjold Library (UN Library).

21. UN Preparatory Commission Press Release No. 158, Dec. 29, 1945, UN Library.

22. Robert A. Caro, *The Power Broker: Robert Moses and the Fall of New York* (New York: Alfred A. Knopf, 1974), p. 771.

23. Chamber of Commerce, *A Guide Book to the City of New York* (New York: Supervue Map and Guide Organization, 1945). La Guardia Field had opened in 1939 and was later renamed La Guardia Airport. Idlewild would later be named John F. Kennedy International Airport.

24. *City-UN Report*, p. 10.

25. *NYHT*, Jan. 6, 1946.

26. *NYT*, Feb. 3, 1965.

27. Ibid., Jan. 9, 1946.

28. *NYHT*, Jan. 9, 1946.

29. William O'Dwyer, *Beyond the Golden Door*, ed. Paul O'Dwyer (New York: St. John's University, 1986), p. 263.

30. *NYHT*, Jan. 9, 1946.

31. Ibid.

32. Manuscript and Archives Division of the New York Public Library (NYPL Archives), Robert Moses Papers, Series 1, Box 27, Folder UNO 1946. First half of quote appeared in letter to Swope, Jan. 16, 1946, and second half in letter to Cass Canfield, Harpers & Brothers, Feb.16, 1946.

33. *City-UN Report*. Text of full letter, dated Jan. 15, 1946, appears in Appendix, XXI.

34. Ibid.

35. NYPL Archives, Moses Papers, Series 1, Box 27, Folder UNO 1946, Jan. 16, 1946.

36. NYC Municipal Archives (NYMA), O'Dwyer-UNO papers, Jan. 22, 1946, note to O'Dwyer from Moses, Box 164, Folder 1773.

37. Cary Reich, *The Life of Nelson Rockefeller: Worlds to Conquer, 1908–1958* (New York: Doubleday, 1996), p. 363.

38. *NYT*, Mar. 3, 1946. Of several articles on the subject, this one headlined "UNO Praises Aid of Rockefeller."

39. Ibid. Additionally, *City-UN Report*, p. 13.

40. *Report and Recommendation of the Inspection Group*, Feb. 5, 1946, UN Library. Also lengthy excerpts, *NYT*, Feb. 5, 1946.

41. Lie, *In the Cause of Peace*, p. 64.

42. O'Dwyer, *Beyond the Golden Door*, p. 263.

43. Lie, *In the Cause of Peace*, pp. 60, 64.

44. *NYT*, Feb. 24, 1946.

45. Ibid., Feb. 25, 1946.

46. Ibid., Feb. 25, 27, 28, and Mar. 1, 1946.

47. O'Dwyer, *Beyond the Golden Door*, p. 264.

48. *NYT*, Mar. 4, 1946.

49. Ibid., Feb. 25, 1946.

50. *City-UN Report*, p. 14.

51. *NYT*, Mar. 25, 1946.

52. Ibid.

53. Lie, *In the Cause of Peace*, p. 66.

54. Ibid., p. 67.

55. Urquhart quote appears in *A Workshop for Peace*, a 2005 United Nations video, produced by Peter Rosen Productions, Inc. and the UN Department of Public Information. The 54-minute video tells the story of the design of the UN buildings, which the lead designer, Wallace Harrison, referred to as a "workshop for peace."

56. Lie, *In the Cause of Peace*, p. 66.

57. *City-UN Report*, p. 18.

58. *NYT*, Mar. 2, 1946.

59. Rockefeller Archive Center (RAC), Nelson A. Rockefeller–Personal Projects–UN, Series III 3L, Box 246. Memo from Nelson to his father, John D. Rockefeller Jr., Feb. 4, 1946.

60. Lie, *In the Cause of Peace*, p. 66; *NYT*, Apr. 2, 1946.

61. *City-UN Report*, pp. 17, 18.

62. *NYT*, Mar. 31, 1946.

63. Ibid., Apr. 5, 1946.

64. *Nation*, Apr. 27, 1946, p. 506.

65. *NYT*, Apr. 6, 1946.

66. Ibid., Apr. 11, 1946.

67. *City-UN Report*, pp. 20, 21.

68. Ibid., Appendix, XXXI, BOE vote, Calendar No. 145, Apr. 11, 1946.

69. *NYT*, Apr. 13 and Apr. 12, 1946.

2. Suburbia Unnerved

1. The *Greenwich Time* episode comes from an author interview with Bernard Yudain, Jan. 6, 2009, and Yudain's oral history, part of the Greenwich, Connecticut, Library Oral History Project (GOHP). In the interview, Yudain told the author he believed Bush had gotten his information from Allen Dulles of the U.S. State Department, later head of the Central Intelligence Agency.

2. *Greenwich* magazine, May 1995.

3. Honorable James D. Hopkins, *Our Voices Were Heard: The Selection of the United Nations Headquarters* (New York: Pace University, 1984), p. 3.

4. *NYT*, Feb. 3, 1946.

5. John Gray and Amadee Cole oral histories, GOHP.

6. Hopkins, *Our Voices Were Heard*, p. 4.

7. *No to UNOville!*, a Greenwich Historical Society (GHS) exhibit from Oct. 24, 2003–Mar. 28, 2004, Section 3/Panel 32: "The Obvious Choice."

8. UNA, S-0532-0001, Report of the Inspection Group's private evening meeting at the Westchester Country Club, January 10, 1946 (UNA has designated no folder no. for this report); the account of the French media reports, *NYT*, Jan. 18, 1946.

9. UNA S-0532-0001 (no folder no. designated).

10. GHS, *No to UNOville!*, Section 3/Panel 32.

11. *NYT*, Feb. 2, 1946. The *Times* that day carried multiple articles about the choice. Tunney's quote is in an article headlined "Site for UNO Stirs Wave of Protests, Evictions Feared."

12. *Greenwich* magazine, May 1995.

13. Alton Ketchum oral history, GOHP.

14. *Time* magazine, Feb. 11, 1946.

15. Yudain oral history, GOHP.

16. Ketchum oral history, GOHP.

17. The Macy chain later became part of the Gannett group.

18. White Plains *Reporter Dispatch*, Feb. 4, 1946.

19. Entire Cole account is from Cole oral history, GOHP.

20. Barrett quote, *NYT*, Mar. 3, 1946; "case of insolent snobbery . . . ," Ketchum oral history, GOHP.

21. *NYT*, Mar. 6, 1946.

22. Lie statement, GHS, *No to UNOville!*, Section 5/Panel 32.

23. Nicholas Fox Weber, *Le Corbusier: A Life* (New York: Alfred A. Knopf, 2008), pp. 482–484.

24. George A. Dudley, *A Workshop for Peace: Designing the United Nations Headquarters* (Cambridge, Mass.: MIT Press; New York: Architectural History Foundation, 1994). Accounts of the two men working together are told throughout the book.

25. UNA, S-0472-0051-09. Account of the Connecticut meeting is a verbatim report.

26. *NYT*, Jul. 30, 1946.

27. Ibid.

28. Ibid., Jul. 31, 1946.

29. Ibid., Jul. 30, 1946.

30. Ibid., Aug. 15, 1946.

31. Ibid., Sept. 8, 1946.

32. Ibid., Aug. 17, 1946.

33. Ibid., Aug. 24, 1946.

34. UNA, S-0472-0051-12. Sir Angus and Rev. Prunty letters.

35. Lie, *In the Cause of Peace*, p. 109.

36. *NYT*, Sept. 13, 1946.

37. Ibid., Oct. 17, 1946. AAUN merged with the U.S. Committee for the United Nations (UNA-USA) in 1964. In 2010, UNA-USA formed an alliance with the UN Foundation, a Washington-based group that advocates for the UN and its causes.

3. Cosmopolitan Charm

1. *City-UN Report*, p. 51.

2. O'Dwyer, *Beyond the Golden Door*, p. 266.

3. *City-UN Report*, p. 51.

4. RAC, Rockefeller family–World Affairs, Series III 2Q, Box 29, Folder 255.

5. *City-UN Report*, Appendix, I.

6. Ibid., Appendix, X. The committee's head, Harriet Aldrich, was Nelson Rockefeller's aunt through her sister Abby's marriage to Nelson's father, John D. Rockefeller Jr.

7. Ibid. Efforts described in detail, pp. 51–61.

8. Lie, *In the Cause of Peace*, p. 72.

9. Ibid., p. 70.

10. RAC, Nelson Rockefeller–Personal Projects–UN, Series III 4L, Box 246. The archive includes letters of invitation to UN representatives for dinner and the show, and subsequent thanks.

11. *Life*, June 10, 1946.

12. *City-UN Report*, pp. 51–61.

13. As it turned out, some Parkway Village units were not immediately needed by the UN, and were sublet to U.S. veterans.

14. *City-UN Report*. A good summation of Moses' housing plans, pp. 44–50; Veterans' group protesting is in Caro, *The Power Broker*, p. 774.

15. Grover Whalen, *Mr. New York: The Autobiography of Grover Whalen* (New York: G. P. Putnam, 1955), pp. 198–199.

16. Robert Moses, *Public Works: A Dangerous Trade* (New York: McGraw-Hill, 1970), p. 541.

17. Caro, *The Power Broker*, p. 1085.

18. *NYT*, Jul. 16, 1946. The World Trade Center project would not be built until the late 1960s, when its construction began in lower Manhattan.

19. *NYT*, Oct. 16, 1946.

20. UNA, S-0472-0051-02. Copy of Lie memo.

21. Le Corbusier, *UN Headquarters: Practical Application of a Philosophy of the Domain of Building* (New York: Reinhold Publishing, 1947), p. 53.

22. Dudley, *A Workshop for Peace*, p. 16.

23. Le Corbusier, *UN Headquarters*, pp. 20, 18.

24. *NYT*, Nov. 2, 1946.

25. Lie, *In the Cause of Peace*, p. 110.

26. *NYT*, Oct. 20, 1946.

27. Ibid., Oct. 19, 1946. Further information from Jan. 3, 2009, *NYT* obituary of Oliver North Lundquist, head of the team that designed the badge. He said the color blue was used because it was the "opposite of red, the war color." Among his later works was the highly recognizable Q-tips box, also blue.

28. Ibid.

29. *City-UN Report*, p. 29.

30. *NYT*, Oct. 20, 1946.

31. *City-UN Report*, p. 32; *NYT*, Oct. 24, 1946.

32. *NYHT*, Oct. 27, 1946.

33. NYPL Archives, Moses Papers, Series 1, Box 27, Folder F, Oct. 19, 1946, a letter to Langdon K. Thorne, requesting that he invite Lie on one of his duck-hunting trips. It was one of several letters Moses wrote to acquaintances requesting a duck-hunting engagement for Lie.

34. *New Yorker*, Oct. 11 and 18, 1946, by Philip Hamburger.

35. Lie, *In the Cause of Peace*, p. 107.

36. *NYT*, Nov. 8, 1946.

37. Ibid., Nov. 2, 1946.

38. *The Yearbook of the United Nations of 1946* (*UN Yearbook, 1946*), pp. 272–273.

39. Ibid., p. 273; *NYT*, Nov. 15, 1946.

40. *UN Yearbook, 1946*, p. 273.

41. NYPL Archives, Moses Papers, Series 1, Box 27, Folder F. Moses memo calling the design team to a meeting to work on construction details, including capacity needs and costs.

42. RAC, Nelson Rockefeller–Personal Projects, UN, Series III 4L, Box 246.

43. NYPL Archives, Moses Papers, Series 1, Box 27, Folder F. Full text of telegram.

44. *NYT*, Dec. 3 and Dec. 6, 1946.

45. William Zeckendorf with Edward McCreary, *The Autobiography of*

William Zeckendorf (New York: Holt, Rinehart and Winston, 1970), pp. 68–69; Financing deadline of Dec. 11, 1946, *NYT*, Letter to the Editor from William Zeckendorf Jr., Oct. 30, 1995, and various.

4. Rockefellers to the Rescue

1. NYPL Archives, Moses Papers, Series 4, Box 91, Folder UN-946, RM Correspondence; a copy of the letter also at RAC, Record Group 4, Series 1114L, Box 246, Folder 2462.

2. RAC, Memorandum written by John D. Rockefeller Jr., Nelson A. Rockefeller–Personal Projects–UN, Series 111 4L, Box 247, Folder 2469. Much of Chapter Four is based on Rockefeller Jr.'s seven-page memo (Rockefeller Jr. memo) which, while undated, he wrote shortly after his gift was accepted by the United Nations on Dec. 14, 1946.

3. William Rockefeller's older brother, John Rockefeller Sr., built a forty-room home, called Kykuit, near his brother's Rockwood Hall mansion. Kykuit was passed on to Rockefeller Jr. upon Senior's death, and later to Nelson Rockefeller. Today, Kykuit is a National Trust for Historic Preservation site, and is open to the public for tours. Meanwhile, the Rockwood Hall property was donated to New York State in 1999, and became part of the Rockefeller State Park Preserve.

4. Reich, *The Life of Nelson A. Rockefeller*, p. 384.

5. Previous twelve paragraphs from Rockefeller Jr. memo, RAC; David's reluctance appears in: Reich, *The Life of Nelson A. Rockefeller*, p. 385.

6. Zeckendorf, *The Autobiography of William Zeckendorf*, pp. 64–65; financing deadline, *NYT*, Nov. 8, 1995, Letter to Editor from William Zeckendorf Jr.

7. Ibid., p. 67, and Robert A. M. Stern, Thomas Mellins, and David Fishman, *New York 1960: Architecture and Urbanism Between the Second World War and the Bicentennial* (New York: Monacelli Press, 1997), p. 606.

8. Zeckendorf, *The Autobiography of William Zeckendorf*, pp. 67–69.

9. Rockefeller Jr. memo, RAC.

10. Zeckendorf, *The Autobiography of William Zeckendorf*, pp. 70–71. There probably was some haggling prior to agreement. On Dec. 17, 1946, James Reston of the *New York Times* wrote an account of the overnight deal, noting prices ranging from $5 million to $15 million, before the final $8.5 million was agreed to. The story, based on sources "who knew what went on," seems likely to have come from Nelson Rockefeller, a personal friend of Reston. On Dec. 20, Rockefeller wrote a note thanking Reston for the article. "It was very swell of you," he said. (RAC, Record Group 1112Q, Box 26, Office of Rockefeller–World Affairs, Folder 229)

11. All from Rockefeller Jr. memo, except Center Theatre comment, which appeared in Reich, *The Life of Nelson Rockefeller*, p. 387.

12. Many sources for text of letter, including *NYT*, Dec. 12, 1946. Under the

arrangement, the land would be sold to the UN, with Rockefeller donating the money.

13. Zeckendorf, *Autobiography of William Zeckendorf*, p. 71.

14. Linda Sue Phipps, in her PhD Dissertation, *"Constructing" the United Nations Headquarters* (Harvard University, 1998), pp. 103–107, points out that Nelson Rockefeller and Harrison had prepared pamphlets, with site plans and renderings of the X-City project, to help the delegates, who had just come from inspecting lush sites in Philadelphia and San Francisco, visualize how the dirty, smelly, blocks of slaughterhouses might be transformed into a respectable, vertical, skyscraper headquarters.

15. RAC, Nelson A. Rockefeller–Personal Projects–UN, Series 111 4L, Box 247, Folder 2469.

5. Rise of a Cityscape Icon

1. Dudley, *A Workshop for Peace*, p. 289. Dudley's 429-page book, published in 1994, is among the few documents that provide personal observations of the UN architects' work. Dudley, a junior New York City architect in 1947, was hired by Wallace Harrison to take "notes" of the architects' meetings, specifying that they not be formal, structured "minutes." As a result, Dudley's collection of notes in *A Workshop for Peace* provide a rich, credible picture of the workings of the UN design team.

2. Dudley, p. 30.

3. Victoria Newhouse, *Wallace K. Harrison, Architect* (New York: Rizzoli International Publications, 1989), p. 5; Dudley, *A Workshop for Peace*, p. 349. In addition to his business relationship with Nelson Rockefeller, Harrison had a connection with the Rockefellers through marriage. The brother of his wife, Ellen, was David Milton, married to Nelson's sister, Abigail, or "Babs."

4. Newhouse, *Wallace K. Harrison, Architect*, p. 115.

5. Accounts of the controversy appear in various Le Corbusier biographies and also in the first of a two-part series in the *New Yorker*, Apr. 26, 1947, by Geoffrey T. Hellman.

6. Dudley, *A Workshop for Peace*, p. 32.

7. Ibid, p. 34.

8. Moses, *Public Works*, p. 495.

9. Dudley, *A Workshop for Peace*, p. 35; Dudley résumé provided by his son, Gus.

10. A 1951 report for Mayor Impellitteri and the Board of Estimate (BOE Report), prepared by Manhattan Borough President Robert Wagner and Robert Moses, p. 3; RAC, Record Group 4, Series III 4L, Box 247, Folder 2468.

11. New York Municipal Archives (NYMA), O'Dwyer-UNO, Box 165, Folder 1780. Memo dated Jan. 13, 1947; *NYT*, Jan. 25, 1947.

12. *NYT*, Jan. 26, 1947.

13. Ibid., Mar. 3, 1947.

14. NYMA, O'Dwyer–UNO, Box 165, Folder 1781.

15. Ibid.

16. Ibid.

17. Samuel Zipp, *Manhattan Projects: The Rise and Fall of Urban Renewal in Cold War New York* (Oxford and New York: Oxford University Press, 2010), p. 55.

18. *NYT*, Feb. 23, 1947.

19. *New Yorker*, Nov. 20, 1954. Article by Herbert Warren Wind; RAC, Nelson Rockefeller–Personal Projects–UN, Series III 4L, Box 247, a memo from Frank Jamieson to Harrison, recounting details of the League competition.

20. Dudley, *A Workshop for Peace*, p. 34.

21. Ibid., p. 346, Appendix A.

22. Bassov's attempt at English, *New Yorker*, Dec. 4, 1954, article by Wind.

23. Dudley, *A Workshop for Peace*, p. 48.

24. *New Yorker*, May 9, 1988. "The Skyline," by Brendan Gill.

25. The film, *A Workshop for Peace*, by Peter Rosen Productions, Inc.

26. Dudley, *A Workshop for Peace*, p. 389.

27. Dudley, *A Workshop for Peace*, p. 56.

28. Ibid., p. 285.

29. Ibid., p. 50.

30. Newhouse, *Wallace K. Harrison, Architect*, p. 120.

31. Dudley, *A Workshop for Peace*, p. 110.

32. *Associated Press*, by Peter Muello, Nov. 2, 2007.

33. Dudley, *A Workshop for Peace*, p. 116. Years later, in a 1985 letter to Dudley, Niemeyer said that on his arrival in New York, Le Corbusier had specifically requested that he not submit any solution of his own and instead collaborate with his (Le Corbusier's) project. "You can create a commotion," Le Corbusier had warned Niemeyer. Ibid., pp. 110, 391. And Linda Sue Phipps, in her PhD dissertation, *"Constructing" the United Nations Headquarters: Modern Architecture as Public Diplomacy* (Harvard University, 1998), writes that in a 1992 interview in his Rio de Janeiro office, Niemeyer told her Le Corbusier had privately asked him not to confuse matters by submitting an independent study, p. 232.

34. Dudley, *A Workshop for Peace*, p. 236.

35. Ibid., p. 266.

36. Ibid., p. 252.

37. Ibid., p. 286.

38. Ibid., p. 289.

39. Ibid., p. ix.

40. Moses, *Public Works*, p. 492.

41. Dudley, *A Workshop for Peace*, p. 393.

42. BOE vote, Calendar No. 141, May 8, 1947, NYMA, Box 165, Folder 1781.

43. Stern, *New York 1960*, p. 614.

44. Zeckendorf, *The Autobiography of William Zeckendorf*, p. 73.

45. Stern, *New York 1960*, p. 614.

46. *NYT*, Aug. 27 and 28, 1947.

47. Zeckendorf, *The Autobiography of William Zeckendorf*, pp. 63, 73, and 76.

48. Pamela Hanlon, *Manhattan's Turtle Bay* (Charleston: Arcadia Publishing, 2008), pp. 126–131.

49. Secretary General Trygve Lie's daughter, Guri, married New York real estate developer, William Zeckendorf Jr., the son of the Zeckendorf who had amassed the large parcel of land on the East River that was purchased by the UN with the $8.5 million donation from John D. Rockefeller Jr. The couple had two sons, Arthur William and William Lie Zeckendorf, both of whom followed their father and grandfather in the real estate business.

50. RAC, Record Group 4, Series III 4L, Box 247, Folder 2468, *1951 BOE Report*, p. 2.

51. *BOE Report*, p. 3.

52. Lie, *In the Cause of Peace*, p. 117.

53. Newhouse, *Wallace K. Harrison, Architect*, p. 138.

54. Ibid., pp. 138, 302.

55. Dudley, *A Workshop for Peace*, pp. 222–223.

56. Newhouse, *Wallace K. Harrison, Architect*, page 130.

57. *NYT*, May 22, 1947.

58. RAC, Record Group 4, Series III 4L, Box 247, Folder 2468, *1951 BOE Report*, p. 5.

59. "An Act of Faith," a UN brochure commemorating the cornerstone ceremony.

60. In the late 1960s, Harrison's firm, Harrison and Abramovitz, designed two apartment towers that were built directly north of the UN site between Forty-eighth and Forty-ninth streets (860–870 United Nations Plaza). According to the apartments' sales brochure, they were "completing the architectural concept envisioned in the original plans for the United Nations."

61. Urquhart interview with author, Apr. 29, 2009.

62. UN Public Information Office fact sheet, rose garden specifics; Columbia University Libraries Oral History Research Office, Mary Lasker oral history, pp. 917– 918. The North Lawn was open to the public from the time of its completion until shortly after 9/11, when it was closed pending security upgrades to its perimeter. On completion of the upgrade, it then reopened to the public in 2006, but closed shortly thereafter when a major renovation of the entire UN campus was undertaken. As of early 2017, the North Lawn remained closed to the public.

63. Stern, *New York 1960*, pp. 617–619; and Newhouse, *Wallace K. Harrison, Architect*, p. 143.

64. NYPL Archives, Moses Papers, Series 4, Box 90, Folder: UN Correspondence.

65. Newhouse, *Wallace K. Harrison, Architect*, p. 143.

66. Ibid., p. 125.

67. RAC, Nelson Rockefeller–Personal Projects, Series III 4L, Box 247, Folder 2468.

68. Ibid.

69. Ibid.

70. Ibid.

71. Weber, *Le Corbusier: A Life*, p. 505.

72. Ibid., p. 757.

73. Aaron Betsky, *The U.N. Building* (London: Thames & Hudson Ltd., 2005), p. 62.

74. Lie, *In the Cause of Peace*, p. 123.

75. *NYT*, Oct. 15, 1952. Text of speech.

76. Since Giuliani, both Mayor Bloomberg and Mayor de Blasio have addressed the General Assembly.

6. Smoothing out the Wrinkles

1. *NYT*, Apr. 21, 1953.

2. In size, the UN's territory is between seventeen and eighteen acres, but nearer to eighteen acres. Therefore, this book refers to the size as eighteen acres.

3. *NYT*, Dec. 16, 1949.

4. Ibid., Dec. 17, 1949.

5. Ironically, the space had traditionally been used for recreation. Since the late 1800s, the property had been an Italian bocce court, where men in the mostly Italian neighborhood played the ancient game of bocce.

6. *NYT*, Oct. 7, 1951.

7. "Isamu Noguchi's Playground Designs," Leslie McGuire, Regional Editor, LandscapeOnline.com, Sept. 2004, retrieved May 15, 2013.

8. Stern, *New York 1960*, p. 626.

9. *NYT*, Oct. 7, 1951.

10. NYMA, Roll 63, MN 22763, Box 107897, Folder 033. Copy of Moses' letter to Eleanor Roosevelt. The Corlears Hook project, eventually named the East River Housing project, was completed in 1956 on thirteen acres of land that included gardens and play areas, none a Noguchi design.

11. UN Photo Library (UNPL) Photo No. 129535 and caption; *NYT*, Apr. 21, 1953. The little playground remained open to the public until 1993, when it was closed because of security concerns in light of the attack on the World Trade Center in February that year.

12. Stern, *New York 1960*, p. 626.

13. Moses, *Public Works*. Lie's quote is in a Lie letter to Moses, reprinted on p. 500. Moses' comments on Lie, p. 106.

14. Moses, *Public Works*, p. 506.

15. Newhouse, *Wallace K. Harrison, Architect*, p. 138.

16. *NYHT*, Aug. 12, 1953.

17. *NYT*, Aug. 12, 1953.

18. *New York Post (NYP)*, Aug. 13, 1953.

19. *NYT*, Aug. 12, 1953.

20. Ibid., Aug. 13, 1953.

21. Ibid., Sept. 11, 1953.

22. Ibid., Feb. 18, 1954.

23. LWA, Wagner Collection, Box 305, Folder 3601, Microfilm 163, Image 53–301.

24. Ibid., Image 0233. Patterson report to Wagner, 1955.

25. NYPL Archives, Moses Papers, Series 4, Box 91, Folder: UN 1946 RM correspondence. In a letter dated Jun. 5, 1946, Moses urges Lie to get in touch with Frederick Ecker, chairman of Metropolitan Life, regarding housing for UN staff at a new complex being built by the insurance company, Peter Cooper Village.

26. UNA, S-0184-0001-17, letter dated Jul. 8, 1946, to Ecker, signed by Arkady Sobolev, as acting Secretary General: ". . . It is understood that such apartments will be occupied only by personnel of this organization in all respects acceptable to your company."

27. *NYP*, May 20, 1943.

28. The UN signed a similar deal with a New York Life Insurance project in Fresh Meadows, in Jamaica, Queens, also segregated. But Metropolitan Life's strident position on race made it the focus of the protests.

29. UNA, S-0542-0008-62. Staff Committee Circular No. 34; NYT, Jul. 25, 1947.

30. UNA, S-0441-0344-01.

31. LWA, Wagner Collection: Box 305, Folder 3602, Microfilm 163, 53–301, Patterson report to Wagner.

32. Ibid.; *NYT*, Aug.14, 1959.

33. The sixteen West African nations were Benin, Burkina Faso, Cameroon, Central African Republic, Chad, Congo, Cote d'Ivoire, Gabon, Madagascar, Mali, Niger, Nigeria, Republic of Zaire (later, Democratic Republic of the Congo), Senegal, Somalia, and Togo.

34. *NYT*, Feb. 28, 1965. Feature story headlined, "Africans in Darkest New York."

35. LWA, Wagner Collection, Box 305, Folder 3606, Microfilm 163, Executive Order 108.

36. NYMA, NYC UN Commission, Series 1, 1962–(1966) 1968, Box 5, Folder 103.

37. Ibid.

38. As of early 2016, the U.S. UN Mission said some 6,500 individuals in the city, including family members, enjoyed full diplomatic immunity, and another 18,000 some limited level of immunity.

39. NYMA, NYC UN Commission, Series 1, 1962–(1966) 1968, Box 5, Folder 103.

40. *Park East* newspaper, Apr. 15, 1965.

41. *DN*, Jun. 23, 1965.

42. NYMA, NYC UN Commission, Series 1, 1962–(1966) 1968, Box 10, Folder 186.

43. Sorensen interview with author, Aug. 5, 2015; Sorensen was married to Ted Sorensen, lawyer, writer, and aide to President John F. Kennedy.

44. The United Nations Foundation was founded in 1998, after Ted Turner, founder of the Cable News Network and owner of the Atlanta Braves, donated $1 billion to support the work of the UN. At the time, it was one of the largest single donations in U.S. history.

45. Dinkins interview with author, Oct. 23, 2015.

46. LWA, Dinkins Collection, Box 6, Folder 70. O'Dwyer's short resignation letter to Dinkins included a thirteen-page attachment, outlining his reasons, which he summarized for the media as relating to human rights abuses worldwide. During his time in the position, he also tangled publicly with the UN over a labor relations issue in its staff cafeteria.

47. *NYT*, Nov. 23, 2007.

48. www.nyc.gov/international, New York Office for International Affairs: Global Partners, history. Accessed Jan. 25, 2016.

49. Tiven declined to respond to the author's repeated requests for an interview.

50. Abeywardena interview with author, Nov. 4, 2015, and various materials provided by the commissioner's office.

7. Learning to Live Side by Side

1. *Vassar Alumnae* magazine, February, 1968, pp. 19–25. Loeb, Vassar class of 1928, wrote an article for the magazine, "The U.N. and the City."

2. Ibid.

3. *NYT*, Dec. 13, 1965.

4. *NYT*, Feb. 9, 1967. Mayor Lindsay's involvement with the committee is in memo at LWA, Lindsay Collection, Box 78, Folder 1475.

5. Dudley, *A Workshop for Peace*, p. 400. Dudley wrote in his notes, "Little did we who liked his quiet good humor expect he would be arrested one evening . . . a spy in the Judith Coplon case." Moses, too, remembered Gubitschev, describing him in his book, *Public Works*, as "a Secret Service man [who] watched [Bassov's] every move. . . . We used to ply Gubitschev with vodka to put him to sleep," p. 494.

6. The Judith Coplon–Valentin Gubitschev case was widely reported in the news media. The story recounted here is generally from the book by Pierre J. Huss and George Carpozi Jr., *Red Spies at the UN* (New York: Coward-McMann, 1965), pp. 7–32.

7. H. Keith Melton and Robert Wallace, *Spy Sites of New York City: Two Centuries of Espionage in Gotham* (Boca Raton, Fla.: Foreign Excellent Trenchcoat Society, 2012).

8. *NYT*, Jan. 7, 1967.

9. *Crain's New York Business*, May 13, 2012.

10. *NYT*, Nov. 14, 1952.

11. Andrew Cordier and Wilder Foote, eds., *Public Papers of the Secretaries General of the United Nations, Vol. 1, Trygve Lie, 1946–1953* (New York and London: Columbia University Press, 1969), p. 485; Lie, *In the Cause of Peace*, p. 65.

12. Suspicions of Communists among the ranks of U.S. UN employees had been fueled in part by the case of Alger Hiss, organizing secretary general of the UN's Charter Conference and a State Department advisor to the early UN site inspection team. In 1948, Hiss was charged with being a Soviet spy and later convicted of perjury in connection with the charge.

13. *Salt Lake City Tribune*, Oct. 9, 1952.

14. Lie, *In the Cause of Peace*, pp. 388, 396, 397. (In the autobiography, Lie devotes a chapter to "The Communist Issue in the Secretariat," pp. 386–405); Michael J. Ybarra, *Washington Gone Crazy: Senator Pat McCarran and the Great American Communist Hunt* (Hanover, N.H.: Steerforth Press, 2004), p. 652. The number of employees fired or put on compulsory leave varies from one account to another. The number Lie uses in his autobiography is eighteen.

15. *NYT*, Nov. 12, 1952.

16. Lie, *In the Cause of Peace*, p. 399; Thant Myint-U and Amy Scott, *The UN Secretariat: A Brief History* (New York: International Peace Academy, 2007), pp. 16–18.

17. Lie, p. 387.

18. Executive Order 19422, issued Jan. 9, 1953, and described as "prescribing procedures for making available to the Secretary General of the United Nations certain information concerning United States citizens employed or being considered for employment on [sic] the Secretariat of the United Nations"; Lie, pp. 401–402.

19. *NYT*, Mar. 31, 1953.

20. UNA, S-0847-0001-08. Lie Private Meetings; *NYT*, Nov. 11, 1953.

21. Brian Urquhart, *A Life in Peace and War* (New York: Harper & Row, 1987), p. 125.

22. *NYT*, Sept. 22 and 24, 1950.

23. Ibid., Jan. 29, 1957.

24. Ibid., Jan. 30, 1957.

25. Ibid., Jun. 23, 1966; *NYP*, Jun. 25, 1966.

26. *NYP*, Jun. 23, 1966; *NYT*, Jun. 24, 1966.

27. Ibid.

28. The king was joined by members of his entourage, and his personal chef, a member of his traveling staff, prepared the dinner.

29. UNPL, Photo No. 75930, Faisal at lunch with delegates; *NYP*, Jun. 24, 1966.

30. Michael Goodwin, *New York Comes Back: The Mayoralty of Edward I. Koch* (New York: PowerHouse Books, 2005), p. 66.

31. Edward I. Koch, with Leland T. Jones, *Mayor: An Autobiography* (New York: Warner Books, 1984), p. 262, 359; NYDN, Feb. 11, 1982; cesspool comment, Associated Press, Sept. 27, 1983.

32. LWA, Koch Collection, Box 080074, Folder 03. Copy of the January 1988 speech.

33. *NYT*, Feb. 10 and 12, 1982.

34. Ibid., Feb. 13, 1982.

35. Pierre-Yves Saunier and Shane Ewen, *Another Global City: Historical Exploration into the Transnational Municipal Moment, 1850–2000* (New York: Palgrave Macmillan, 2008), p. 127, New York City chapter by Soffer.

36. LWA, Koch Collection, Box 270, Folder 04, letter from Thai UN Ambassador, Jul. 30, 1984.

37. Sorensen interview with author, Aug. 5, 2015.

38. *NYT*, Sept. 24, 1985.

39. Ibid., Oct. 20, 1985.

8. Autumn in New York

1. *NYT*, Oct. 22, 1995.

2. Ibid.

3. Ibid.

4. NYMA, Giuliani Papers, Box 30235, Publications, "New York City and the United Nations: Celebrating a 50-Year Partnership."

5. Previous seven paragraphs, Sorensen's recollections, Sorensen interview with author, Aug. 5, 2015.

6. *NYT*, Oct. 25, 1995.

7. *NYDN*, Oct. 25, 1995.

8. *NYT*, Oct. 25, 1995.

9. *NYDN*, Oct. 25, 1995.

10. Ibid., Oct. 26, 1995.

11. *NYDN*, Oct. 27, 1995.

12. Ibid., Oct. 26, 1995.

13. *NYT*, Oct. 25, 1995.

14. *NYDN*, Oct. 26, 1995.

15. Sorensen interview with author, Aug. 5, 2015; Giuliani declined the author's request for an interview for this book.

16. Bogucki interview with author, Oct. 2008, and Dec. 9, 2015.

17. For years, the U.S. president stayed at the Waldorf Astoria whenever he was in New York City, including for the UN General Assembly session. But after the Waldorf was purchased by a Chinese entity in 2014, President Obama moved to the nearby Lotte New York Palace. The White House said a number of factors entered into the decision, including security. (*NYT*, Sept. 11, 2015). As of early 2017, the Waldorf was closed for several years for renovation.

18. Shop owner, Isaac Bashiry, conversation with author, Jul. 29, 2015.

19. Shop owner, Charlie Belghiti, conversation with author, Sept. 15, 2015.

20. Bogucki interview with author, Oct. 2008, and Dec. 9, 2015.

21. *NYT*, Sept. 17, 1960.

22. Ibid., Sept. 20, 1960.

23. Arkady N. Shevchenko, *Breaking with Moscow* (New York: Alfred A. Knopf, 1985), p. 106.

24. According to Khrushchev aide Arkady Shevchenko, the pier choice turned out to have been a problem created by Khrushchev's own people, who had let the United States know the Soviets didn't want to spend much money for a New York berth.

25. In 1963, the Soviet Mission moved to East Sixty-seventh Street.

26. *NYT*, Sept. 22, 1960.

27. Various accounts, including Shevchenko, *Breaking with Moscow*, p. 108; 1961 *World Book Encyclopedia* Supplement summary, p. 217; and *NYT*, Oct. 13, 1960.

28. *NYT*, Sept. 17 and 24, 1960.

29. Shevchenko, *Breaking with Moscow*, p. 107.

30. *NYT*, Sept. 21, 1960.

31. Urquhart, *Hammarskjold* (New York: Alfred A. Knopf, 1972), p. 458.

32. Shevchenko, *Breaking with Moscow*, p. 106.

33. "Ask Dag," UN Dag Hammarskjold Library, from UN Department of Public Information. As of 2016, Castro's 1960 speech remained the longest in the history of the opening General Assembly sessions. In more recent years, the lengthiest was in 2009, when Libyan leader Muammar el-Qaddafi spoke for one hour and thirty-six minutes.

34. *NYT*, Sept. 16, 1960. NYPD discusses security precautions.

35. *Time*, Oct. 26, 1970.

36. LWA, Lindsay Collection, Box 20, Folder 236. Copy of letter dated Sept. 19, 1970.

37. LWA, Wagner Collection, Box 060224A, Folder 2. Congressional Record, House of Representatives, Apr. 5, 1962, p. 6000.

38. Ibid., p. 5992.

39. Ibid.

40. *NYT*, Apr. 6, 1962.

41. LWA, Lindsay Collection, Box 20, Folder 236. Copy of letter dated Sept. 19, 1970.

42. Ibid., copy of letter dated Sept. 23, 1970.

43. Ibid., copy of letter dated Sept. 25, 1970.

44. LWA, Lindsay Collection, Box 19, Folder 234. Lindsay letter to Deputy Under Secretary of State, William MacComber Jr., Mar. 1, 1971; also *NYT*, Jul. 13, 1971.

45. Letter from Mayor Beame to President Ford, dated Nov. 18, 1974. WikiLeaks.org, dated Nov. 20, 1974 and accessed Jan. 1, 2016.

46. *NYT*, May 9, 1980.

47. LWA, Koch Collection, Box 230, Folder 7. Testimony of Mayor Koch before the Commerce, Justice, State, the Judiciary and Related Agencies Subcommittee of the House Appropriations Committee on Apr. 11, 1984, concerning Diplomatic Police Protection Reimbursement. In the full text, Koch reviews history of the reimbursement issue.

48. "Diplomatically Speaking: Report of the New York City Commission for the United Nations and Consular Corps," 1978–1986, issued 1987, p. 4. Copy from Sorensen.

49. Sorensen interview with author, Oct. 29, 2015, and Jan. 10, 2016.

50. "Diplomatically Speaking: Report of the New York City Commission for the United Nations and Consular Corps," 1989. Copy from Sorensen.

51. "United Nations Impact Report 2016," a study by the New York City Mayor's Office for International Affairs and the Economic Development Corporation, based generally on fiscal 2014 data, and released on Dec. 6, 2016, www.nyc.gov/international. Also related EDC report, www.edc.nyc/UNImpactReport2016, accessed Dec. 6, 2016.

52. *NYT*, Sept. 2, 2000.

53. Ibid.

54. UNPL, Photo No. 118199 and caption.

55. Abeywardena interview with author, Nov. 4, 2015; various news reports.

9. Tussle over Tickets

1. LWA, Lindsay Collection, Box 20, Folder 237.

2. "Diplomatically Speaking: Report of the New York City Commission for the United Nations and Consular Corps," 1978–1986, issued 1987.

3. "The Economic Impact of the Diplomatic Community on the City of New York," a study prepared by the New York City Commission for the United Nations and Consular Corps, December 1989. The report showed that in 1988, there were $1.5 million in unpaid fines. The number varied throughout the years, but for the year 1996, the number was $5 million, according to *NYT*, Mar. 11, 1997.

4. *NYT*, Jan. 1, 1997, and various news reports at the time.

5. Ibid., Mar. 11, 1997, summarizing the situation. Various other news reports at the time.

6. Ibid., and Apr. 4, 1997.

7. LWA, Giuliani Collection, Box 02/04/02, Folder 0511, 14-page "UN Note by Legal Counsel: New York City Diplomatic Parking Program," dated Mar. 20, 1997, and sent from the UN to the New York City Commission for the United Nations and Consular Corps, and then forwarded to Deputy Mayor Randy Mastro; also *NYT*, Apr. 12, 1997.

8. *NYT*, Apr. 11, 1997.

9. Ibid.

10. Ibid., Apr. 4, 1997.

11. Ibid., Apr. 1, 1997.

12. Ibid., Apr. 12, 1997.

13. Ibid., Apr. 11, 1997.

14. Ibid. By the author's count, *NYT* carried at least twenty articles on the DPL controversy during the month of April 1997; other New York newspapers reported it similarly.

15. LWA, Giuliani Collection, Box 02/08/012, Folder 0339. Press statement dated Apr. 11, 1997.

16. LWA, Giuliani Collection, Box 02/04/021, Folder 0511. Letter from Deputy Mayor Mastro to President of the Society of Foreign Consuls, Kay Baxter-Collins.

17. *NYT*, May 21, 1997.

18. Ibid., Apr. 18, 1997.

19. Ibid., May 21, 1997. Richardson later served two terms as governor of New Mexico.

20. *NYT*, Apr. 19, 1997.

21. LWA, Giuliani Collection, Box 02/08/012, Folder 0339. Press Statement dated Apr. 28, 1997; and various press reports.

22. New York City Municipal Archives, Giuliani, Box 30235, Publication Title: "New York City and the United Nations: Celebrating a 50-Year Partnership."

23. Sylva moved on to chair the City's preparations for the celebration of the fiftieth anniversary of Israel.

24. *NYT*, Mar. 3, 2000.

25. *NYT*, Aug. 23, 2002.

26. "Diplomatic Parking: A Policy of Safety and Fairness," included in "Managing the Local and the Global," City Office for International Affairs, 2013, accessed Aug. 21, 2014, at www.nyc.gov/html/ia. Later, federal legislation was passed that called for withholding U.S. foreign aid to countries that owe money for parking tickets, although it was unclear to what extent the law was ever applied.

27. Ibid.

28. Ibid.

29. "United Nations Impact Report 2016," a study by the Mayor's Office for International Affairs and the Economic Development Corporation, p. 21, accessed Dec. 6, 2016, www.nyc.gov/international.

30. *NYT*, Feb. 20, 2002.

10. Trio Created

1. *NYDN*, Oct. 29, 1975.

2. *NYT*, Nov. 20, 1975, various reports, with headlines: "Fiscal Panel Acts . . . ," "Albany Meetings Seek . . . ," and "A Word from Ford."

3. United Nations Photo Library, UN photo and caption, NICA 249139.

4. LWA, Lindsay Collection, Box 78, Folder 1475. Memo to Lindsay from Richard Rosen, Nov. 7, 1966, outlining issues with UN's need for expansion.

5. Ibid.

6. *NYT*, Dec. 6, 1966.

7. Moses, *Public Works*, p. 504. Moses writes that by June 1967, there was a tentative agreement to put a thirty-story tower on the city-owned property west of the ventilating building.

8. Ibid., p. 503, letter dated Dec. 20, 1966.

9. LWA. Lindsay Collection, Box 113, Folder 2136.

10. Moses, *Public Works*, p. 502.

11. Ibid., and p. 503.

12. LWA, Lindsay Collection, Box 113, Folder 2136. Ironically, Wallace Harrison, chief of the architectural team that designed UN headquarters, had, in the 1930s, been the architect of the Pepsi-Cola plant.

13. Moses, *Public Works*, pp. 502–503.

14. Stern, *New York 1960*, p. 460.

15. Fund for Area and Planning Development brochure, dated Apr. 1968. Obtained by author from UNDC.

16. *Turtle Bay Gazette*, Spring 1968.

17. *NYT*, Apr. 21, 1968.

18. Historical summary, prepared by UN (B. de Fondauiere), April 2000, via Katherine Grenier, UN Capital Master Plan; *NYT*, Nov. 4, 1968.

19. LWA, Lindsay Collection, Box 20, Folder 237. Memo dated Nov. 26, 1969, to Lindsay from Michael Dontzin, assistant counsel.

20. *NYT*, Apr. 10, 1971.

21. Ibid., Nov. 12, 1969. Two articles, one by Kathleen Teltsch and the other by Ada Louise Huxtable.

22. UNDC brochure of plans, dated Nov. 1969: "The UN Center: A Development Program for UN-related Activities," obtained by author from UNDC.

23. *NYT*, Feb. 15, 1970.

24. Ibid., Nov. 15, 1969.

25. *NYT*, Dec. 20, 1969.

26. Stern, *New York 1960*, p. 636.

27. Ibid.

28. *NYT*, Feb. 15, 1970.

29. Ibid., Jun. 13, 1971.

30. Ibid., Dec. 21, 1972.

31. UNDC response to author inquiry, Jan. 29, 2016.

32. Stern, *New York 1960*, p. 403.

33. Historical summary, prepared by UN (B. de Fondauiere), April 2000, via Katherine Grenier, UN Capital Master Plan; Stern, *New York 1960*, p. 414.

34. Portions of Chapter 10 were adapted from a description of events in Hanlon, *Manhattan's Turtle Bay: Story of a Midtown Neighborhood* (Charleston: Arcadia Publishing, 2008).

11. Making a Mark

1. *NYT*, Oct. 29, 1979.
2. Ibid., Jun. 17, 1984.
3. Ibid.
4. Ibid., Jun. 18, 1984.
5. Ibid., Jun. 23, 1984.
6. Ibid., Sept. 17, 1988.
7. Stern, *New York 1960*, pp. 628–629.
8. Ibid., p. 405.
9. Stern, *New York 2000*, pp. 406–407.
10. Ibid., p. 407–409.
11. Ibid., p. 628.
12. Author observation of houses; Qatar purchase, *Real Deal*, Jun. 20, 2013.
13. Curtis interview with author, Nov. 5, 2015, and Oct. 12, 2016.
14. Stern, *New York 2000*, pp. 408–409.
15. Transcribed interview with Niemeyer, by Louis F. Reuter, IV, in Niemeyer's office, Apr. 20, 2006. Provided to author by Reuter.
16. Perkins Eastman, architects, press release issued Mar. 7, 2016.
17. Judith Berdy, president of the Roosevelt Island Historical society, interview with author, Feb. 2015.
18. Barbara Davis, New Rochelle historian, interview with author, Oct. 15, 2016.
19. "United Nations Impact Report 2016," a study by the Mayor's Office for International Affairs and the Economic Development Corporation, released Dec. 6, 2016, and based generally on data collected during fiscal 2014. www.nyc.gov/international. Also related EDC report online, at www.edc.nyc/UNImpactReport2016, accessed Dec. 6, 2016.
20. NYMA, New York City Commission for the United Nations, Series 1, Box 10, Folder 182, Office of the Mayor, 1965 Report, Special Projects; Stern, *New York 1960*, p. 635; *NYT*, May 25, 1958; *NYT* Jun. 24, 1958.
21. Coincidentally, it was the same pier that had irritated Premier Nikita Khrushchev of the Soviet Union when his ship was assigned to dock there in 1960.
22. LWA, Wagner Collection, Box 26, Folder 507, City Hall press release dated Dec. 28, 1965; *NYT*, Dec. 29, 1965.
23. United Nations International School brochure, and www.unis.org, accessed Feb. 29, 2016.
24. Stephen Schlesinger interview with author, Jan. 26, 2016.
25. Ibid; Arthur Schlesinger Jr., *A Thousand Days: John F. Kennedy in the White House* (Boston: Houghton Mifflin, 1965), pp. 464–465.
26. "New York and the United Nations," a report by the Special Committee on the United Nations of the Association of the Bar of the City of New York,

issued December 2001, Lawrence Moss, principal author and founding chair of the Committee.

27. Bing interview with author, Nov. 3, 2015, and Nov. 10, 2016.

28. Curtis interview with author, Oct. 12, 2016; Mark Thompson, Community Board 6 member and former president, Nov. 20, 2015; and Jesus Perez, CB6 manager, Oct. 18, 2016.

29. Curtis interview with author, Oct. 12, 2016.

30. "New York and the United Nations," New York Bar Assn. report.

31. "United Nations Impact Report 2016," a study by the New York City Mayor's Office for International Affairs and the Economic Development Corporation, based generally on fiscal 2014 data, and released on Dec. 6, 2016, www.nyc.gov/international. Also related EDC report, www.edc.nyc/UNImpact Report2016, accessed Dec. 6, 2016.

32. Bus shelter advertising, installed Oct. 2016.

33. Twitter, Oct. 31, 2016; Van Oosteram interview with author, Jan. 15, 2016.

34. Dinkins interview with author, Oct. 23, 2015.

35. *NYT*, May 25, 1992; employee numbers also in "Economic Impact of the Diplomatic Community on the City of New York," New York City Commission for the United Nations and Consular Corps, 1989.

36. David Dinkins, *A Mayor's Life: Governing New York's Gorgeous Mosaic* (New York: Public Affairs, 2013), p. 270.

37. *NYT*, May 25, 1992.

38. Ibid., Nov. 1, 1992.

39. Ibid.

40. Dinkins interview with author, Oct. 23, 2015.

41. *NYT*, Jul. 18, 1993.

42. *Our Town*, May 18, 1994.

43. UNDC response to author inquiry, Jan. 29, 2016.

44. By 2016, Bonn was home to offices for some one thousand UN or UN agency–related staff, up from just a handful of employees in the early 1990s, according to the UN Public Information Office, Feb. 15, 2016.

45. *Our Town*, May 18, 1994.

46. LWA, Koch Collection, Mar. 5, 1981, memo to City Planning Commissioner Theodore Teah, telling him he was opposed to the parks swap; *NYT*, Jan. 22, 1981, recap of long-running story.

47. History of playground on East End Hockey Assn. website, www.eastendhockey.com, accessed, Feb. 5, 2016.

12. Quandary over Age

1. Meeting of the Turtle Bay Association (TBA), Sept. 13, 2004. Author in attendance.

2. *Turtle Bay News (TBN)*, Summer 2004.

3. UNDC, Jan. 29, 2016, e-mail response; *NYT*, Sept. 20, 2002. It was an idea that dated back to 1995 when La Salle Partners had prepared a "UN Planning Study of Long-Term Facilities Alternatives" for the Giuliani administration. (LWA, Giuliani Collection, Box 02/11/014, Folder 0540.)

4. *TBN*, Summer 2004.

5. *TBN*, March 2003 and June 2003.

6. Letter from Councilmember Moskowitz, printed at her request in *TBN*, Fall 2004.

7. *Architect*, February 2008 interview with Michael Adlerstein, UN Capital Master Plan (CMP).

8. Author on tour of UN facilities, Feb. 7, 2006, and Apr. 7, 2006.

9. *NYT*, Apr. 20, 2004. Tony Raymond, foreman quoted.

10. UN CMP Timeline, on UN CMP website, http://www.un.org/wcm/content/site/cmp/, accessed Oct. 15, 2015.

11. UN Secretary General report on CMP (A/55/117), Jun. 28, 2000. E-mailed to author by CMP office, Oct. 27, 2015.

12. Associated Press, Jul. 28, 2000.

13. *NYT*, Oct. 24, 1999.

14. UNDC response to author's inquiries, Jan. 14, 2016; UN CMP Timeline, CMP website; and various news reports. The hotel space in UNDC One and Two had been sold to a private hotel operator in 1997.

15. UN CMP Timeline, CMP website, SG report to General Assembly, A/57/285.

16. U.S. General Accountability Office, May 2003, Report on United Nations' Early Renovation Planning; and U.S. GAO, Nov. 2006, Report on United Nations' Renovation Planning, with recap of financing options.

17. *NYT*, Aug. 21, 2003, and Feb. 14, 2004; UNDC response to author's inquiries, Jan. 14, 2016.

18. *New York Observer*, Feb. 6, 2006, story by Matthew Schuerman, quoting Megan Quattlebaum, associate director of Common Cause.

19. Bing interview with author, Nov. 3, 2015.

20. *New York Sun (NYS)*, Dec. 6, 2004.

21. *NYS*, Mar. 8, 2005.

22. *NYT*, Dec. 3, 2004.

23. *NYS*, Dec. 6, 2004.

24. Ibid.

25. *NYS*, Dec. 16, 2004.

26. *NYDN*, Dec. 8, 2004.

27. *NYT*, Jan. 6, 2005.

28. *NYS*, Mar. 8, 2005.

29. Ibid., Jun. 27, 2005.

30. *Crain's*, Jul. 18, 2005, as well as multiple other news reports at the time.

31. *NYS*, Jun. 27, 2005.

32. UN Press Release, SG/A/931, issued Jul. 19, 2005; Reuter interview with author, Nov. 23, 2015.

33. *TBN*, Fall 2005.

34. *DNA Info*, Sept. 29, 2005.

35. *NYS*, Feb. 4–6, 2005 issue.

36. *NYT*, Oct. 16, 1998, and Dec. 20, 1998, by Charles V. Bagli; further details of neighborhood opposition, Hanlon, *Manhattan's Turtle Bay*, pp. 143–145.

37. Trump testimony before the Federal Financial Management, Government Information, and International Security Subcommittee of the Senate Homeland Security and Government Affairs Committee, Jul. 21, 2005, http://www.gpo.gov/fdsys/pkg/CHRG-109shrg23164/html/CHRG-109shrg23164.htm. Accessed Oct. 12, 2015 (Senate Subcommittee testimony); Schori reference appears in testimony and also in *NYT*, Dec. 8, 2000.

38. Ibid.

39. Donald J. Trump, with Tony Schwartz, *Trump: The Art of the Deal* (New York: Random House 1987), p. 200.

40. Ibid., p. 210, and various news reports.

41. Associated Press, Jul. 21, 2005, by Devlin Barrett, and transcript of Senate Subcommittee testimony on same date.

42. Louis Reuter interview with author, Nov. 23, 2015, and chronology of his UN tenure provided to the author by Reuter. The Reuter meeting with Trump was on Nov. 29, 2005.

43. Reuter chronology, and follow-up e-mail with author, Jan. 23, 2016.

44. Reuter interview with author, Nov. 23, 2015; and Reuter chronology.

45. Ibid.

46. Some two years later, Trump again spoke out about the renovation project, telling *AP's* UN reporter John Heilprin on Feb. 7, 2008: "It's a total disgrace," . . . "It shouldn't cost more than $750 million" . . . and then asking "What's happening to all that money?" From that date forward, however, it appeared, from a reading of press reports, that Trump never publicly criticized the UN's plan again.

47. Bolton comment, *Washington Post*, Mar. 9, 2005; Biden, opening statement at Bolton hearings, U.S. Senate Committee on Foreign Relations, Apr. 11, 2005, www.foreign.senate.gov.

48. When Oscar Niemeyer, the Brazilian architect on the original UN design team, heard about a possible plan to build a permanent building on the UN North Lawn, he called it "architectural heresy!" He told UN architect Louis "Fritz" Reuter, who interviewed him in his Rio de Janeiro office on April 20, 2006, "It would be a horrible precedent to agree to change significant projects. Imagine a new papal consolidation building in Bernini's St. Peter's Square in Rome!"

49. Author present during "dirty tour" and Reuter's summation, Apr. 7, 2006.

50. *NYT*, Apr. 18, 2006. Warren Hoge interview with Reuter and Bolton.

51. Author interview with Reuter, Nov. 23, 2015. Two months after his resignation, Reuter returned to New York Presbyterian Hospital as Senior Vice President-Facilities Development and Real Estate.

52. UN CMP Timeline, on UN CMP website, accessed Oct. 15, 2015.

13. Renewal of a Cityscape Icon

1. George Dudley background from conversation with his son, Gus Dudley, Aug. 13, 2015; George Dudley resume. The Albany Mall project was led by Wallace Harrison's firm, Harrison and Abramovitz.

2. Adlerstein interview with author, Apr. 16 and 22, 2015.

3. The U.S. General Accountability Office, in a report dated May 14, 2015, concluded that the primary reason the UN's Capital Master Plan was over its original $1.88 billion budget, approved by the General Assembly in 2006, was because of unplanned security upgrades and delays and expenditures related to Hurricane Sandy in Oct. 2013.

4. Adlerstein interview with author, Apr. 16, 2015.

5. Ibid. Coincidentally, Sheldon Solow was the same developer who was said to be trying to woo the UN to rent permanent office space in a tower he planned on the site of the old Con Edison generating plant.

6. UN Doc. A/55/117.

7. "Managing the Local and the Global," City Office for International Affairs, 2013. Accessed Aug. 21, 2014, at http://www.nyc.gov/html/ia/html/home/home.shtml; also *NYT* Feb. 15, 2003. Tiven declined to respond to the author's numerous e-mail and telephone requests for an interview, made between Nov. 2015 and Sept. 2016.

8. Tiven letter to UN Under Secretary General Angela Kane, dated Sept. 8, 2008, and recapping previous communications with UN on the subject. Accessed via link in *New York Sun (NYS)*, Sept. 10, 2008. The letter states that the City first approached the UN about fire and safety inspections in early 2006. However, a later report issued by the City's Office for International Affairs in December 2013 and posted on its website, said, on page 14, that the first request was in 2005.

9. UN Capital Master Plan timeline. www.un.org/wcm/content/site/cmp. Accessed Sept. 15, 2015.

10. WikiLeaks.org, dated Apr. 11, 2007, and accessed Jun. 1, 2015.

11. Tiven letter to UN Under Secretary General Alicia Barcena Ibarra, dated Jul. 30, 2007, reported in *Washington Post (WP)*, Aug. 11, 2007.

12. *WP*, Aug. 11, 2007.

13. *NYT*, Nov. 23, 2007, Tiven interview with Anthony Ramirez. Separation and compartmentalization info included in *NYS*, Nov. 13, 2007.

14. Adlerstein interview with author, Apr. 22, 2015.

15. Tiven letter to UN Under Secretary General Kane, dated Sept. 8, 2008,

recapping events; also WikiLeaks.org, dated May 19, 2008, and accessed Jun. 1, 2015; UN estimate of 40 percent, from Barcena letter, dated Nov. 5, 2007, and reported in *NYS*, Nov. 13, 2007.

16. Adlerstein conversation with author, Nov. 3, 2015.

17. Tiven letter to UN Under Secretary General Kane, dated Sept. 8, 2008.

18. Sign shown to author by UN CMP office, Apr. 22, 2015.

19. Sherrill Kazan, president of World Council of Peoples for the United Nations, interview with author, Nov. 6, 2015.

20. Adlerstein interview with author, Apr. 22, 2015.

21. WikiLeaks.org, dated Mar. 17, 2009. The visits for school children resumed in Dec. 2013, according to UN Public Information Office Jan. 27, 2016, e-mail.

22. UN News Service, April 16, 2008.

23. Edward B. Marks, *A World of Art: The United Nations Collection* (Il Cigno Galileo Gallilei, Roma, 1995), p. 158. Another early exterior donation was the Peace Bell, given to the UN by the UN Association of Japan in 1954, two years before Japan would become a UN member.

24. UN Capital Master Plan timeline. www.un.org/wcm/content/site/cmp. Accessed Sept. 15, 2015.

25. "United Nations Capital Master Plan" booklet, distributed in conjunction with North Lawn Conference Building ground-breaking, May 5, 2008.

26. Barwick interview with author, Nov. 11, 2015.

27. Information from UN CMP office.

28. Ibid.

29. Adlerstein interview with author, May 27, 2015.

30. Werner Schmidt, UN CMP office.

31. Zettel, from Marti Ahtisaari, *The United Nations at 70: Restoration and Renewal* (New York: Rizzoli International Publications, 2015), p. 52; Carter Wiseman interview with author, Oct. 20, 2016; Barwick interview with author, Nov. 11, 2015.

32. Schmidt, UN CMP office.

33. Adlerstein interview with author, Apr. 22, 2015, and Schmidt.

34. "United Nations Capital Master Plan" booklet, distributed in conjunction with North Lawn Conference Building ground-breaking, May 5, 2008.

35. Communication from Adlerstein, Feb. 10, 2016.

36. Councilman Dan Garodnick interview with author, Dec. 1, 2015.

37. "Legislative and MOU Framework," distributed at Sept. 8, 2011 community meeting hosted by elected officials, and attended by author; various news reports.

38. Krueger interview with author, Oct. 15, 2015.

39. Kavanagh interview with author, Nov. 30, 2016.

40. Heritage Foundation report, "The Building You're Buying the U.N.," dated Oct. 3, 2011, and an earlier report, dated Sept. 12, 2011, questioned the

financial implications of the deal to the U.S. government, which pays 22 per-cent of the UN regular, operating budget.

41. http://www.nycedc.com/project/east-midtown-waterfront, NYC Economic Development Corporation website, accessed Jan. 22, 2015. Author also attended elected officials' briefings on Sept. 8, 2011, and Apr. 12, 2012, and a community workshop to address section of the esplanade, Jul. 26, 2011. Also, interviews with Krueger, Oct. 15, 2015, and Kavanagh, Nov. 30, 2016.

42. Steve Simon, New York City Parks Department, Chief of Staff, Borough of Manhattan, interview with author, Feb. 9, 2016; program produced for the ribbon-cutting ceremony, Sept. 18, 2016.

43. LWA, La Guardia Collection, Box 26C3, Folder 3, prepared script for WNYC *Talk to the People* broadcast, Dec. 16, 1945; Audio: WNYC Archives ID 71130. Foreseeing the upcoming UN decision on a site, La Guardia concluded the UN "will naturally come to New York City"; Lie, *In the Cause of Peace*, p.123. He wrote of the site choice, "What had once been a dream was now reality."

Sources

Archives

GHS	Greenwich Historical Society *(accessed 2009)*
GOHP	Greenwich Connecticut Library Oral History Project *(accessed 2009)*
LWA	La Guardia and Wagner Archives, La Guardia Community College, City University of New York *(accessed 2012–2016)*
MAS	Municipal Art Society, Greenacre Reference Library *(accessed 2013)*
NYHS	New York Historical Society *(accessed 2009)*
NYMA	New York City Municipal Archives and Library *(accessed 2008–2013)*
NYPL Archives	Manuscript and Archives Division of the New York Public Library *(accessed 2008, 2009)*
RAC	Rockefeller Archive Center *(accessed 2009)*
UNA	United Nations Archives and Records Management Section *(accessed 2008, 2009)*
UN Library	United Nations Dag Hammarskjold Library *(accessed 2008)*

Periodicals

AP	*Associated Press*
Arch. Record	*Architectural Record*
Architect	*Architect, Journal of the American Institute of Architects*
Art News	*Art News*

Crain's	*Crain's New York Business*
CT	*Chicago Tribune*
DNAInfo	*DNA Info*
Greenwich	*Greenwich*
GTime	*Greenwich Time*
Life	*Life*
NA	*Nation*
New Yorker	*New Yorker*
NY Observer	*New York Observer*
NYDN	*New York Daily News*
NYHT	*New York Herald Tribune*
NYP	*New York Post*
NYSun	*New York Sun*
NYT	*New York Times*
Our Town	*Our Town*
Park East	*Park East News*
Real Deal	*Real Deal*
SLT	*Salt Lake City Tribune*
TBG	*Turtle Bay Gazette*
TBN	*Turtle Bay News*
Time	*Time*
Vassar	*Vassar Alumnae*
WP	*Washington Post*
WPR	*White Plains Reporter Dispatch*

Books

Abrams, Charles. *Forbidden Neighbors: A Study of Prejudice in Housing.* New York: Harper & Brothers, 1955.

Acheson, Dean. *Present at the Creation: My Years in the State Department.* New York: W. W. Norton & Company, 1969.

Ahtisaari, Martti, and Carter Wiseman. Foreword by Ban Ki-Moon. *The United Nations at 70: Restoration and Renewal.* New York: Rizzoli International Publications, 2015.

Bacon, Mardges. *Le Corbusier in America: Travels in the Land of the Timid.* Cambridge, Mass: MIT Press, 2001.

Ballon, Hilary, and Kenneth T. Jackson. *Robert Moses and the Modern City: The Transformation of New York.* New York: W. W. Norton & Company, 2008.

Barros, James. *Trygve Lie and the Cold War: The UN Secretary-General Pursues Peace, 1946–1953.* DeKalb, Ill.: Northern Illinois University Press, 1989.

Betsky, Aaron, and Ben Murphy, photog. *The U.N. Building.* London: Thames & Hudson Ltd., 2005.

Biondi, Martha. *To Stand and Fight: The Struggle for Civil Rights in Postwar New York City*. Cambridge, Mass.: Harvard University Press, 2006.

Borstelmann, Thomas. *The Cold War and the Color Line: American Race Relations in the Global Arena*. Cambridge, Mass.: Harvard University Press, 2001.

Brands, H. W. *American Dreams: The United States Since 1945*. New York: The Penguin Press, 2010.

Caro, Robert A. *The Power Broker: Robert Moses and the Fall of New York*. New York: Alfred A. Knopf, 1974.

Chamber of Commerce. *A Guide Book to the City of New York: 1945*. New York: Supervue Map and Guide Organization, 1945.

Collier, Peter, and David Horowitz. *The Rockefellers: An American Dynasty*. New York: Holt, Rinehart and Winston, 1976.

Cordier, Andrew, and Wilder Foote, eds. *Public Papers of the Secretaries General of the United Nations, Volume 1, Trygve Lie, 1946–1953*. New York: Columbia University Press, 1969.

Deery, Phillip. *Red Apple: Communism and McCarthyism in Cold War New York*. New York: Empire State Editions, an imprint of Fordham University Press, 2014.

Desmond, James. *Nelson Rockefeller: A Political Biography*. New York: The Macmillan Company, 1964.

Dinkins, David N., with Peter Knobler. *A Mayor's Life: Governing New York's Gorgeous Mosaic*. New York: Public Affairs, 2013.

Dudley, George A. *A Workshop for Peace: Designing the United Nations Headquarters*. Cambridge, Mass.: MIT Press; New York: The Architectural History Foundation, 1994.

Eichelberger, Clark M. *Organizing for Peace: A Personal History of the Founding of the United Nations*. New York: Harper & Row, 1977.

Fasulo, Linda. *An Insider's Guide to the UN*. 2d ed. New Haven, Conn.: Yale University Press, 2009.

Feller, Abraham H. *United Nations and World Community*. Boston: Little, Brown and Company, 1952.

Freeman, Joshua B. *Working-Class New York: Life and Labor Since World War II*. New York: The New Press, 2000.

Gaglione, Anthony. *The United Nations Under Trygve Lie, 1945–1953*. Lanham, Md.: Scarecrow Press, 2001.

Giuliani, Rudolph W., with Ken Kurson. *Leadership*. New York: Hyperion, 2002.

Goodwin, Michael, ed. *New York Comes Back: The Mayoralty of Edward I. Koch*. New York: PowerHouse Books, 2005.

Hanlon, Pamela. *Manhattan's Turtle Bay: Story of a Midtown Neighborhood*. Charleston, S.C.: Arcadia Publishing, 2008.

Hazzard, Shirley. *Defeat of an Ideal: A Study of the Self-Destruction of the United Nations*. Boston: Little, Brown and Company, 1973.

Hopkins, Honorable James D. *Our Voices Were Heard: The Selection of the United Nations Headquarters*. New York: Pace University, 1984.

Huss, Pierre J., and George Carpozi Jr. *Red Spies in the UN*. New York: Coward-McCann, 1965.

Isitt, Mark, and Ake E:son Lindman, photog. *United Nations: The Story Behind the Headquarters of the World*. Stockholm, Sweden: Bokforlaget Max Strom, 2015.

Jackson, Kenneth, ed. *The Encyclopedia of New York City*. New Haven and New York: Yale University Press and New York Historical Society, 2010.

Janello, Amy, and Brennon Jones, eds. *A Global Affair: An Inside Look at the United Nations*. New York: Jones and Janello, 1995.

Jenger, Jean. *Le Corbusier: Architect, Painter, Poet*. New York: Harry N. Abrams, Inc., 1996.

Kessner, Thomas. *Fiorello H. La Guardia and the Making of Modern New York*, New York: McGraw-Hill, 1989.

Kirtzman, Andrew. *Rudy Giuliani: Emperor of the City*. New York: William Morrow, 2000.

Koch, Edward I., with Leland T. Jones. *All the Best: Letters from a Feisty Mayor*. New York: Simon & Schuster, 1998.

Koch, Edward I., with William Rauch. *Mayor: An Autobiography*. New York: Warner Books Edition by arrangement with Simon & Schuster, 1984.

Langewich, George J. *New York City: A Short History*. New York: New York University Press, 2002.

Le Corbusier. *UN Headquarters: Practical Application of a Philosophy of the Domain of Building*. New York: Reinhold Publishing, 1947.

Lie, Trygve. *In the Cause of Peace: Seven Years at the United Nations*. New York: The Macmillan Company, 1954.

Lipsey, Roger. *Hammarskjold: A Life*. Ann Arbor, Mich.: University of Michigan Press, 2013.

Marks, Edward B. *A World of Art: The United Nations Collection*. Rome: Il Cigno Galileo Galilei, 1995.

Meisler, Stanley. *United Nations: The First Fifty Years*. New York: The Atlantic Monthly Press, 1995.

Melton, H. Keith, and Robert Wallace. *Spy Sites of New York City: Two Centuries of Espionage in Gotham*. Boca Raton, Fla.: Foreign Excellent Trenchcoat Society, 2012.

Mires, Charlene. *Capital of the World: The Race to Host the United Nations*. New York: New York University Press, 2013.

Morgan, Ted. *Reds: McCarthyism in Twentieth-Century America*. New York: Random House, 2004.

Morris, Joe Alex. *Nelson Rockefeller: A Biography*. New York: Harper & Brothers, 1960.

Moses, Robert. *Public Works: A Dangerous Trade*. New York: McGraw-Hill, 1970.

Mouat, Lucia. *The United Nations' Top Job: A Close Look at the Work of the Eight Secretaries-General*. North Charleston, S.C.: CreateSpace Independent Publishing Platform, 2014.

Myint-U, Thant, and Amy Scott. *The UN Secretariat: A Brief History*. New York: International Peace Academy, 2007.

Neal, Steve, ed. *Eleanor and Harry: The Correspondence of Eleanor Roosevelt and Harry S. Truman*. New York: Scribner, 2002.

Newhouse, Victoria. *Wallace K. Harrison, Architect*. New York: Rizzoli International Publications, 1989.

O'Dwyer, William. *Beyond the Golden Door*. Edited by Paul O'Dwyer. New York: St. John's University, 1986.

Phipps, Linda Sue. *"Constructing" the United Nations Headquarters: Modern Architecture as Public Diplomacy*. PhD Dissertation. Harvard University, 1998.

Purnick, Joyce. *Mike Bloomberg: Money, Power, Politics*. New York: PublicAffairs, 2009.

Reich, Cary. *The Life of Nelson A. Rockefeller: Worlds to Conquer, 1908–1958*. New York: Doubleday, 1996.

Rodgers, Cleveland. *Robert Moses: Builder for Democracy*. New York: Henry Holt and Company, 1952.

Rodgers, Cleveland, and Rebecca Rankin. *New York: The World's Capital City*. New York: Harper & Brothers, 1948.

Saunier, Pierre-Yves, and Shane Ewen, eds. *Another Global City: Historical Exploration into the Transnational Municipal Moment, 1850–2000*. New York: Palgrave Macmillan, 2008.

Schlesinger, Arthur M. *A Thousand Days: John F. Kennedy in the White House*. Boston: Houghton Mifflin, 1965.

Schlesinger, Stephen C. *Act of Creation: The Founding of the United Nations*. Boulder, Colo.: Westview Press, 2003.

Shevchenko, Arkady N. *Breaking with Moscow*. New York: Alfred A. Knopf, 1985.

Smith, Richard Norton. *On His Own Terms: A Life of Nelson Rockefeller*. New York: Random House, 2014.

Soffer, Jonathan. *Ed Koch and the Rebuilding of New York City*. New York: Columbia University Press, 2012.

Stern, Robert A. M., David Fishman, and Jacob Tilove. *New York 2000: Architecture and Urbanism Between the Bicentennial and the Millennium*. New York: The Monacelli Press, 2006.

Stern, Robert A. M., Thomas Mellins, and David Fishman. *New York 1960: Architecture and Urbanism Between the Second World War and the Bicentennial*. 2d ed. New York: The Monacelli Press, 1997.

Stettinius, Edward R., with Edward Reilly. *Roosevelt and the Russians: The Yalta Conference*. Westport, Conn.: Greenwood Press, 1970, 1949.

Truman, Harry S., with Monte M. Poen. *Letters Home by Harry Truman*. New York: G. P. Putnam's Sons, 1983.

Truman, Harry S., with Robert H. Ferrell. *Off the Record: The Private Papers of Harry S. Truman.* New York: Harper & Row, 1980.

Trump, Donald, with Tony Schwartz. *Trump: The Art of the Deal.* New York: Random House, 1987.

United Nations. *Basic Facts about the United Nations.* New York: United Nations Department of Public Information, 2011.

United Nations. *Report to the General Assembly of the United Nations by the Secretary General on the Permanent Headquarters of the United Nations.* United Nations, Lake Success, New York, July 1947.

Urquhart, Brian. *Hammarskjold.* New York: Alfred A. Knopf, 1972.

———. *A Life in Peace and War.* New York: Harper & Row, 1987.

Weber, Nicholas Fox. *Le Corbusier: A Life.* New York: Alfred A. Knopf, 2008.

Whalen, Grover. *Mr. New York: The Autobiography of Grover Whalen.* New York: G. P. Putnam's Sons, 1955.

World Book Encyclopedia. Chicago: Field Enterprises, 1960, and various accompanying annual supplements through 2015.

Wurst, James. *The UN Association-USA: A Little Known History of Advocacy and Action.* Boulder, London: Lynne Rienner Publishers, 2016.

Ybarra, Michael J. *Washington Gone Crazy: Senator Pat McCarran and the Great American Communist Hunt.* Hanover, N.H.: Steerforth Press, 2004.

Zeckendorf, William, with Edward McCreary. *The Autobiography of William Zeckendorf.* New York: Holt, Rinehart and Winston, 1970.

Zipp, Samuel. *Manhattan Projects: The Rise and Fall of Urban Renewal in Cold War New York.* Oxford and New York: Oxford University Press, 2010.

Sources for the sidebars that appear throughout the text

UN-U.S. Headquarters Agreement: www.usun.state.gov, Host Country Affairs, Treaty Obligations, Headquarters Agreement: PL 80–357, and conversations with David Stewart, Georgetown University, and retired U.S. State Department legal advisor.

"Walk Right In": Dinkins comment from interview with author.

Secretary General at Home: *The New Yorker,* Oct. 11 and 18, 1946; *NYT,* Aug. 1, 1954, and Jan. 1, 2007; James Wurst, *The UN Association–USA: A Little Known History of Advocacy and Action* (Boulder, Colo.: Lynne Rienner Publishers, 2016).

UN Economic Contribution to New York: "United Nations Impact Report 2016," study by the New York City Mayor's Office for International Affairs and the Economic Development Corporation, based generally on fiscal 2014 data, and released Dec. 6, 2016, www.nyc.gov/international and www.edc.nyc/UNImpactReport2016; and Beame report: *NYT,* Dec. 5, 1977; 1989 Koch report: "The Economic Impact of the Diplomatic Community on the City of New York" (the report also refers to 1981 report); Giuliani report: LWA,

Giuliani Collection, Box 02/11/1/014, Folder 0540, memorandum dated Aug. 18, 1995, from David Gmach to Jane Steiner and Clay Lifflander, Subject: Analysis of the Economic Benefit of the Diplomatic Community.

    Restoring and Renovating: UN Capital Master Plan office.

Index

Mark Naison and Bob Gumbs, *Before the Fires: An Oral History of African American Life in the Bronx from the 1930s to the 1960s*

Robert Weldon Whalen, *Murder, Inc., and the Moral Life: Gangsters and Gangbusters in La Guardia's New York*

Joanne Witty and Henrik Krogius, *Brooklyn Bridge Park: A Dying Waterfront Transformed*

Sharon Egretta Sutton, *When Ivory Towers Were Black: A Story about Race in America's Cities and Universities*

David J. Goodwin, *Left Bank of the Hudson: Jersey City and the Artists of 111 1st Street*. Foreword by DW Gibson

Britt Haas, *Fighting Authoritarianism: American Youth Activism in the 1930s*

Pamela Hanlon, *A Worldly Affair: New York, the United Nations, and the Story Behind Their Unlikely Bond*

For a complete list, visit www.empirestateeditions.com.